P9-DFK-094

THE COMPLETE BOOK OF
EXERCISEWALKING

THE COMPLETE BOOK OF
EXERCISEWALKING
GARY D. YANKER

Contemporary Books, Inc.
Chicago

Library of Congress Cataloging in Publication Data

Yanker, Gary.
    The complete book of exercisewalking.

    Includes index.
    1. Walking.   2. Physical fitness.   I. Title.
GV199.5.Y36   1983   613.7'1   83-2081
ISBN 0-8092-5535-9

Copyright © 1983 by Gary D. Yanker
All rights reserved
Published by Contemporary Books, Inc.
180 North Michigan Avenue, Chicago, Illinois 60601
Manufactured in the United States of America
Library of Congress Catalog Card Number: 83-2081
International Standard Book Number: 0-8092-5535-9

Published simultaneously in Canada by
Beaverbooks, Ltd.
150 Lesmill Road
Don Mills, Ontario M3B 2T5
Canada

To Ginny

CONTENTS

ACKNOWLEDGMENTS

First of all, thanks to my heroes: Gary Bitner, Peg Sinclair, T George Harris, Lynn Laurenti, Hara Estroff Marano, Maria von Pawelsz, Bill Reiss, Virginia Rice, Maria Marioni, and Donavan Vicha for helping me with all my walking activities including the preparation of this book.

Walkers and authors alike need benefactors, confidants, and supporters—here are some of my most important ones: Jim Powell, Mary Moore Hamrick, Drew Mearns, Bruce Bassett, Harold Gessner, Wendy Black, Lynn Hayes, Jerry Gorman, Dr. Russell Warren, Tom Singleton, Marty Batchelor, John Harris, Bob Lipson, Juraj Chmel, Timothy Augello, Fawn Evenson, Dr. Michael Pollock, Dr. David Levy, David Balseley, Elizabeth Yanker, Joann Dolan, Helen Thalman, Bud Siemon, Bill White, Joe Filipowski, the Ostromeckis, Tom and Kathy Owens, Nancy Evans, Marilynn Tanner, Theresa Dziorney, Bill Carey, Chris Anderson, Foy J. Shaw, Larry Williams, Peter N. Yanker, and Diana Adams.

My special thanks to the members of the Ocean Hiway Association who gave me lodging and support on my 1,100-mile walk to test and demonstrate the health-giving effects of walking: Lou Rodia (Cape May, NJ), Barbara Cutler (Bethany Beach, DE), Mr. & Mrs. Russell W. Everett (Chincotegue, VA), Martha Everett (Chincoteague Island, VA), Kenneth Burton (Chincoteague Island, VA), Brooks Russell (Tasley, VA), Randall Higinbotham (Cape Charles, VA), Lorraine Smith (Chesapeake Bay Bridge Tunnell, VA), Jim Mathews (Norfolk, VA), Alive Sykes (Kill Devil Hills, NC), John Harris (Nags Head, NC), Dabrey Coddingson (New Bern, NC), John Singleton (Morehead City, NC), Mary Fox (Wilmington, NC), Mike DeSherbinin (Brunswick County, NC), Zeb Thomas (Myrtle Beach, SC), Robert Sippel (Georgetown, SC), Abe Fogel (Georgetown, SC), Captain Sandy Jones, John Roberts, and Don Sottile (Charleston, SC), Jim Jordan (Brunswick, GA), Judy Picard and Bob Nelson (Jacksonville Beaches, FL), and all the other kind persons on the coast between New York City and Jacksonville.

Also thanks for helping to all my European walking friends: Inge Kobow, Sybil Ehman, Heidi Apel, Jean Marie Bottequin, Erich and Ingrid Schymik, Brigitte Smith, Margit Dix, Susanne Bollman, Martin von Pawelsz, Sigrid Gutzmann, Dr. Herbert L. Schrader, Frank Apel, Mr. Sroka (Ambassador Hotel, Hamburg), Mohamed Salem, Fritz Schuster, Familia Happel, and Dr. Werner Jopp.

Photo and illustration credits go to: Michael Hartnett, Virginia Rice, Marilynn Tanner, Thomas Iannaccone (Harvin), Bob Acree, Bill McGowan, James W. Leslie, Thomas Stankiewitz, and Al Campbell (Minolta).

PREFACE

This book is written primarily for those of you who already walk for exercise. It's no secret that exercise and diet experts recommend walking as the exercise of the '80s and that already there are 50 million of us who have made walking their favorite exercise activity. Most of us don't need lessons on how to walk but rather on how to use walking as an exercise. If I called my book just *Walking* you might have concluded, "I know how to do that already so why do I need a book?" *Walking as Exercise* is another title I considered, but that might suggest walking is hard work, and that's not my purpose. *Exercisewalking* says it better, just as "jogging" became the exercise word for the sport of running. I have written this book with the intention of both preserving the joy of walking and taking into account the wide variety of walking styles and activities.

I believe walkers need an exercise book which give them a scientific understanding of what they are getting out of their walking beyond the sheer enjoyment of it. Because walkers are health conscious and fitness conscious, they want to know if walking can really do the job for them. I believe it can. The knowledge contained in this book will show you how it works.

I have tried my best to keep the fun in walking, but it's a serious business, too. It's probably the only sure way to stay fit and active all through your life. You'll soon learn how walking has its own special and compelling logic in addition to its well-known emotional benefits. So, enough with generalities. Let's get to the specifics.

Exercisewalking means converting the walking you already do—strolling, hiking, backpacking, stair climbing, brisk walking—into exercise routines while preserving the fun of the activity. By using and integrating new knowledge about walking techniques and exercise values as part of everyday and weekend walking, you will be able to practice exercisewalking unconsciously just like you do regular walking. And finally, *exercisewalking* means taking the basic "walking action" or movement and using it in a variety of ways as a training device for the highest fitness levels and conditioning for other exercises and sports—if that's what you want.

I want to caution you, however, this is a book for moderates. Walkers are not fanatics like other sports or exercise enthusiasts. Walking itself calms you down and gives you an even-handed view of life and exercise.

Walking is both emotional and logical. In this book science and art walk together toward a common goal. The logic of this book is like the logic of exercisewalking: the marriage of health and joy.

Although the major emphasis of this book is to allow each reader to create his or her own exercise program using walking as the core exercise, it does include routines that can be fashioned into a variety of exercise programs. It never loses sight of the art of walking nor does it exclude anyone on the basis of age, for walking is truly the lifetime exercise.

Finally, to be a truly *complete* book of exercisewalking, it provides up-to-date information on foot care, shoe care, and walking equipment, clothing, aids, and supplies. If I've left anything out, come see me at the next American Event Walk held in your city and let me know—I'll be glad to walk with you.

February 1983
New York City

INTRODUCTION: FOUR WALKING LESSONS

Many books about walking have been published, but they have generally approached the subject in the traditional manner as an "art" and as a leisure pastime, dealing with geographical routes, equipment, and nature study. The idea of walking as a sport and exercise has not been sufficiently developed in any of these books. Yet public interest in this subject has been greatly aroused, particularly in terms of walking as an alternative exercise that avoids the risk of injury associated with jogging.

My own experience with walking taught me four lessons that convinced me of walking's benefits to such a degree that I sought out scientific data to prove them.

My First Walking Lesson

I developed a passion for walking at age 13 during my freshman year in high school in the town of Neustadt in West Germany's Black Forest region. I went to Neustadt from a Catholic grammar school in Maywood, New Jersey. I still carried with me a nice layer of baby fat. Until that point in my life I had mostly been chauffeured around in a station wagon, so I was in poor physical shape for a young boy. During that freshman year in Germany I was introduced to more walking and to more different kinds of walking than I had ever imagined.

A small health resort town with about 7,000 inhabitants, Neustadt lies in a valley with mountains on all sides. The German family I lived with had no automobile, so I walked almost everywhere I went: in and around town and to and from school, soccer practice, and gymnastics practice. It was not uncommon for my roommate, Hans, and me to take a daily hike up a mountain after school or to visit a relative's farmhouse in some outlying region. On Sundays we might hike to a tea dance through the forest (a 2½-hour walk to another Black Forest village) or stroll around the whole town with school friends after church. Even a date with a girlfriend involved a stroll, perhaps to the ski jumping park at the edge of town. Having also joined the German Boy Scouts, I hiked with them on weekends—sometimes as much as 20 miles a day.

In the summer we often went *wassertreten*, walking barefoot in a cold mountain stream followed by a brisk walk or run on the freshly cut mountain meadow. While your feet felt cold in the water, they soon heated up afterward on the meadow. Neustadters claim this is great therapy for circulation and nerves.

The amount of walking activity in Neustadt did not decline in the winter. Neustadt had beautiful ski slopes but no ski lifts. So we walked up the mountain with skis on our shoulders and used our poles for walking sticks. I also learned to ski jump that year and spent plenty of time walking steep inclines to get to the top of the jump. Walking up every slope I skied down in that one year improved my skiing ability from moderate to excellent.

I returned to the United States from Germany to find that President Kennedy had thrown down a challenge for all Americans to walk 50 miles in one day to prove that they were physically fit. I took up the challenge and walked 75 miles from my home in New Jersey to my grandmother's farm in upstate New York.

Over the next 15 years my walking activity declined. I shifted my physical activity to team sports in high school and college, keeping in shape by training for, and playing, football, soccer, and crew. I still walk occasionally, particularly as training for the ski season. During law school and graduate business school as well as during my first year of law practice my physical conditioning plummeted.

I concentrated on doing well in school and career and had no available team sport activities to keep me in shape. I became extremely dissatisfied with my physical condition and grew even more frustrated when I realized that an occasional tennis game, basketball game, or workout in the gym would not substantially improve things. My law practice often demanded as much as 70–90 hours a week. I wanted to excel in my profession, so giving up working time was out of the question.

I gained 60 pounds. I started smoking and was soon up to two packs of cigarettes a day. I wanted to lose weight, but eating was one of the ways I relieved nervous tension. I had developed this bad habit in graduate school, where I ate candies and cakes during my coffee breaks while studying for exams.

Then, in a moment of extreme anxiety, I remembered my walking experience in Neustadt and recalled how walking had strengthened my body and made my fat melt away. The next weekend I set out on a walk to my grandmother's farmhouse, only this time from my home in Manhattan. I walked 100 miles over a three-day weekend. I started out slowly and built up speed. I proceeded at my own pace, wanting to ensure that I would complete the walk no matter what. Whenever I became tired I took a rest.

The first day was easy, the second harder, and the third very difficult. My feet and the rest of my body were in agony when I arrived. I lost five pounds in those three days and tightened my stomach muscles. With that one important walking act I began my road to recovery. The walk gave me a feeling of accomplishment and self-confidence. With this newfound strength I was able to start exercising again and start a weight-loss diet.

Having seen immediate results from walking I started changing my lifestyle in Manhattan. I gave up taxi rides: instead I walked to and from work, and I often took brief walks to get my mind off food and calm my hunger pains. Going out for a walk during lunchtime got my mind off the stress of dieting. I took more weekend walks, not 100 miles long but half-day walks around Manhattan of six to twelve miles. During these periods I went off my diet, knowing that the extra miles of walking would keep me from gaining any weight back. Eating a normal, well-balanced diet gave me the physical strength to endure. After two months the amazing results were in: I had lost 60 pounds and now felt like a new man.

It's been 10 years since that dramatic weight loss, and except for perhaps five to ten pounds, those 60 pounds have never been regained. I now control my weight through walking, knowing that I can balance out any temporary weight gain with extra miles. No matter how hectic life gets or how time-consuming work becomes, with walking, I will always be able to regain and maintain my physical fitness. And that is a lesson I recommend to you—whatever sport or exercise you've tried or given up on, walking is your security for gaining control of your physical fitness. It will always be an activity you can do for the rest of your life.

My walking story does not stop here or with this one lesson. Walking soon became more than a basic exercise conditioner and weight-control method for me.

My Second Walking Lesson

Four years after my big weight loss I found myself in the throes of a hectic career. Having switched jobs and taken on the additional responsibility of my own business and outside law clients, I found that work had become so important to me that I figured I had had only 119 hours a week or 17 hours a day for working, 168 hours in a week minus one hour a day for eating and six hours a day for sleeping. This would give me the opportunity to work 6,171 hours a year if I didn't take Sundays off and took only one day at Christmas. When fellow lawyers closed their law books at 6:00 P.M. and went home I closed my door and burned the midnight oil on my other law and business projects. I had no wife or children, so this was possible to do without any competing commitments.

Work consumed me, and I sacrificed almost all my free time to it, including weekends, vacation time, and evenings. I became a workaholic, living an extremely stressful existence. My sanity and basic health were maintained with walks cleverly squeezed in during various parts of the day, so that walking never interfered with my work commitments. I even walked with my clients and subordinates while giving them advice and instruction.

After three years of this kind of schedule I asked myself whether it was all really worth it. My life was rapidly passing me by because I concentrated only on my career. My friends had all given up on me, since I turned down their invitations to parties, weekend outings, and trips to the islands. But one old friend, Tim, from high school finally convinced me to take a break. He readily agreed when I suggested we take a 100-mile walk to visit his mother in Rhinebeck, New York. We took that walk along the Hudson River through small towns and villages. Stopping at bars and restaurants along the way, we talked about old times and enjoyed ourselves tremendously. The walk was over before we knew it and, although our muscles were sore, we immediately planned another walk down the New Jersey and Delaware coast on the Fourth of July weekend. That second walk was so pleasant that it gave us another chance to talk about old times, think of the future, and forget about the problems back in New York City. It was an escape and an adventure; we met many new people along the way down the coast who were interested in hearing about our long walk.

On the fourth day I called my New York office and announced that I was going to extend my vacation and keep walking a few more days. My secretary was very surprised, remarking that it was not like me to miss a day of work. "You sound so calm and relaxed, like a different person," she said.

By the seventh day of the walk I was relaxed and feeling fit. I noticed a remarkable strength and vigor coming over me with each additional day.

This newfound strength reminded me of the days spent surfing at the beach in high school. I inexplicably dropped to do push-ups and sit-ups along the way. My body began to crave the physical exercise. Blue sky, barefoot walking in the surf, spotting fish and birds (and some pretty girls) not only relaxed me but awakened in me an awareness of the physical world inside and outside of my body.

My second lesson from walking was that it makes you relax and get in touch with yourself and the outside world. But I also learned much more, for as you will see, walking changed my life.

My Third Walking Lesson

The bug of long-distance walking bit us on our 250-mile walk. The idea of walking across the United States seemed crazy at first, but it began to grow on us. Tim and I began speculating what it would be like if we kept on walking the whole coast of the United States. We imagined that it would be as much fun as the first segment. Such a walk would in fact give us an extended vacation or even a year off. Tim and I resolved to do it.

We spent the next year and a half planning a 5,000-mile long-distance walk from New York City to San Francisco via a coastal route. We mapped out the route of towns we would pass along the Atlantic Coast through the South; along the Gulf of Mexico; through the deserts of Texas, New Mexico, and Arizona; and up the California coast.

Just dreaming about the walk became a pleasurable experience. The logistics of such a walk became quite a job. While we planned to do some camping, we wanted to walk with light packs, so we could really use the trek as an exercise. We would use the walk to meet up with old friends or have them join us along the way. We also arranged to stay with friends and acquaintances along the route.

As the logistical plan formed we thought it would be a good idea to test walking's health-giving effects, so I contacted my university's sports coach, who recommended a group of doctors willing to do the physical testing as a research project. As the day for planning the stepoff date approached, tension heightened.

Six months prior to this I had started training with a race walking coach to learn the walking techniques and formulate a training regimen I could practice on our trek. I also read every book and article on walking I could find. A shoe manufacturer agreed to provide us with shoes and some financial support for expenses in return for feedback on the shoes' performance as well as some local publicity for the company.

Then a series of setbacks occurred. My employer was unable to grant a year-long sabbatical. After much agonizing I made the decision and resigned. (Quite a turnaround from calculating the number of hours a year I could work.) One month before we were scheduled to start, Tim became very sick and had to be hospitalized. When I learned that he would be in the hospital for many months I decided to make the walk by myself, relying on the hope that friends would join me to walk part of the way.

At this writing I have completed 1,100 miles of the walk (having walked from New York to Jacksonville, Florida). During that walk my body underwent an amazing transformation. I noticed it as I was walking, and you can see it in some of the pictures of me in this book. Later, medical tests revealed dramatic improvements in my cardiovascular conditioning, muscle strength, and body composition. I not only lost 11 pounds, but my body composition changed from flabby to muscular—my body fat was reduced by five percent.

This transformation was so amazing that it motivated me to test walking's effectiveness for body shaping and strength producing. Although my trek concentrated 1,100 miles into 49 days of walking, an exercisewalker can easily walk this distance in six to twelve months while staying at home with just four to eight miles of walking a day. Thus, my third walking lesson: four to eight miles a day can add up to a dramatic change in the shape of your body and the state of your mind.

My Fourth Walking Lesson

While walking I also had time to reflect on the walking action and to practice my walking techniques. As I walked and talked with people along the way, the purpose of my walk expanded from being merely personal adventure to demonstrating and explaining the health-giving benefits of walking to people I met along my route. I talked with, and listened to, persons of all ages and from all walks of life (press reps, sporting goods retailers and manufacturers, retirees, school children, athletes, soldiers, businesspersons interested in walking as an exercise and its benefits compared to other sports and exercise. I heard many stories of other walkers, including long-distance walkers who used walking to stay in shape, and began researching walking from all perspectives: medical, how-to, sport, exercise, recreation, literature, technique.

In the meantime I was also commissioned to do a number of magazine articles on the subject for American and European health and general interest magazines. I started giving press interviews and walking demonstrations. I not only read about physical fitness subjects but also studied the market for walking shoes and other products. I talked to sporting goods manufacturers, athletic coaches, and other walking enthusiasts. It soon become clear to me that my own interest in walking coincided with a growing public interest. That interest had grown by leaps and bounds in the wake of the physical fitness and jogging boom in the United States and the resurgence of interest in walking in Europe, especially among the young people in Germany and northern Europe. A number of opinion polls show that more than 50 million Americans already choose walking as their exercise and undertake group walks for that purpose.

Despite these polls in favor of walking many of the walkers I talked to enjoyed their walking but were not sure about the exercise value of it or whether it was really vigorous or comprehensive enough to substitute for jogging. Further, they weren't sure how much of it they had to do to get results.

I began to notice more and more articles on the subject as well as a greater number of references to walking in other people's exercise books. It was uncanny that the turning point for increased interest in walking as an exercise came about 1980, the same year I had undertaken my long-distance walking adventure. My interest in walking seemed to be a kind of coincidental bellwether for America's interest in walking. Analyzing it more carefully, I realized that it was really the jogging boom of the '70s which had turned much of this attention to walking. People who tried jogging and didn't like it or were injured were looking for an alternative. Recreational walkers were more than ever concerned about their health and fitness and how their walking could help them maintain this. I gradually started turning walking from a hobby or avocation into a full-time occupation, realizing that walking was at the dawn of a new age and that my love for, and knowledge of, it could help bring walking to the forefront of America's fitness revolution. I decided to learn everything I could about it, particularly the science and exercise part, in preparation for making the best possible case for walking.

My enthusiasm for walking, however, wasn't shared by all athletes and sports professionals. While endorsing walking as a good starter program for more vigorous exercises and sports, they relegated the role of walking to a rehabilitative tool for

Brisk walking at full tilt on the streets of Munich.

those recovering from illness or injury. While they were positive in their recommendations for walking, walking wasn't viewed as an exercise and sport for somebody who was serious about sports or really wanted to get into top physical conditioning. In trying to be kind to walking they inadvertently gave walking a bum rap. They were prejudiced against walking. They had not considered enough styles or variations of walking but only the normal and brisked-paced versions done every day on the street. They didn't seem to recognize the real power of walking, that walking as a dynamic action can be practiced in different ways. With weight training up inclines, with greater speeds for greater distances and longer periods, and in combination with other sports and exercises, walking action is a more dynamic, even a super, exercise. My gut reaction was that walking was better than it had been rated. My own long-distance walk had proved that, too. Long-distance walking is similar to the walking we do throughout a lifetime, but bunched up in shorter time periods.

It seemed logical, but the proposition needed scientific backup if people were going to believe it and apply it to their walking or walk seriously as a regular and reliable exercise. Further, it became clear that the critics of walking focused only on the functional walking and not on the other types, like hiking and climbing. So I decided to gather all the evidence, synthesize and make the most comprehensive case for walking as an exercise that I could.

My fourth walking lesson was that there is more to walking than meets the eye, and scientific analysis is needed to see the whole picture.

Lessons for You

In general *The Complete Book of Exercisewalking* will prescribe walking exercise programs that can easily be integrated into your daily life without much sweat, fuss, or elaborate equipment and preparation. Tips on "walking for miles" will show how exercisewalking can be integrated into specially tailored programs based on miles.

This book will serve as a basic manual for learning how to convert your existing walking activities into exercise. It will do this first by showing you the unique qualities of the walking action and what are good walking techniques (Chapters 1 and 3). How walking will benefit your health and physical fitness is explained in Chapter 2. Chapter 4 describes and illustrates stretching and strengthening exercises to prepare you for exercisewalking.

Chapter 5 discusses the seven basic principles that underlie the *exercisewalking concept*, and Chapter 6 helps you determine whether your walking activities qualify as exercise by providing measuring methods with which you can analyze your walking. In Chapter 7 walking styles—from strolling to climbing—are discussed, and start-up, progressive, and maintenance programs are described.

In Part IV, Chapters 8–12, routines for fitting exercisewalking into your daily life are given, from using walking as the core of a total athletic program to using advanced routines such as long-distance walking.

Part V, Chapters 13 and 14, help you put all this information together into a lifetime program.

Everything exercisewalkers need for a lifetime of walking—equipment and apparel—is discussed in Part VI.

PART 1

THE ART AND SCIENCE OF WALKING

When I first tried to place my Walking column with newspaper syndicators one skeptical editor responded, "A column about walking? That's like writing a column about sitting! Everybody does it. So what?"

Walking means different things to different people. The newspaper editor reacted to the functional definition of *walking*, which says that it is a means of transportation. Because people use walking as a practical way of getting places, they do not think of it as a form of exercise. They take it for granted as an everyday movement like any other—opening a door, getting dressed, or driving a car. They also consider *exercise* an uncommon or special activity, limited to push-ups or running, that is not done regularly.

Perhaps the newspaper editor was not aware of the "art of walking" practiced by poets, philosophers, essayists, and novelists like Thoreau, Emerson, Goethe, Dickens, and Burroughs. In farther distant times the "art" had religious roots in the pilgrimages made to the Holy Lands (which began with Peter the Hermit's walking tour of France and Germany in 1095 AD) and

1

philosophical roots in the peripatetic school of Plato and Aristotle. For all, walking cleansed the spirit, clearing away cobwebs from the mind and improving thought and discourse.

This approach to walking has been articulated beautifully by great poets and writers and is still practiced today by walking artists like Colin Fletcher and Peter Jenkins. These artists walk at their own pace and like this self-paced walking best. The art of walking, for them, is walking for its own sake, for the pleasure of it, and for the unexpected discoveries that walking has brought to them. The destination of their walks is secondary to the journey itself, which frequently is a journey to the inner self anyway. Such an art is the complete opposite of functional walking.

The words of these walking artists describe their art better than I can:

Edna St. Vincent Millay: "It's little I care what path I take, And where it leads it's little I care. . . ."

Cervantes: "The road is always better than the inn."

Stevenson: "Wealth I ask not, hope nor love, Nor a friend to know me; All I ask, the heaven above And the road below me."

Ralph Waldo Emerson: "No man is suddenly a good walker. Many men begin with good resolution but they do not hold out. . . .These we call apprentices.

"Few men know how to take a walk. The qualifications. . .are endurance, plain clothes, old shoes, an eye for Nature, good humor, vast curiosity, good speech, good silence and nothing too much." (*Notes on Walking*)

Walking artists have never really agreed on the importance exercise played in their walking. Thoreau took the hard line against it: "[T]he walking of which I speak has nothing in it akin to taking exercise, as it is called, as the sick take medicine at stated hours—as the swinging of dumb-bells or chairs; but is itself the enterprise and adventure of the day." (*Excursions*)

Other walking artists were not so harsh:

Oliver Wendell Holmes: "[T]he pleasure of exercise is due first to a purely physical impression and secondly to a sense of power in action. The first source of pleasure varies, of course, with our condition and the state of the surrounding circumstances; the second, with the amount and kind of power, and the extent and kind of action. In all forms of active exercise, there are three powers simultaneously in action: the will, the muscles and the intellect. Each of these predominates in different kinds of exercise. In walking, the will and the muscles are so accustomed to work together and *perform their task with so little expenditure of force,* that the intellect is left comparatively free. The mental pleasure in walking, as such, is the sense of power over all our moving machinery." (*The Autocrat of the Breakfast Table,* emphasis mine)

Without the benefit of modern scientific studies, Holmes made a significant comment on the relative ease with which we walk, the efficiency of the walking motion. Of course, these walking artists, who lived before the invention of the elevator, escalator, and telephone, did their joyful walking on top of their functional walking. In effect, they did double the amount of walking that most modern men do; thus they could easily prescribe walking without a care.

Because of the sedentary lifestyle that has been created by modern technology, modern man cannot benefit from only the art of walking. The "art" must now share walking with the scientists and their interest in its exercise value.

The science of walking is the systematic study of walking, which breaks it down into a body movement with various parts, for the purpose of analyzing the action itself and the relationship of walking activities to the general health of humans. In the case of walking as an exercise studies have shown how a walking program can contribute to physical fitness and overall health. As you will discover in the next two chapters, far from being common and simple, walking is a complex activity that is so unique and complicated that scientists have been unable to duplicate it with any mechanical device. Instead, they must content themselves with an understanding of its various components.

It was inevitable that science would catch up with the art of walking. Walking brings so many benefits so effectively because it is a joy to walk without care. As I see it, the art of walking makes the exercise more enjoyable and the exercise benefit justifies devoting more time to the art.

THE BIOMECHANICS OF WALKING

Most of us cannot remember the details, but it took quite a bit of experimenting and learning before we got up from the crawling position and learned how to walk. Walking is most likely a learning process rather than the maturing of some inborn reflex. Most animals are quadrupedal and coordinate their movements so at least three of their feet are always on the ground, thereby giving them a high degree of stability. The human walker, however, gets along at least some of the time supported only by one foot—quite an accomplishment of biomechanics when you think about it.

In fact, at least one study of the development of the walking mechanism in children shows that, contrary to the conventional theory that they can walk by age two, children are still mastering the art of walking at ages seven to nine. (Popova, 1935) As children grow in physical size they are continually experimenting with their neuromusculoskeletal system and improving the neural controls over their bodies for walking.

To harness the walking action as an exercise and to improve your walking techniques you may have to learn walking all over again. This is only proper, for if we are to give walking its proper place among other sports and exercises, we must not only understand it but have a healthy respect for it.

The Biomechanical Definition of Walking

The study of walking has not been made easy because of one basic fact of life: *all individuals walk differently*. Each walking style is as idiosyncratic as one's signature, perhaps as unique as a fingerprint. Certainly we know from observation and personal experience that we can recognize many people from the way they walk. Thus, throughout this book, you will see that when we talk about any aspect of walking—or even exercises in general—we speak of averages, knowing full well that the averages must still be applied to individual walking styles.

Gaitologists, those who study walking styles, know that a whole group of factors influence the style of walking. Primarily, genetic factors have a great influence. But in addition, height or build, the shoes worn, mental attitude, and walking environment all affect walking style. So any scientific test of walking must take these differences into account.

Walking does not refer to any specific single movement, as a *bicep curl* does. Walking is rather a series of body movements that are all part of one package called the *walking cycle*. Despite the aforementioned variations in walking styles, we can still observe types of movement in human locomotion that, although executed a little differently, are still basically similar events or occurrences during the cycle of forward motion.

Human walking is a body action of forward locomotion while in the erect position, supported first by one leg and then by the other. As the body passes over each supporting leg, the other leg simultaneously swings forward in preparation for the next support phase. At all times during the forward movement one foot or the other is on the ground. (This is essential if the motion is to be called *walking*.) There is also a brief period when both feet are on the ground, called the *double-support phase*. As the walker goes faster, these double-support periods become shorter.

In running, the double-support periods are replaced by periods in which the forward-moving person is airborne, with both legs off the ground. What distinguishes walking from running and all

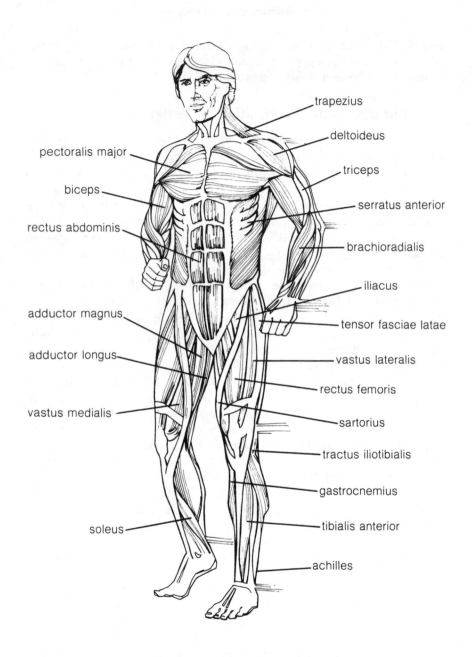

pectoralis major

biceps

rectus abdominis

adductor magnus

adductor longus

vastus medialis

soleus

trapezius

deltoideus

triceps

serratus anterior

brachioradialis

iliacus

tensor fasciae latae

vastus lateralis

rectus femoris

sartorius

tractus iliotibialis

gastrocnemius

tibialis anterior

achilles

Muscular Anatomy of a Walker.

other body locomotions is that one foot is always in touch with the ground and at least once during the walking cycle both feet are on the ground simultaneously. These two prerequisities are what makes walking universally recognized as such, no matter who's doing it—man, woman, or a disabled person with a prosthetic device.

The walker's body moves not in one but in three directions. With each step the body rises and falls and weaves slightly from side to side, all in a highly systematic and harmonious fashion. In addition, while the body appears to be moving continuously forward in a straight line, it is slowing down and speeding up again with each step.

You can prove this to yourself by carrying a plate filled with water while you walk and observing how difficult it is to keep the water from sloshing back and forth. What's really causing the instability in the pan of water is the acceleration and deceleration of the legs. As the stepping foot starts out ahead of the body it begins to slow down before being placed on the ground. This also slows down the body motion. And as that foot passes under the body and goes to the rear it starts to accelerate again. Likewise, as the body passes over the supporting foot it rises and then descends. Finally, while the walker is supported by one foot his pelvis shifts to the side of his other foot and then back again. It's not really a lateral shift but a rotational one about the axis of the joints. The pelvis lists, rotates, and undulates as the body moves forward. The shoulders and arms also rotate in the opposite direction of the moving leg. Thus, nearly all parts of the body are in motion at some time during the walking action.

What makes this action so amazing is that the human body can actually integrate all these separate actions of the various segments and keep from falling down—and on top of all that, do it rhythmically in continuous motion.

Consider this: walking is a dynamic action that uses almost all of the body's 206 bones and 650 muscles.

Bones

To understand walking, we must first learn how walking starts with the bones. The spine is the foundation of the walking action; 26 articulated vertebrae yield and bounce back with each walking stride. The weight of the body proceeds down the spine to the pelvic girdle. From there the femur or thighbone, the strongest of all bones, carries body weight to the tibia (shinbone) and fibula. The fibula is the long slender bone attached above and below the side of the tibia. The feet are attached to these bones and act as platforms for the whole body. Each foot contains 26 bones, which distribute the body weight like a tripod on the base of the big and little toe and on the heel. An ideal support phase exists when body weight is balanced over the arches and the feet remain parallel.

The bones are strong and rigid because of their composition, which is half mineral (calcium, phosphorous, etc.), one-quarter collagen, a type of protein fiber, and one-quarter water. Bones are held together by bands of elastic tissue called *ligaments* and are fitted together at the joints, which are lined with cartilage and synovial fluid. The largest joint connects the leg bone with the hipbone, which enables the walker to maintain his stride.

Muscles

Muscle moves bones by contracting and expanding. A contraction muscle pulls the bone forward, and an extensor muscle pulls it back. All the muscles of the lower body assist in walking. When we start to walk, the calf muscles relax, and the body sways forward to overcome inertia. The front thigh muscles contract quickly to swing the leg forward and to pull up the foot and prevent it from dragging before the heel strikes. When the heel strikes, all thigh and lower leg muscles contract to stabilize the knee and ankle until the body weight is moved forward by the calf muscles. Thereafter, the hip muscles on the outside of the thigh swing the thigh forward to stabilize the leg. The trunk muscles in the abdomen, side, back, and chest contract to hold the body erect so the legs can swing. To counterbalance the leg swing the opposite arm swings forward by the contraction of the flexor muscles in the shoulder and forearm on the forward swing and the extensor muscles contract on the return swing.

The rear leg pushes the body forward and immediately swings itself forward to strike the ground heel first. The body continues to roll forward across the ball of the foot until another push-off is

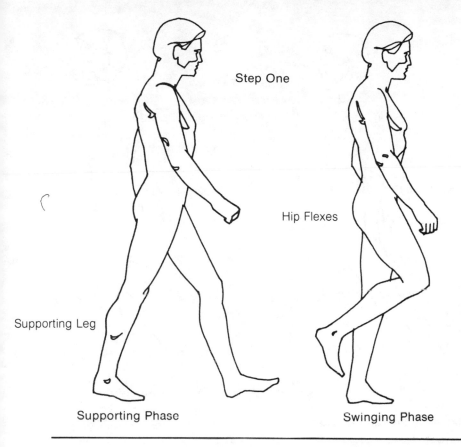

Step One

Hip Flexes

Supporting Leg

Supporting Phase   Swinging Phase

Phasic Action of Some Walking Muscles.

Most muscles are active at the beginning of the swing and stance phases. During the midstance and midswing there is minimal activity even though this is the period of maximum angular displacement. Thus the principal action of the muscles is to accelerate, then decelerate the legs.

The hip abductor muscles (*gluteus medius and minimus*) are activated during the supporting (stance) phase when the pelvis drops on the non-weight bearing side. The femur is being slightly abducted. By being elongated, the abductors stabilize the pelvis.

The *iliacus* lengthens as the hip is extended at the termination of the stance phase and also contracts at the beginning of the swing phase to start the hip flexing.

9

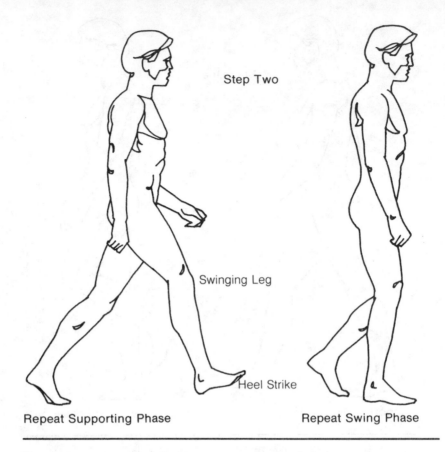

Step Two

Swinging Leg

Heel Strike

Repeat Supporting Phase   Repeat Swing Phase

The *gluteus maximus* muscle is being stretched before its maximum contraction period which occurs right after the heel strike. This assures the greatest extension of the hip placing the muscle in an elongated position right before it has to achieve its greatest force.

The *tensor fasciae latae* contracts once during the end of the swing phase and then again at the beginning of the stance phase along with the contraction of the *gluteus maximus* preventing the posterior displacement of the *iliotibial tract* into which the greater portion of the *gluteus maximus* is inserted. This also assists with hip flexion.

The *quadriceps* (thigh muscles including rectus femoris, sartorius, and the vastus group) are active only during the early part of the stance phase during the knee flexion. During higher speeds of walking the *quadriceps* contract to prevent abnormal knee flexion and start the knee extension after the toe-off.

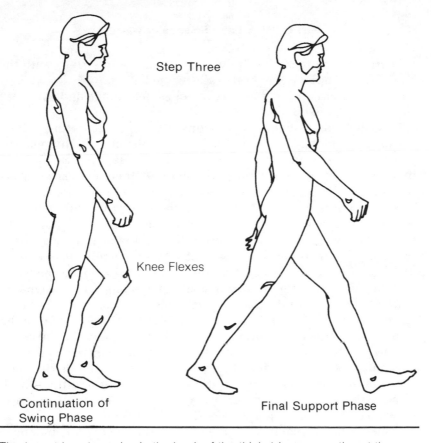

Step Three

Knee Flexes

Continuation of
Swing Phase

Final Support Phase

The *hamstrings* (muscles in the back of the thighs) become active at the termination of the swing phase. They are being elongated as they act to decelerate the swinging leg. The hamstrings continue their activity in the early part of the stance phase to assist the *gluteus maximus* in extending the hip.

The *adductors* are activated during the beginning and end of the swing phase.

The *triceps surae* (calf muscles) contract only long enough for the heel to lift off after they have been fully stretched making the contraction nearly isometric, thereby achieving maximal force with a minimum of energy expenditure. The *peroneals* also act with, and at the same time as, the calf muscles.

The *tibialis anterior* and the toe extensor muscles show maximum activity right after the heel strike. They also become active again after the toe off to dorsiflex the foot.

11

executed by the rear foot. It swings forward and strikes with the heel. This completes the first walking cycle.

The act of breathing expands the chest and lungs and activates the diaphragm, abdomen, and ribs.

Muscular movement is responsible for circulating blood throughout the body. The heart is the major muscle that accomplishes this feat. In conjunction with the lungs, the heart pumps blood to the brain and torso of the body. Although a very powerful muscle, the heart was not designed to do the job alone; it *can*, but this causes an extra burden for the heart over the long run. Arteries and veins are equipped with one-way valves that force the blood to move in one direction, either toward or away from the heart. Thus, other muscular activity—especially in the arms and legs—assists in circulating the blood by squeezing the veins and arteries, forcing it to move along its one-way-designated course. The effect that muscles other than the heart have on blood circulation is called *peripheral heart action* (PHA). PHA is an important factor in explaining why exercise is good for the heart.

Walking also involves balance and muscle control, and muscles, such as the *sartorius* and the *quadriceps* in the thighs, near the legs and help us to maintain our balance. In addition, fluid-filled structures in the inner ear give us our sense of balance. However, with all this equipment, we're still not ready to walk: we must still overcome the force of gravity. The body is balanced when its center of gravity, the hips, are over its supported base, the feet. Thus, we maintain equilibrium when we stand still. But we're off-balance when we take a step.

The Walking Cycle

Walking is not one specific action, but a series of actions called the walking cycle.

A complete walking cycle is from heel contact of one foot to heel contact of the other foot and finally back to heel contact of the starting foot, or, in plain language, three steps forward. (See pages 9–11.) In a complete cycle each leg is involved in the supporting phase for 60 percent of the cycle and in the swing phase for 40 percent of the time, but these phases overlap when the body weight has moved onto the supporting leg and the swinging leg touches the ground. The faster the walk, the less the phases

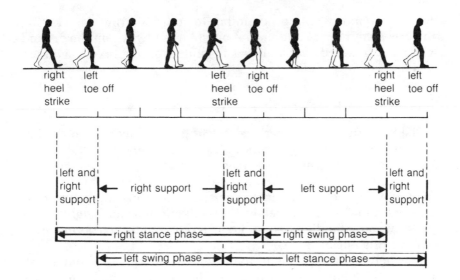

right	left		left	right		right	left
heel	toe off		heel	toe off		heel	toe off
strike			strike			strike	

left and right support — right support → left and right support ← left support → left and right support

|← right stance phase →|← right swing phase →|
|← left swing phase →|← left stance phase →|

Anatomy of the Walking Cycle.

overlap. The overlapping of the support and swing phases distinguishes walking from running or jumping because at no time in walking are both feet off the ground.

The *supporting (stance) phase* begins when the heel strikes the ground after the swinging leg is extended in front of the body. (See page 13.) The foot then rocks forward from heel to toe. The forward motion is maintained by the horizontal momentum of the body and the contraction of the muscles in the supporting leg.

The *swing phase* of the walking cycle starts with the push-off by the ball of the rear foot. The hip flexes with the knee and ankle, thereby shortening the leg so that it will clear the ground. The swinging leg passes under the body, and the knee begins to extend. The heel strikes the ground before the toe because the ankle is flexed. The heel strike again marks the end of the swinging phase.

In running the runner actually flies through the air as he moves forward, and both feet can be off the ground at the same time. On the other hand, walking is similar to roller skating, ice-skating and cross-country skiing in that one foot is always on the ground while the forward foot is lifted to slide, roll, or take a walking step.

The Sinusoidal Path of the Walker

The path that the walker's center of gravity, located in the hip area, follows during the walking cycle is *sinusoidal*. Namely, it approximates a sine curve (see illustration) and as such is smooth and undulating. The normal amount of vertical displacement (i.e., up-and-down movement) is not more than five centimeters and falls only below the walker's normal height, measured when standing. Here is how the body parts move to achieve this effect:

The pelvis rotates about four degrees to the left and right, alternately, about a vertical axis. This rotation angle increases with increases in speed. The pelvic rotation elevates the ends of the successive arcs somewhat less abruptly, thereby reducing impact on the walking surface. The pelvis on the opposite side of the weight-bearing leg lists downward about five degrees, permitting the pathway of the arc of the center of mass to move forward without going too far upward. This enables the body to move over the supporting leg in the stance phase of the walking cycle. Finally, the knee of the supporting leg also flexes as the body moves over it and continues to flex until the beginning of the heel-strike of the other foot. After the heel-strike, the knee begins to flex again and continues to do so until the striking foot is flat on the ground.

While contributing to decreasing the amount of vertical displacement of the body's center of gravity, pelvic rotation, pelvic list, and knee flexion are not enough to prevent sudden changes in vertical displacement. The motion of the ankle and foot are really the most important factors in ensuring a curved pathway with a low arc.

When the heel strikes, the body's downward motion is decelerated by a slight flexion of the knee against the resistance of the quadriceps. When the heel makes contact with the ground and begins to roll forward, the foot is plantar flexed against the

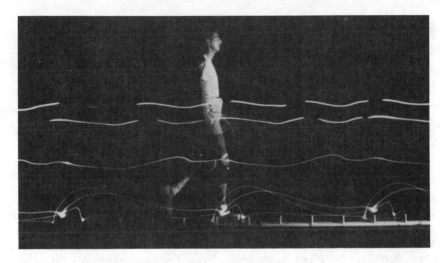

Using continuous light techniques, the paths of targets on the leg and foot of the walker show a smooth, almost sinusoidal pattern.

resisting *tibialis anterior* muscle, thus decelerating the downward motion further. All these phases of muscle action and joint flexion work together to ensure smooth deceleration. In fact, the leg and body are gradually let down with this special action.

After the center of mass has passed over and in front of the foot, its fall is then delayed by the elongation of the supporting leg through the extension of the knee, the plantar flexion at the ankle, and the supination of the foot. All contribute to a smooth passage in an almost sinusoidal pathway, as shown in the interrupted light study shown above.

What all of this demonstrates is the biomechanical principle that differentiates the walking action from actions performed in jogging and running. By being airborne at various parts of the running cycle, the runner actually rises above his normal body height. Rather than forming a smooth, sinusoidal path, the runner forms a path of valleys and peaks that account for the jolting action that will eventually cause injury to the runner. These pathways are compared in the illustrations on page 00.

You can prove the veracity of this claim by finding a low ceiling or tunnel that corresponds to your height and by walking under or through it. You won't bump your head. I wouldn't advise running through it, however.

You have just learned the walking action. As you can see, it is a complicated dynamic action that uses the entire body. What other body movement can make this claim.

Thank heaven you didn't have to comprehend the complexities of the walking action when you first learned it as a baby. The mere thought of it could unnerve anyone and keep us all crawling the rest of our lives.

While the walking action is dynamic, it is still not an exercise until put to that purpose. Further, the walking action can be controlled and made efficient through proper techniques and body alignment. The next chapter will continue to bring walking out of your subconscious into your conscious mind. You know the art of walking; now you will learn the science of walking as an exercise. But first let's try to motivate you by presenting all the real benefits of walking for exercise.

2

THE HEALTH AND FITNESS BENEFITS OF WALKING

When my friend Tim and I walked 250 miles from New Jersey to Delaware, Tim was a chain-smoker who went through two to three packs a day. He brought his cigarettes along on the walk. I felt like suggesting that he use the walk vacation to give up smoking, but I knew that lecturing to Tim did not pay. He was a free spirit, an artist-composer who did what he wanted and pursued his pleasures the way he felt best. So I said nothing and privately watched him smoke during the eight-day walk.

As we increased our walking distance from 18 to 25 miles a day I noticed that Tim smoked fewer cigarettes a day. It did not seem to be a conscious decision—the fresh air and increased oxygen intake worked naturally to depress his appetite for cigarettes.

On the fifth and sixth days of our hike Tim would put out a cigarette after smoking only half or three-quarters of it and mutter that it didn't taste right. I pointed out what was happening to Tim, and he was surprised and encouraged to break the habit completely. During the next two days he replaced the smoking habit with the walking habit.

What happened to Tim is a good example of what I call the natural powers of walking. By merely increasing the amount of daily walking, without regard to techniques or exercise regimens, anyone can benefit greatly. Of course, this is not the whole walking story, because adding techniques and converting normal walking activities into exercise can reap many benefits.

There are really two basic types of walking: natural and dynamic. Both can be forms of exercise providing fitness and health benefits. Natural walking is the kind we all do without regarding as exercise. We just do it for fun or function. The speed of the natural walker falls between one and three miles per hour. It's the art of walking if we take a walk for its own sake without any particular destination. It's functional walking if it gets us to a place we want to go. Either form is just what comes naturally.

Dynamic walking is walking with a greater level of metabolic expenditure than natural walking. It's the kind of walking we do to get into shape for a particular purpose. The speed of the dynamic walker is often above 3 mph and up to 10 mph. But it's not only speed that makes the difference—duration of the walk, incline of the walking surface, and work effort also add metabolic expenditure to the walking activity. Some dynamic walkers go slowly but carry a big weight load. Other dynamic walkers travel up inclines, and still others raise their legs higher (to walk on sand, snow, or rocky terrain for instance).

This book will show you all the ways to make your walking more dynamic. But not all exercisewalking will be dynamic walking. In fact, most walkers will still do most of their exercisewalking using the natural style. Natural or self-paced walking is also an exercise, and it is healthful in its own way. Above all, walking must be fun. The fun factor is the most important one in any exercise program you want to stay with.

The benefits of walking, which follow in this chapter, refer both to natural and dynamic walking. I like to think that the health part of health and fitness applies to natural walking and the fitness part applies to dynamic walking.

Walking Is the Lifetime Exercise

Walking is the exercise that will be accessible to you throughout your life. Walking helps build up your basic body strength when you are young. And at the other end of life it helps you prevent your body from deteriorating rapidly. In the middle years walking can serve to help you maintain your health and fitness. It can also intervene in a physical or emotional crisis, helping to nurse you back to health and build your physical fitness back up. If you want to really go gung-ho, the basic walking action can be your bodybuilding and aerobic conditioning exercise; thus walking by itself can fulfill all your exercise needs throughout life.

Finally, you will not be able to get through life without a minimal amount of walking anyway. If your walking muscles atrophy, your whole body atrophies. So you may as well give walking your fullest attention; it's the best life insurance policy you can get.

Walking Is the Most Efficient Exercise for Improving Overall Physical Fitness

Physical fitness is the generally accepted purpose of exercise and is defined as a state of body efficiency that enables a person to work actively with his body for a long period of time without fatigue and to respond to sudden physical and emotional demands with an economy of heartbeats and only a moderate rise in blood pressure. When measuring a person's state of physical fitness, we look at cardiovascular stamina, musculoskeletal strength, and a general sense of well-being.

An exercise is efficient in producing physical fitness if it can help keep the body healthy and free from disease without producing injury. Physical exercise should be progressive and not tend to overstrain the body. It should start at a natural pace and gradually work toward greater stamina, strength, and well-being.

With exercise and physical fitness defined, we can now look at how walking fulfills these terms as no other form of exercise can. Walking is its own training exercise and requires no prior conditioning even when a person is out of shape. When a sedentary person first attempts to jog or run, he *walks*. Walking also has less potential for injury than jogging or running and does not involve a high degree of physical exertion from the start.

There are other forms of exercise that might be more comprehensive than walking—that is, exercises that engage more muscles in a uniform, continuous action. Rowing in the Olympic style provides a sliding seat and a pumping foot action in a single motion. But it is difficult to start this form of exercise at low fitness levels and at low intensity. Rowing is also limited by the expense of equipment and the geographical and weather factors involved with launching a boat.

Swimming has also been mentioned as a comprehensive exercise but is limited by the lack of antigravity forces that make walking so naturally efficient. Water reduces the weight of the individual's body, unlike the surface on which a walker walks. Bicycling similarly reduces the effects of gravity by supporting the body mechanically.

Cross-country skiing is another candidate but is limited for the most part to the winter and therefore is not practical as year-round exercise. Walking can be done indoors if one doesn't want to face the challenge of walking in snow.

Aerobic dancing is an excellent form of exercise that is usually limited to the indoors. However, this is a vigorous activity that requires a gradual breaking in at a fitness level higher than that required of walking. You also need some form of training and/or instruction in proper techniques.

Thus, we are left with walking, which is simple and comprehensive. More muscles are exerted in a continuous, uniform action than in any other form of exercise not mentioned above. And as you progressively increase the work effort of walking, your return is an increase in physical fitness. In fact, at higher levels of walking, when you consciously go against the biomechanical efficiency of the walking action—for example, expending more calories to walk at the same speed that makes running metabolically efficient—you are safely increasing stamina and strength.

Walking Is a Safe and Injury-Free Exercise

Walking is a virtually injury-free exercise. In fact, joint and muscle injuries and strains are perhaps the primary reason why people choose walking as an exercise. Such injuries result from improper joint alignment, strenuous exercises like jogging, and overused and overdeveloped muscles. Walking reduces the angular stresses on the body joints because the feet remain parallel to each other in a wider gait. The walker's parallel leg movement is the natural movement for the joints, which were built for a forward/backward motion and not a side-to-side angular motion.

In jogging the feet come into contact with the ground along a straight line below the center of the body, causing an abnormal change of motion in the knee joint. The angular stresses on the jogger's knee joints cause a condition called *runner's knee,* a type of bursitis that accounts for approximately 25 percent of injuries. The impact of each jogging step on the body's shock-absorption system is 3½−4 times a person's weight, while the shock impact of the walking step is only 1½ times body weight. This is a significant difference for preserving the body's musculoskeletal and internal organs from injury.

Walking develops better balanced leg muscles on both the front and back of the leg. Muscular development in joggers' and skaters' legs is uneven. Overdeveloping some leg muscles while leaving others in a relatively weaker state results in the stronger muscles overpowering the weaker ones, causing them to be strained to the point of inflammation and even rupture. "Shin splints," or injured muscles in the front and lower leg, is a condition that results from overdeveloped calf muscles, which overpower the muscles at the front of the lower leg.

Walking Is the Most Natural Body Movement

Walking is the most natural function of the human body. Because of the structure, shape, and flexibility of the spine, we are better constructed for walking than for sitting, standing, or running. The human body is a perfect walking machine. When we walk, the skeletal and muscular systems perform harmoniously together and create a near-perfect balance between gravity's pull and our forward motion.

Walking is as natural as breathing: it is the most efficient, energy-conserving method of locomotion for the human species. Walking is the perfect exercise for everyone. Sport scientists say that each sport has a perfect body type who can competitively perform that particular sport best and feel most comfortable and natural while doing it. Running, the competitive equivalent of jogging, requires an ectomorphic body type, which has lean, thin, muscles and thin bones weighing two pounds for each inch of height. Approximately 10–15 percent of the population has such a body type. The remaining 85–90 percent of the population are not considered to be the perfect body type to run competitively. Walking, on the other hand, has no such restrictions, and everyone can have the same ability.

Walking Can Be Done in a Variety of Styles and Speeds

A walker has a choice of several styles or speeds of walking. These various styles include strolling (the slowest form), everyday walking, hiking, walk-climbing, speedwalking, backpacking, snowshoeing, and racewalking.

Walking Is Inexpensive

Walking does not involve the expense and inconvenience or the need for equipment and setting aside special time periods for training that jogging, rollerskating, tennis, skiing, and weight lifting do.

Walking Is the Best Family and Group Exercise

Health and fitness start with the family. The parents teach the children good habits, which they carry on with them into later life. While there are various kinds of sport and game activities available, none can be shared more easily by a group than walking. I learned to walk with a group as a teenager, first with the Boy Scouts, then with my family on after-dinner strolls. As a high school freshman in the Black Forest I also learned about boy–girl walks to tea dances.

To be able to walk and visit with your friends and family is not only an important socializing habit but a healthy one, too. With other exercises, the level of intensity is always high, requiring— no matter what the best intentions—separate exercise and rest intervals. With walking it is easier to adjust yourself to the group and keep talking while you walk. This also means you will be able to fit your walking exercises into more parts of your life because they will serve both an exercising and a socializing purpose.

When sports or exercises are complicated or individualized

they tend to be abandoned after a while or not even taken up in the first place. This occurs because these activities pull us away from our friends and family.

Of course there is a certain amount of walking you will want to do alone, and you will see later in this book how walking permits one to break away occasionally.

Walking Is the Bridge to Fitness in Other Sports

A walker can start slowly and gradually build to a high level of fitness. Thus, walking is recommended as a starter program and as interval training for many other exercise and sports training programs, including running, skiing, soccer, and mountain climbing. Chapter 13 will go into more detail on this subject.

Walking Improves the Heart and Circulation

In our quest for aerobic fitness we often forget about the basic health of our heart. Bouts of aerobic training often leave us extremely inactive in between. While it is better to stick with our exercise goals on a continuous basis, unrealized good intentions and poor planning leave us with large accumulations of inactivity. It's better during these periods to walk even if it is at low intensity just to keep our blood circulating, thereby helping prevent arteries and blood vessels from deteriorating and cutting off the oxygenated blood from the heart. Such deterioration can lead to heart diseases like myocardial infarction, in which a section of the heart muscle actually dies. Keeping your blood circulating is probably the best preventive medicine for arterial blockages. Our bodies were not built for staying still. They must remain active to stay healthy. Walking is the most common and accessible form of activity to keep the blood circulating and carrying oxygen to the various body parts.

Cardiologists often refer to the leg motion of walking as the second heart. While we are walking, the contraction of the thigh, buttocks, and calf muscles helps to squeeze blood back up toward the heart from the feet and legs where, because of prolonged sitting or standing, it tends to pool. By improving the circulation, walking lowers the blood pressure and serum cholesterol and triglycerides levels. Walking increases the flow of blood through the arteries by dilating the blood vessels and allowing the heart to work more efficiently at a slower rate. Walking also helps prevent varicose veins.

In addition to developing cardiovascular fitness, walking is often used as an integral part of medical programs to cure and prevent heart-related diseases.

Walking Is Aerobic

Walking exercises have the capacity to raise aerobic fitness levels like other continuous, rhythmic sports and exercises. Even natural or normal walking can do this for those who are badly out of shape. But after this basic level, walking must be made more dynamic if cardiovascular improvements are to continue. Dynamic walking offers a number of alternative ways to aerobic fitness, such as increasing the speed to brisk or fast walking, increasing the weight load or work effort, and increasing the duration of walking. Parts II and III of this book are devoted to making your walking serve you as an aerobic conditioner.

Walking Strengthens Muscles and Tissues

Probably more muscles are used in walking than in any other exercise. In addition to the leg and thigh muscles, walking also develops the buttocks (gluteus maximus) and the abdominal muscles. If the upper arms are used as part of the walking exercise, shoulders, triceps, and forearms will also be developed during the walking cycle. The walking action also helps strengthen the skin by making it thicker, stronger and more elastic. Skin responds to regular exercise in the same way that muscles, tendons, and ligaments do.

How Walking Strengthens Muscles, Tissues, and Body Frame

1. *Strengthens Buttocks.* These muscles are the first muscles to become firm because of the pulling action of the leg at foot plant.

2. *Strengthens Front of Thighs and the Shins.* Thighs and shins become quite strong and firm from the pulling action phase of walking.

3. *Strengthens the Back of Leg Muscles.* Calves and hamstring muscles are built up from pushing off with back leg.

4. *Strengthens Upper Body Muscles.* Triceps, forearms, shoulders are strengthened and toned because of the dynamic action of the arms. Will also give a woman a firmer and higher bustline because pectoral muscles that support breast become stronger.

5. *Improves All-Over Development.* Walking causes adaptive increases in muscle mass and muscle endurance. Long and lean muscles are built up for endurance and lean athleticism.

6. *Strengthens Bone Composition.* Walking's healthful physiological stress in the form of an exercise sends an electrochemical change through your bones, causing them to rebuild themselves by increasing bone density. Walking also helps prevent demineralization.

7. *Strengthens Your Skin.* Walking will make your skin thicker, stronger, and more elastic. Skin responds to regular exercise in the same way that your tendons and ligaments do.

8. *Strengthens Your Abdominal Muscles.* These are strengthened when you practice with your head and back erect and buttocks tucked in.

The walking motion itself contributes to the strengthening and toning of the skeletal muscles as well as the heart muscle. Each step is like a repetitive exercise of the leg muscles. These include the contraction and extension of the calf, iliotibial, quadriceps, and buttocks muscle so that between 1,500 and 3,000 leg muscle flexes occur during every mile walked. The weight of the body gravity force produced by gravity and the acceleration and deceleration of the limbs against the inertial force provide the resistance or workload to make the muscles work. Of course, as the body muscles used in walking become conditioned for a lot of walking a greater workload will be needed to provide further conditioning effects.

Walking specifically improves the capacity of muscles in several ways:

- *Strength* refers to the force of the individual muscular contractions. When the muscles are working they contract or twitch. The stronger the muscle, the heavier the weight it can lift. Muscular strength refers to the power output of each muscle and to its size.

- *Power* refers to the time it takes the muscle to do the work; it is strength combined with speed.
- *Endurance* refers to the number of times a muscle can contract or repeat the work effort before it becomes exhausted or fatigued. Muscular endurance refers to the muscle's ability to perform a number of times against resistance for the longest possible period of time. Muscular endurance is not only dependent on the individual muscle's development but also on the strength of the cardiovascular system to deliver fresh, oxygenated blood to the performing muscle, staving off the fatigue that results from the buildup of lactic acid. This buildup means that the oxygenated blood supply was not sufficient for the amount of work performed.
- *Muscular flexibility* refers to the muscles', joints', and tendons' ability to stretch and move quickly, gracefully, and efficiently as the muscles perform their work.

Walking Improves Body Composition and Helps Reduce Weight and Body Fat

Walking decreases the appetite by redirecting the flow of blood away from the digestive tract and stimulating the tract's use of blood fats instead of blood sugar. A diet program without exercise is considered undesirable because weight loss results in losing lean muscle tissue as well as body fat. Thus, weight loss without exercise leaves the body flabby.

Experience shows that without exercise mere dieting leads to a yo-yo effect, or swinging phenomenon, with the weight lost through crash diets being added back again since only the dieter's eating habits have been changed. Exercise like walking not only helps one lose weight but provides a good balance for overeating. The extra calories can be walked off with extra miles.

Physical activity includes a wide range of human activity, starting with reclining, sitting, standing, and then walking. These are all natural activities, but walking is definitely the most active one when measured in terms of caloric expenditure. It is the opposite of sedentary activity, characterized by or requiring much sitting or a habitual sitting posture. Another form of sedentary activity and worse, from the exercise point of view, is reclining. Also a less active behavior is standing without moving.

If you compare the energy demands of walking with those of reclining, sitting, and standing, you will quickly observe a dramatic difference. Reclining is often equated with the basal metabolic expenditure rate, also referred to as the basic or resting metabolic rate. This rate is the amount of calories your body burns just to stay alive and functioning. Sitting or standing quietly boosts the caloric expenditure approximately 25 percent over that of reclining—about 1.22 Kcal per minute as a mean average. This small increase reflects the low amount of muscle activity required for standing and sitting.

Surprisingly, there is little difference between standing and sitting in terms of caloric expenditure. Waitresses don't get much exercise in their jobs because they stand a lot. Standing, of course, produces more fatigue than sitting because of the extra weight the body must support that the chair does not support. But this fatigue is not the same kind that muscular activity produces.

When you start walking, a dramatic increase in caloric expenditure results because your body must work to move the individual body segments, accelerating and decelerating them, and also do this work against the force of gravity. It's interesting to note that the antigravity work factor present in walking is not present in other exercises such as bicycling, rowing a boat, or even swimming. This is because the body's weight is supported by the vehicle. It's as if you stayed in the seated position and just started moving. The energy increase of even very slow and level walking (i.e., at 1 mph, which is really almost a shuffle) is almost three times the caloric expenditure of standing and sitting. And it increases even more dramatically with the increase of walking speed. Just in the natural walking speed range of 1–3.5 mph, which is also known as the comfortable walking speed, it goes to 276 percent at 1.5 mph, to 316 percent at 2 mph, to 460 percent at 2.5 mph, 525 percent at 3 mph and 598 percent at 3.5 mph (and 762 percent at 4 mph), all compared to the alternative of sitting or standing.

You might think that these dramatic percentage increases can't be very significant since more vigorous activities like running and rope skipping would increase the caloric expenditure even more. This is certainly true, but you can't maintain these activities all day long like you can sitting, reclining, standing and walking. More intense activities, while providing a higher per-minute caloric expenditure, can only be maintained practically by most people for 30–60 minutes. If you want to maintain these activities continuously you would have to raise your level of fitness dramatically.

Walking Is Easier to Stick with than Other Exercises

Walking is easier to do than most exercises and is more fun. Even many professional athletes hate the running aspects of training because they are intense, painful, and not as exciting as the sport they are training for. Many beginning exercisers give up out of pain and boredom. Tests measuring the dropout rate of walking versus jogging exercise programs showed a 25 percent dropout rate for walking against 35–40 percent for jogging.

Walking for many exercisers is more interesting because it is conducted at a speed that enables the exerciser to talk and visit with his friends, explore natural surroundings, or even reflect on creative problems. While experienced and professional joggers claim many of these benefits for themselves, the majority of people must work too hard while jogging to get these pleasurable benefits. The intensity of the jogging activity makes talking with fellow joggers a physical feat in itself.

I have recently observed a yo-yo effect among my exercising friends and also among certain professional athletes. They adopt a vigorous training schedule for their marathon running race or for a swimming meet, training 40–60 hours a week. After they compete their training often drops to zero until months later, when they train for the next meet.

Walking Relieves Stress and Enhances Creativity

Walking relieves stress by steering us away from our daily problems. Plato said that walking is so relaxing "it could almost relieve a guilty conscience." Walking exercises relieve the tension in our bodies through the contraction and expansion of the muscles. High-intensity exercises like jogging, however, may have their own specially created stresses, particularly among beginners who are being asked to work beyond their capabilities. This produces mental as well as physical stress.

Walking works to reduce stress in the following ways.

- It provides a break—a minivacation—from constant stress.
- Physical exertion and concentration on the walking activity helps you forget about your daily problems, reduces anxiety, and thereby reduces your blood pressure.
- Walking helps elevate a person from a depression by developing a feeling of accomplishment. It requires patience and helps bring self-control into your life. Walkers have been known to give up such bad habits as overeating, drinking, nonproductive arguing, and smoking.
- It is believed that walking increases two chemicals in the brain known as endorphins and norepinephrines, which appear to have a mood-elevating effect.
- By improving the blood circulation, walking helps bring more oxygen to the brain, leading to a euphoric feeling.
- Walking improves creativity and problem-solving ability because the increased oxygen supply to the brain resulting from walking improves thinking ability and memory, lengthens concentration spans, and heightens clarity of thought. Since the oxygen supply in the brain is probably the highest during the walking period, the period would seem to be the most fertile period for new ideas and solutions. It may be no accident that many of the greatest thinkers—da Vinci, Plato, Aristotle, Rousseau, Kant, and Einstein—were also avid walkers.

Christopher Morley in his essay, *The Art of Walking* (published first in 1917), listed the great creative thinkers in the walker's hall of fame as Tennyson, FitzGerald, Matthew Arnold, Carlyle, Kingsley, Meredith, Richard Jeffries, George Borrow, Emily Bronte, Walt Whitman, G. M. Trevelyan, Hilaire Belloc, Edward Thomas Dickens, Edward Lucas, Holbrook Jackson, Pearsall Smith, Thomas Burke, Wordsworth, Coleridge, DeQuincey, Goldsmith, Vachel Lindsay, Keats, and others, concluding: "[s]ometimes it seems as though literature were a coproduct of legs and head."

Walking Assists in the Growth Development of Children and Fighting the Aging Process in Adults

Despite their natural proclivity toward physical activity, many children suffer from the same sedate behavior as adults. This results from modern conveniences and attractions such as television, station wagon, and telephone. It is the responsibility of parents to teach good exercise habits and help with the exercise activities of children, particularly before reaching school age. Parents should also watch out that schools provide for physical fitness programs and provide additional exercise activities if there is any shortfall.

Walking and the proper teaching of walking techniques will help the child first learn to walk properly and will result in better posture for that child and the avoidance of improper walking. It also will help control the weight of children in the critical years when overeating and overweight can lead to additional fat cell formation and development of bad health habits permanently affecting the child's later life. The hiking and walking skills taught children by their parents will translate into a love for the outdoors and for staying active.

There is a great deal of evidence to support the concept that we *learn* to be active. Children who walk to school instead of ride are in better physical condition and have a more active outlook on life, which translates into better self-control and a desire to participate in sports and remain active. Walking also smooths out the activity gaps between school sports seasons. Children can also use walking to get into shape for sports seasons. Running and more vigorous training devices may be too intense and stunt growth, particularly before age 16.

Walking is the exercise you can do your whole life. You don't have to stop because it is strenuous or produces injuries. If the person can stick with it, walking will help retard the aging process. Walking stimulates bone-growing cells and slows down the bone demineralization process, particularly in the legs. Thus, bones become stronger and are less likely to break. Walking also retards the emphysemalike changes in lungs, giving an older person a far greater breathing capacity. Walking exercises permit greater intake of nutritional food and better blood circulation that nourish cells while preventing obesity. In addition, rheumatoid arthritis and osteoarthritis can be retarded with walking. Walking makes and keeps older people more mobile, which is the key to being able to maintain one's independence from medical facilities and wheelchairs.

Some Walking Enthusiasts Claim Walking Even Improves Sexual Performance

As a person builds up his or her walking capabilities, the muscles become firm and strong, and the hips become more flexible. Sexual performance and creativity are thus enhanced. In addition, through walking, stamina and drive are increased, and the body becomes slim and alive, and the mental faculties keep a person in better touch with his or her senses.

Disadvantages of Walking Examined

The most significant disadvantage claimed for walking is that it has only limited value as a cardiovascular conditioner because it does not raise the heart level sufficiently (i.e., to more than 120 beats per minute) to achieve a training effect. This criticism has been disproven by medical tests where improvements in cardiovascular fitness were observed. Walking can be practiced in a wide range of speeds and levels of exertion, allowing persons at all fitness levels to improve their heart and circulation.

This criticism of walking's limited aerobic effect is based on only one style and one speed. The heartbeat rate with walking spans the whole range of zones below, in, and above the training zone. Furthermore, walking practiced at a low-intensity level can achieve similar results to those of high-intensity exercises if the former is practiced over a longer period. In other words, intensity of effort and duration of effort are interchangeable to a significant degree.

It is also claimed that walking does little for upper-body strength and the abdominal muscles, and that walking tightens up the hamstring muscles located at the back of the legs. Upper-body strength can be improved by swinging the arms rhythmically while walking or doing supplementary exercises that will be explained in Parts II and III. My own walking tests show in fact that walking does improve your stomach muscles significantly. Furthermore, certain types of walking, like marching and climbing, raise the leg level high enough to be the equivalent of stomach curls. Finally, most exercises and sports produce tightness of muscles. Stretching muscles before and after you exercise will eliminate the tightness walking may give them.

PART II

AN EXERCISE-WALKER'S CLINIC

This exercise clinic is devoted to the technical aspects of walking. You may have already unconsciously learned some of the skills covered in this part of the book but have forgotten them. You may never have learned others correctly in the first place. Chapter 3 will introduce you to all the skills you need to get the most from walking. In Chapter 4 are some basic techniques for stretching, warm-up, cool-down, and strengthening joints and muscles.

The concept of a clinic comes from the Greek word, *kleneke*, meaning art. It was first used by physicians to instruct classes of medical students and residents, demonstrating techniques and treating patients in front of the class. Today we have painting and writing clinics, marriage clinics, and running clinics, among many others. Any group situation in which the instructor gives advice on specific problems through demonstrations and has students practice what was shown can be called a clinic.

My walking clinic, like early Greek classes, is almost always conducted outdoors in as scenic a setting as possible. Although strict concentration is required to benefit from such instruction, the atmosphere of the clinic is informal, and the students are

These walking clinic photographs
perfectly illustrate how natural
surroundings and people of varied
backgrounds can be brought
together for their health
and enjoyment while learning
how to walk better.

encouraged to socialize and help each other by observing and correcting technical points. I take a more flexible approach with these clinics than you might find in other sports clinics. And no wonder, since you don't have to reserve court time, join the crowd at an exercise salon, or find a special track or field for practice. That is the beauty of walking: it can be done just about anywhere a group can congregate and hear and watch one another.

My exercisewalking sessions are usually one or two hours long, depending on the size of the class. The following outline of a typical session should give you an idea of how much time you should devote to its various components:

- 20 minutes of stretching and warm-up exercises,
- 20 minutes of instruction and practice of individual walking techniques,
- 45 minutes of workout exercises, and
- 15 minutes of cool-down.

In Chapter 3 we will discuss and describe the various walking techniques that are covered in my clinics during the second 20 minutes of a session. Once these techniques are mastered a majority of the session is devoted to the workout during which I watch each member of the class to ensure that they perform the techniques and exercises correctly. But of primary importance is time spent before and after instruction and workout to properly warm up and cool down. Chapter 4 will cover all you need to know to warm up effectively and get the most from exercisewalking or any other exercise regimen you choose. It will also cover strengthening exercises.

With this book I hope you will be able to study the photos and diagrams and to practice as you come across each technique in Chapter 3 and each exercise described in Chapter 4. Once you have mastered the technical points, you will be able to set the book down and apply them to your everyday walking. I have organized my material so you can teach walking techniques to yourself and to family and friends in a kind of miniclinic of your own. You can hold your clinic anyplace you want, whether it's in your backyard, at the city park, or on the trail of a state or national forest. You can structure it anyway you enjoy most as long as you remember to perform warm-up stretches before and after your technical practices, exercises, and routines. You have to have fun—and with walking that is the best part—to make the clinic effective.

With this part of the book you will begin to convert your everyday walking into a form of exercise that you will want to continue for the rest of your life.

3

WALKING TECHNIQUES

As discussed earlier, we do not finish learning how to walk until ages seven to nine. For some of us this was our grammar school of walking, where the teachers were our parents, though much of the walking was self-taught through trial and error and motivation. Most of us graduated successfully from this primary school of walking, but studies have shown that 25 percent flunked and still suffer improper walking form—duck-footed walking, pigeon-toed walking, poor posture, or favored-limb walking. The techniques that I will discuss in this chapter will address these problems as well as serve as a refresher course for the rest of the walking population who desire to get the most from this extraordinary body movement.

People often ask me why it's necessary to break down walking into specific techniques. While many people are naturally correct walkers, they often make mistakes when they do a lot of walking. When you are tired you must concentrate more on what you are doing and cannot rely on instincts alone. Furthermore, there are plenty of people who walk incorrectly and have done so for years. The incorrect walkers must literally relearn walking from the ground up.

Technique as applied to exercisewalking physiology means the body skills necessary to accomplish the exercise of walking itself. While many people walk properly by nature, if you ask them to describe what they are really doing, they probably couldn't tell you. That's because they execute their walking techniques without conscious thought. Learning walking techniques generally means understanding and applying the most efficient, scientifically determined movements and using them as body skills. You should learn and understand walking skills so that you will be able to explain them to others. The techniques you will learn in this chapter can also be used as exercises if they are practiced or repeated a number of times.

In Chapter 1 we defined the walking action; now we will refine it into a technique and then an exercise. Understanding, learning, and practicing the walking technique will help you control and extend your natural walking motion and enhance its exercise potential by widening your stride, increasing your speed, raising your level of endurance, and developing proper body alignment. Walking, like other sports and exercises, involves good techniques for efficient performance and avoidance of injuries, and developing good walking techniques will make your walking more dynamic and active. It will enable you to use walking for exercise purposes. These scientific walking techniques are derived not only from the experience of passionate walkers but also from athletic coaches, competitive and long-distance walkers, and scientists who have studied the walking action.

The techniques developed by these people have sharpened and defined the walking motion to make it function more smoothly and efficiently and to provide the walker with economy of movement and increased speed and endurance.

Remember, technique is not style; it is a basic synchronized movement. In Chapters 4 and 5 you will learn how to apply these techniques to your various walking styles and activities, but right now, you need to learn the techniques of walking.

Practice each of these techniques separately and slowly in the beginning before trying to put them together into one continuous walking motion. By practicing each technique over and over

Proper, relaxed posture.

Stiff, improper posture.

Left arm is naturally bent
and swinging back as left
leg strides forward.

Faster walking naturally
brings the arms to a 90-
degree angle to shorten
the swinging action.

again, you will program your body to do it properly. Soon this conditioning effect will make the individual movements reflexive so that you can again walk subconsciously and naturally but with greater precision. Even while doing your walking exercises, continue to practice your walking techniques. You may wish to focus on specific techniques in which you are weak and correct recurring errors.

Note: You may wish to read the section on strengthening exercises (pages 65–78) before practicing these techniques.

Technique #1

Holding Proper Posture while Walking

You have to work to keep your walking posture perfectly upright, balanced, and relaxed. As you practice your walking technique, you'll need to correct your sagging or contorted posture and bring it upright again. I suggest that you work with an observer or have someone film or videotape you from the side while walking.

Assume an erect posture with your toes pointing forward and your feet parallel to one another, approximately two to four inches apart. Your eyes and head should be pointing forward. Your head should remain level, not pointing downward or leaning from side to side. Your shoulders should be relaxed and back and not hunched up. The buttocks should be tucked in firmly. Sounds easy when you're standing still, but try to maintain this straight relaxed posture in the upper body while walking. It will take practice. When you do a lot of walking the strain tends to contort the body. Have someone observe you while you're walking fast, and you'll see what I mean. Your body will tend to lean forward when walking fast or when walking for a long period of time. This shortens your stride and after a while causes needless fatigue and back pain.

Also, when you are walking very fast your shoulders tend to raise themselves and bunch up around the neck. When walking longer distances or for longer periods of time you put your head down to look at the ground immediately beneath you. Bending the head down leads to unnecessary neck and back pains. To remain erect you must cast your eyes four or five yards forward.

Other walkers tend to lean from side to side, and a few lean too far backwards. Practicing walking with good posture and alignment from the beginning will make it easier for you to maintain your posture naturally and subconsciously.

Technique #2
Maintaining Parallel and Synchronized Movements for Arms, Legs, and Breathing

As mentioned above, your toes should be pointed forward, and the feet should move parallel to each other and be no more than two to four inches apart. The arms should be allowed to swing naturally in an arc about the shoulder. If you let this swinging motion happen naturally, you will see that the arm opposite the forward swinging leg will swing forward in a rhythmic, pendulumlike movement. This is a natural, flowing movement. Some people consciously or subconsciously hold the arms by their sides and do not let them swing with the leg motion. For normal walking style, the arms hang straight down and swing like a pendulum. For a faster walking style the arm is bent at a 90-degree angle, shortening the pendulum swing to conform to the quicker leg movements.

Breathing motion, exhale/inhale, is also synchronized with the leg–arm motion. While walking slowly you should breathe slowly and rhythmically and inhale for the first step and exhale for the next step and so on. When walking faster, you can inhale on two steps, exhale on the next two steps, and so forth. You set the cadence of your breathing.

Breathe Count Example

Normal Walking Speed

    Two Count: left, right   and   left, right

                   inhale   **exhale**

Fast Walking

    Four Count: left, right, left, right and left, right, left, right

                i n h a l e   **e x h a l e**

You can make up your own variations as long as your breathing remains rhythmic and is synchronized with your leg and arm movements. Breathing rhythmically also requires concentration and practice. When practicing, it is useful to count cadences out loud or to yourself. After a while, however, it will become second nature.

Technique #3
Heel Strike and Placement

Many walkers don't realize that they land on their heels first when walking. This landing, called the *heel strike,* must be done properly to be effective and produce proper body alignment. To start, you must find a gait or width of foot placement that allows for the width of your thighs and the general weight carried by your body. Ideally, the heel and subsequently the entire foot should be placed with toes pointed in the direction of travel, not more than two inches apart. Wider placement is undesirable because it will cause the body to sway from side to side, producing inefficient extraneous motion similar to the waddling of a duck. While you should remain flexible about which width you choose, be aware that efficient walking is done with a narrower width so that the legs don't have so far to travel and only straight back/straight forward motions are made. As you walk faster, your feet will almost touch each other.

The proper heel strike involves placing the heel at about a 40-degree angle from the ground. The foot and leg are then at a 90-degree angle with each other. The back edge of the heel should strike first. Your foot should be lifted slightly to the outside so that you will be able to roll on that side to the toe. Before rolling forward on your foot, practice walking on the outside of your heels to further emphasize this important phase of the walking motion. Setting your ankle slightly to the outside will help prevent an undesirable internal rotation of the leg, which may lead to knee pains and injuries. Sloppy walkers often land flat-footed on the whole surface of the bottom of their foot. This not only slows down the walk but causes proper leg muscle development and body alignment to be lost.

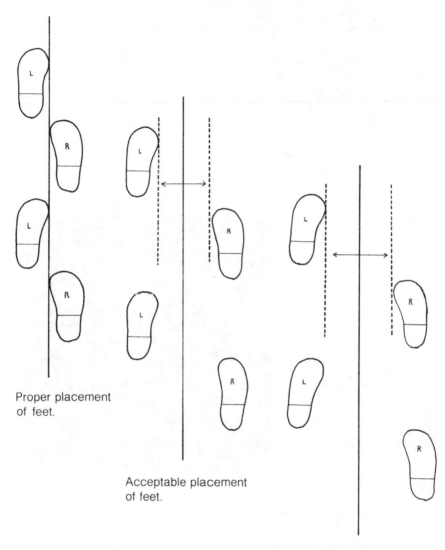

Proper placement
of feet.

Acceptable placement
of feet.

Wide foot placement
that is acceptable when
carrying a heavy pack.
Width depends on
weight of pack.

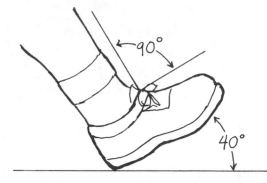

Heel-toe angle
of the heel strike.

Set your ankle slightly to
the outside to prevent an
internal rotation of the leg
that could lead to knee
pains and injuries.

Technique #4
Leg Pull/Heel–Toe/Roll–Push

This technique is begun from the support phase of walking. To get there from a standing position, swing your leg forward on the heel and freeze in this position. Your back leg should be balanced on the ball of your rear foot. Although this position is difficult to hold for more than a few seconds, it is good to practice holding it with each step while further lengthening your stride and trying to maintain proper upper body balance and posture.

The leg pull involves lifting the rear foot by pushing off with the toe straight back and pulling the leg forward under the body, slightly bending the knee as it passes. Next, stretch out the leg and bend the ankle before placing the heel down. As the back leg pulls, the forward foot rolls from the outer edge of the heel along the outside edge of the foot and pushes off when it reaches the ball of the foot. While the heel–toe/rolling motion is taking place, the rear leg has passed by the forward leg, putting it in the position for its own strike and toe-off. Do this technique gently, or you will push off in the wrong direction.

Freezing in this position gives you an appreciation for the muscles involved in the support phase of walking. The next series of photos will focus on integrating the actions involved in walking.

When practicing the leg pull and heel–toe/roll–push, it is best to let the arms fall and only concentrate on this one technique. You can even let the head drop from time to time to check that you have placed the heel properly. Look back also at your toe-off position. Many beginners don't push straight back with the ball of their feet but to the side. This causes a loss of energy and parallel movement. At the toe-off, the leg should be fully extended. Likewise, at the heel strike, the front leg should be fully extended.

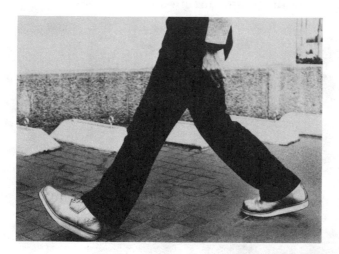

Heel plant at 40-degree angle.

Back edge of heel should strike first.

Now try to put it all together. When practicing techniques, you should first try to concentrate on each one separately. Then integrate two at a time before finally trying them all at once. The result should be a fluid and rhythmic motion. When you've managed to synchronize all the walking techniques, look at your shadow on the side of the street or a wall while walking and note whether your head bobs up and down. Try to keep your head and body at one level throughout the walking cycle.

After you have learned the techniques, you should try to feel

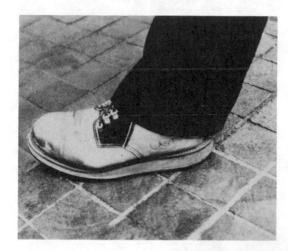

Roll on the outside edge of the foot from heel to toe.

Thrust with the right leg toe off gives you forward acceleration.

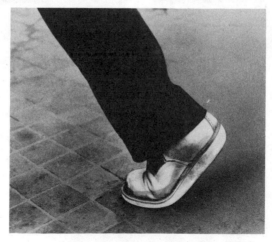

A Breakdown of the Walking Action

- Hold your head and back erect with buttocks tucked in tightly. Walking tall gives you a higher center of gravity.

- Reach out with your hip, knee, and heel, pointing your toes in the direction of travel.

- Plant the heel of your forward moving foot at a 40-degree angle— leg and foot are at a 90-degree angle.

- Back edge of the heel should strike first. Your ankle should be set slightly to the outside.

- Pull forward with the leading leg while pushing straight back with the other leg until the toe off.

- The toe off with the rearward leg gives your acceleration.

- Each leg performs two separate actions to pull the body forward over the leading leg. Once over that leg, the other action is that same leg pushing the body forward.

- In the "swing phase," the leg is not PUSHING OR PULLING, BUT REACHING FORWARD after the toe off to become the supporting leg again.

- Use the arms in a smooth and powerful style.

- Eliminate up-and-down and side-to-side movements.

rather than observe your walking movements. Since trying to look at yourself will throw off your alignment, try instead to mentally visualize or feel each technique as you move forward.

Imagine while you're walking that your hips are or your trunk is moving along in a straight line and that your leg is lifting and pulling under the body. Imagine too that your toes are pointed forward just before the ankle bends and that the toe is up before the heel strikes. When the heel rolls on the outer edge of your foot to your toe, visualize a rolling motion almost as if your shoes were built with rockers. Feel how all your leg muscles are pulling and pushing, contracting and expanding, while all this happens. Don't forget to tuck in the buttocks, as they tend to stick out after awhile from the pulling and straining. Now look again at your upper body posture. Don't give up. It will take practice. In the end you will be grooving your walking muscles just like other sportsmen groove their muscles for greater precision.

These techniques are basic and can be utilized with any walking style and practiced during any walking activity. Feel free to modify the techniques with respect to width or stride, arm motion, the force of the heel strike, and the push-off. Otherwise, the techniques will remain the same for the wide range of walking styles and activities. There are some additional techniques that will help you improve your speed, rhythm, and leg strength for walking.

Technique #5
Stride Stretch

While walking, you should practice reaching out with the forward-moving leg. One way to do this is to rotate the hip down and forward, reaching out with the leg a few extra inches than you're normally used to doing. By maintaining your erect posture while walking, you'll keep your center of gravity higher, which will give you a fuller leg extension. Stride length and speed are related. Studies show that the average stride grows from 89 percent of body height for the average walker to 106 percent of body height for the fast walker. Stretching exercises will also help you prepare the muscles and tendons for an increased stride.

The side stretch.

Technique #6
Arm Swing and Breathing

This is a racewalking as well as a sprinter's technique, which you needn't do as vigorously as when you do your walk sprinting exercises. Your arms should be bent at a 90-degree angle, and your hands should make a loosely clenched fist. The arms should swing, just brushing your side in a straight forward/straight backward motion. On the forward motion they should swing as high as the chest. On the back swing the elbow should almost reach shoulder level. Before trying them while walking, practice your arm swinging and breathing by standing still. Synchronize your arm swing with your breathing like you did with your leg swing. Count cadences to yourself in either 2/4 or 4/4 time.

Inhale on left-arm swing.   Exhale on right-arm swing.

Technique #7
The Straight-Arm Swing Variation

Of course, you don't have to use the bent-arm swing technique in every exercisewalking situation, particularly when fast walking speeds are not part of your routine or if you are not doing any of the heavy arm workouts like those described later in Chapter 12. Because it's a longer and therefore slower pendulum, the straight-arm swing technique is preferable at low and moderate walking speeds. However, when weights are used on hands or wrists, the bent-arm swing is preferable, even at low walking speeds.

You can execute the straight-arm swing by keeping the arm slightly crooked at the elbow. With walking speeds of 1–3 mph the arm swings forward at a 30- to 45-degree angle and back at an angle that is slightly less. As you increase your speed, the angle will become larger. Of course, you can accentuate this angle as you see fit.

Let the arm hang naturally when starting the swing. Like a pendulum, it will compliment your walking pace. As your arm swings upward, the inside will turn slightly outward. By pumping your straight arms you will, as with the bent-arm swing technique, be able to help propel yourself forward.

The straight-arm swing technique has the advantage of being applicable to everyday walking situations by allowing you to do your exercisewalking without standing out in a crowd. The straight-arm swing also gives your shoulder muscles more exercise because swinging a straight arm takes more effort than swinging a bent one.

Technique #8
Walk Climbing

Since you will be doing a fair amount of walking up hills, stairs, and other inclines, you should learn the proper techniques now. There's a tendency in normal walking to take stairs and hills on the balls of the feet, omitting the heel strike. This will produce sore calf muscles and Achilles tendons. Therefore, walk up hills by placing your heel down first, even though it feels like you are pressing it down. You will feel the calf muscle stretch when you are doing this.

Flat-footed walking is not a proper technique and will only make the walk climber tire faster because he is trying to balance himself on only one part of his feet. Therefore, press the heel back as shown in photos. Note: You will find that you lean your body forward to counterbalance an incline. While leaning forward is an acceptable technique, it will vary with the degree of the incline.

Walking on the Downside

There are also special walking techniques and skills you use when descending an incline. First keep your posture erect, though you will have to lean backward to compensate for the sharp grade on some inclines. (On most stairs, where the descent is graded, you can maintain a fully erect posture throughout.) Place the heel strike down first. As with ascending, don't get caught in

Walk climbing.

the trap of walking on the balls of your feet. With stair and some hill-walking descents you will not be able to flex your ankle as fully as on flat ground in the heel-toe roll. Therefore, be prepared to walk flat-footed down stairs. This is acceptable as long as you don't go any farther forward and step on the balls of your feet. Going downhill, flat-footed walking will be less of a problem.

Brake Step

On really steep inclines, especially over rugged terrain, it will be necessary to turn your foot sideways and use it like a brake. Walking straight down such inclines can be dangerous, and you should use the "brake step." Of course, your step length will shorten on most downward walks. And you will be using more of the muscles on the front of your leg to assist with the braking action. Try to walk down every incline you walk up. This way you'd use both the front and back muscles of your legs in an even manner.

Rest Step

This is a special stepping technique used for ascending (and sometimes descending) at high altitudes. It differs from the normal walking steps in that you do not swing through with the toeing off leg but merely bring it up to the forward leg and no farther. Once even, you again extend the leg just placed down forward. Once it is set, you bring the back leg even with the forward one. This forward motion amounts to a series of slow half-steps creating a rest period in between each step, thereby extending the period of the double-support phase. You'll soon find out that at high altitudes this is the only way to keep going forward.

Exercises to Improve Techniques

Sometimes the only way to learn a new technique properly is to exaggerate it. This is certainly the case with the following four technique exercises that serve a double purpose to improve your technique and also to stretch and make more flexible the joints and tendons you will use in executing your walking techniques.

The Arm Pump

We have already seen how pumping the arm and synchronizing breathing while standing improves the same action while walking.

The Goose Step

While the Stride Stretch is used both as a stretching and a stride-lengthening technique, it can be supplemented with a hip-extending or hip-walking exercise called the Goose Step. With the stride stretch you learned the importance of the hips in dynamic walking. By extending the hips as well as the legs you can lengthen your stride and thereby increase your speed. To get a feel for how your hips help move your legs farther along, try goose-stepping with stiff legs, raising them as high and as far as you can. Repeat these goose-stepping exercises as you do your heel and toe walks, and you will notice how it feels to stretch your stride by using more hip action when you walk. I recommend that you do this exercise out of sight of onlookers who may misunderstand your purpose and take offense.

The Heel and Toe Walks

These are two exercise techniques (see page 57) that will help develop ankle flexibility and improve the heel-toe and toe-off techniques. Once you get into the heat of walking or get tired after a long walk, there is a tendency to place the foot down flat rather than on the heel first. The rolling motion also is often skipped when the foot and ankle become tired and stiff. The heel walk is a good exercise for improving flexibility and teaching yourself the full motion of the heels and ankles. The toe walk is the complement to the heel walk and helps with the toe-off phase.

The Leg-Lift Technique

Like marching in place, the leg-lift technique is the walker's equivalent of jogging in place but involves higher leg lifts that sometimes reach as high as the chest. Once you've practiced the technique you'll be able to walk more effectively over rugged terrain. Leg lifting involves three height levels. Low is 6–12 inches off the ground, medium is 12–24 inches, and high is so high that the top of your thigh is touching your chest. In Chapter 11 we'll show you how leg lifting can also be used on a progressive basis. This is quite strenuous and should be done in a series of exercise techniques for muscle building and aerobic training.

Leg-lifting techniques not only strengthen the stomach muscles but, if done for periods of 5–12 minutes, constitute by themselves an aerobic fitness exercise. Leg lifts are better than jogging in place because you control the velocity and pressure of your foot hitting the ground. You also are able to lift your legs higher, giving your leg muscles a greater range of motion. If the leg lifts are done with outstretched legs, they are also good for stretching the hamstring muscles.

Techniques for Correcting Special Problems

Before starting each training session you might take an inventory of your progress in mastering walking techniques. This

Heel walking.

section will cover some common problems you will encounter in the execution of proper technique and provide some tips for solving those problems.

Slouch Walking

As we already discussed, maintaining proper posture is difficult even while standing or sitting. And it certainly becomes a challenge when walking for exercise. Posture problems come from two principal sources: bad habits and the weakening of stomach and back muscles from being out of shape. The act of trying to maintain correct posture is itself an exercise, albeit an isometric one.

Slouching will further aggravate any back problems you may have. While done out of alignment any body movement puts extra weight on the skeletal structure instead of the body muscles. The displaced center of gravity tends to unnaturally jog the vertebrae, leading to a sore neck and sore back soon after you have walked a few miles.

The solution is not simple and will require constant attention, particularly if you have poor posture to begin with. The following are some tips to help you correct slouch walking and improve your overall posture on a permanent basis:

1. Don't look down toward the ground while walking. Focus your eyes 10–15 feet in front of you. If your head is bent and not straight, your neck and shoulders will follow. All these parts are attached, so bending one bends the others.

2. Hold in your stomach muscles. Usually weak stomach muscles are the basis of back problems. You can do this even while breathing. It's also probably the easiest way to strengthen these muscles. But it also tends to straighten your posture as you do it. After awhile you won't even notice that you are holding in these muscles; they will hold in themselves when the stomach muscles are no longer contributing to holding up the back and spine, the weight of the body begins to rest on the lower back and then starts to lean forward to help prevent stress.

3. Tuck in your buttocks even while standing still. With the buttocks tucked in, the walking action will not only naturally lengthen your stride but will also help keep your

posture straight. Whenever you notice yourself slouching, tuck in your buttocks and hold that posture. This will contribute greatly to posture improvement and maintenance.

4. Hold your shoulders back. If, after you have applied and practiced the stomach and buttocks tuck, you still have slouching problems, you should practice holding your shoulders back and simultaneously hold your head high but not back. When you wear a backpack for some of the walking exercises described in this book, you'll notice that the load of the pack will also pull your shoulders back.

Backpackers with heavy packs can slouch, too. They often do this in a vain attempt to carry the body forward with the heavy pack by leaning forward. You have to develop good posture independently of outside artificial devices but with your own muscles and determination to straighten up. The only exception to straight posture is in hill walking, where some forward lean will be allowed to compensate for the imbalance the incline causes. Backpacks that put you off-balance and require forward leaning are too heavy and require a pack frame to distribute some of the weight to the trunk of your body.

Duck-Footed and Pigeon-Toed Walking

Walking with parallel leg and foot movements will help to correct these two problems, depicted on the step charts on page 60. However, the problems may be more pronounced with persons who have walked this way all their lives. Persons who are overweight often develop duck-footed walking because their fat thighs force them to do this. My recommendation is to walk with a wider stance—particularly the one shown on page 43, recommended for backpackers—until the thighs are trimmer. Practicing the heel walk described on page 56—walking on the outer edges of the heels—will also help correct this condition.

Pay particular attention to walking on the outer edges of your heels. Walking in old-style snowshoes may also cause you to walk duck-footed. Recently manufacturers have been making walking-style snowshoes, which are built narrower so that the shoes can pass by one another. These are better for exercisewalking.

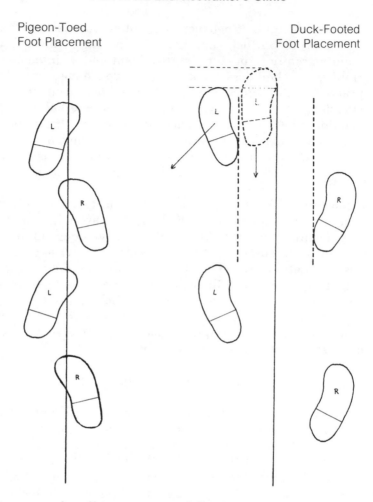

Pigeon-Toed
Foot Placement

Duck-Footed
Foot Placement

Pigeon-toed walking is not as difficult to correct as duck-footed walking. For this problem I suggest you exaggerate pointing your toes. After the toe-off and before the heel strike, picture in your mind how you are controlling the forward direction of your feet by pointing them straight in the direction of your travel.

Favored-Leg Walking

If you hear a thump-thump sound when you walk, you are probably favoring the thumping leg over the other one. By practicing your heel–toe roll and your posture-building exercises you should bring your body into balance so that the weight is evenly distributed over both your legs. Hearing the thumping, you know too that you have to shift your weight to the thump side. By concentrating on the forward flow of your legs and placing each heel strike purposefully you will have to improve your basic walking stance. Get it into proper balance so you can correctly execute these movements.

Lifting

Lifting is the opposite of slouching. In other words, you are letting your body rise up and down in an exaggerated manner. You've probably seen or experienced this type of walking—it looks like Frankenstein's monster trying to race or speed walk. What's really happening is that you are trying to lift your body up to move it forward. But it doesn't work because you are going more up and down than forward. Usually your shoulders hunch up and you start walking on the balls of your feet while skipping the heel–toe roll.

The solution to lifting problems is to slow down. If you have to lift your body to get more speed, you are neglecting other walking techniques. By dropping back to a slower speed and concentrating on your techniques, particularly the application of the heel–toe roll and the placement of the heel strike, you can eliminate lifting. You will replace the vertical, lifting action with more hip thrust and heel–toe roll. Once you have established this basic form, you can work on increasing your speed.

There's one exception to this solution—the walk sprinting routine on page 164. There, you are allowed to walk as fast as you can as part of a speed routine to see how fast you can get your legs moving. As you practice walk sprinting in conjunction with other walking techniques you will see how you can bring your body lifting under control.

Shuffling and Scraping

You probably heard it at least once in your life: "Pick up your feet!" Well, that admonition doesn't go away when you're exercisewalking. The klutzes among us trip, stumble, and sometimes fall if we hit a bump or some other unevenness on the trail or road. But for the more sophisticated low-leggers, it's the occasional scraping sound. Both problems indicate that our feet are traveling too close to the ground. For the scrapers and shufflers the solution requires a conscious mental effort to raise the height of our legs on the lift-off. For the stumblers a more radical solution is recommended. See the leg-lifting exercises prescribed on page 56. For the occasional scrape, however, remember that no one can account for every unforseen bump in the road.

Leg lifts or marching in place can also be a good cure for chronic shufflers and scrapers (see page 170).

Tired from Too Much Technique

Sometimes when your legs feel tired you don't have to stop walking. Here's a little trick to give yourself a "walking massage." After completing your heel strike, instead of straightening up the leg, bend it to sink down a few inches and then up again. Do this on the other leg just after it completes the heel strike. It reminds me of how Groucho Marx walked in his comedy films, and it works great for refreshing your legs if they're sore from lots of walking.

You can walk quite a distance using this method of bending slightly down in the knee with each step. Or you can alternate doing it for a few steps with the right leg only and then the left. It will contract your leg muscles in a different way, thereby providing a massaging effect for your sore muscles. Do this type of walking until your legs feel better and resume your normal style.

A Note to Parents

Teaching children walking techniques can start during the period when you teach them how to walk (i.e., ages 9 months to two years old). But it can also continue throughout the formative years of their gait development (up to age nine). With toddlers it is important to observe their walking development, looking out for parallel leg movements. Teach your children to avoid pigeontoed or duck-footed walk behavior and play with them to make learning to walk fun. Above all, have patience.

A child just learning to walk is in a very sensitive and precarious position. The motion is brand-new, and the child should not be rushed or made to learn too fast. Don't make the child's natural curiosity for experimentation into a structured and regimented series of lessons. Allow the child room to experiment on his own. And give the child lots of encouragement, support, and praise. Don't be too technical with the child. Your job is really to encourage and to provide overall guidance so that your child doesn't develop any bad walking habits.

Children of ages three to six have already learned the basics of walking but should still be watched for bad habits. You can get more technical here, but make it into a game rather than serious classroom-type work. Try it as show and tell. Say, "Watch what Mommy's doing. Can you do that, too?" Children at this age should be encouraged to walk, of course, within the confines of the backyard, apartment, or country place. Walking games like "So Many Times Around the House or Backyard" can be devised to encourage walking. If the parents are doing their daily exercisewalking, they can bring these preschoolers along. Let them try the techniques. But again, do not force them. At this age walking should not be the only physical activity children pursue. It should be part of game playing, ball-playing, and other activities to make the child active.

Children of ages seven to nine are in school and can become very active walkers and learners of walking techniques. Now they can definitely accompany their parents on fitness walks and practice walking techniques right along with them. This is the age range for instilling in them the benefits and pleasures of walking and its importance in leading an active life. They should learn that being carted around in a station wagon is for babies. They should be given as many opportunities to walk as possible. Some children will be joining the Scouts and begin to apply walking techniques to their hiking and other outdoor activities.

Youngsters of ages 10–12 should be participating in a comprehensive exercise program and can become full participants with the parents in learning the walking techniques. While running at this age is permissible, long-distance running should not be used to supplant long walks. The latter are safer.

Walking for fitness as well as health can be introduced to the preadolescent child. The child will have the ability to learn and even to teach the walking techniques. He or she will also have a healthy respect for walking as an exercise. Walking should be treated as a choice and not a requirement, however. The child should be free to engage in a wide variety of activities, still having a healthy respect for using walking instead of motorized transportation whenever possible. Also, parents should work with scout troops and schools in emphasizing walking techniques as part of outdoor and fitness training.

Parents and children can participate in many natural walking opportunities that will stimulate the child's interest in walking and walking techniques. Almost every weekend some kind of walking activity is held in most communities, whether it is a hike, a bird walk, or a walkathon. These will serve as great opportunities to practice walking techniques with your children.

4

STRETCHING AND STRENGTHENING CALISTHENICS

On one of my long-distance walks I learned the value of warming up before, and cooling down after, a strenuous hike. By trying to increase my walking from 25 to 30 miles a day I began to neglect my "basic four" stretching exercises, which I had used religiously for the previous weeks. The result of this experiment was soon felt—*by my third stretchless day I had developed shin splints*. A *shin splint* is the pain that occurs in the front of the lower leg when the calf muscles of the back lower leg overpower the relatively weaker muscles in the front. This tightness in the lower leg is so painful that every step hurts. Shin splints usually take two or three weeks to heal completely.

Shin splints are not that common with normal walking or hiking, but I neglected to stretch and pushed too hard for long distance. Although I had no choice but to continue my walk, I had to endure more days of walking injured than I would have had I taken the extra time to stretch each morning and evening. Instead of building up to 30 miles a day, my daily mileage—when I walked at all—fell to 12–15. Believe me, it's a helluva way to learn a lesson about the importance of warming up and cooling down for sessions of exercising, whether walking, running, or whatever.

Thus, exercise experts have long recommended stretching before and after periods of exercise for good reason. Doing so warms up your muscles and limbers up your joints and tendons. Stretching will help you perform better by giving you a wider range of upper-body movements while you are exercisewalking. Stretching exercises warm up the muscles so they slide on each other rather than tear during vigorous activity; they also get your heart pumping faster. After an exercise session stretching serves to keep overcontracted muscles from getting stiff and sore.

While the walking action is, in a sense, its own stretching exercise, an exercisewalking workout longer than 15 minutes or at a speed of more than four mph will cause muscle tightening. Certain calisthenics will not only warm up muscles but stretch them for a wider and more relaxed walking stride. Such light exercises tend to gear the body for further vigorous activity. As you progress to higher repetitions of calisthenics, your muscles will be strengthened and toned on top of the benefits you receive from the walking action itself.

Basic Four Stretching Exercises

The basic four stretching exercises are particularly useful for walkers because they help to widen the walker's stride for a quicker pace. The first stretching exercise is the *Achilles and Calf Stretch* and stretches parts of the leg that you use in pushing off in the toe-off phase of the walking cycle. The second basic stretching exercise is the *Standing Hamstring Stretch*, which stretches the muscles in the back of the thighs. These muscles tend to tighten up when doing a lot of walking. The third stretching exercise is the *Quadriceps Stretch*, which is excellent for the front thigh muscles and gives you the ability to extend your leg for a wider walking stride. The fourth basic stretch is the *Flying Lunge*, which helps increase your stride and opens up your chest cavity.

These basic stretching exercises should be done before any kind of vigorous workout and squeezed in at the end of a workout, or before and after a long walking day. If a leg muscle feels tight or inflexible whenever you are walking, don't hesitate to stop and use one of these exercises to stretch it—this is called "first aid," and it cures what could develop into a serious problem.

Achilles and Calf Stretch

The Achilles tendons and the calf muscles work together to propel the legs and very often tighten up if not properly warmed up prior to extended activity. Stand facing a tree or wall with one leg forward and the other leg back. Keeping the backward heel flat on the ground and the knee straight, lean forward slowly and note the pulling sensation in the back of that calf. Hold this position for 10–15 seconds and release slowly. *Do not bounce.* Perform 10–15 times, then reverse leg positions, or alternate positions for a total of 20–30 times.

Standing Hamstring Stretch

There are four hamstring muscles in the thigh, two on the inside and two on the outside. Because all four have to be stretched, touching the toes does not adequately fulfill your needs and may put unnecessary stress on the lower back.

To stretch the hamstrings properly, raise one leg on the back of a chair or park bench so it is approximately two feet off the ground. (This height will vary for each individual's needs, so determine what object to use on the basis of sturdy support and ready availability as well as height.) With the heel supported and the knee straight, turn the foot inward and lean toward the toes until you feel a good stretch. Hold the position for 10–15 seconds and release slowly. There's no need to touch toes. Rotate the leg so your toes are straight up and lean forward again, holding for 10–15 seconds. You should feel the stretch move from the outside of the back of the leg to the middle. Release slowly; then turn your foot outward and lean into the stretch again. Hold for 10–15 seconds and feel the stretch move to the inside of the hamstring muscle. Release slowly and do the same for your other leg, stretching at the three stations just described.

Achilles and Calf Stretch done in a forest (above) and in the city.

Standing Hamstring
Stretch done in the city
(above) and on the trail.

69

Quadriceps Stretch for
right and left legs.

Flying Lunge Stretch with daypack for extra stress.

Quadriceps Stretch

Your quadriceps muscles stabilize the knees and lift the legs during the swinging phase of the walking cycle. For a proper stretch stand erect and balance on one foot with that leg straight. Reaching behind you, grasp your other leg by the ankle. Gently pull on the ankle to stretch your thigh. Repeat for your other leg.

The Flying Lunge

A difficult but very worthwhile stretching exercise, the Flying Lunge helps increase your stride length by stretching your pelvic area and the tops of your thighs. The "flying" part of the movement stretches your abdominals and opens up your chest cavity. This stretch is difficult for most people at first, but you will learn to love it because it also tests your sense of balance as well as some of the leg muscles you will use in your exercisewalking routines.

To perform the Flying Lunge, take a long step back with one of your legs. Hold your arms out for balance and keep both feet pointed straight ahead. Keeping your back straight and hips untwisted, lunge forward until your forward knee is above your toes and raise your arms overhead. As you perform this move-

ment, let gravity do the work by keeping your pelvis tucked in.
Stretch farther, keeping the front knee over the toes and breathing into the position. Hold for 20 seconds or so. Then lower your arms and pull out of the lunge, relax, and repeat for the other leg.

Warm-Up and Cool-Down

The stretching exercises just described are the basic, absolute minimum stretching exercises you need to do to warm up and cool down for exercisewalking workouts. You will hit the primary walking muscles and can be on your way if time is an important factor. If you wish to improve your flexibility and upper-body strength, however, you should consider a wider variety of light calisthenics. And there are literally hundreds of such movements to choose from. Exercise books of all kinds borrow from dance, yoga, and gymnastics, and from Army boot camp and the Mounties. I won't go into detail on which ones you should choose—it's entirely up to you—except to say that you should look for a balanced assortment that stretches all of your major muscle groups equally.

The purpose of warming up and cooling down is to stretch the major joints and muscle groups from head to toe with special emphasis on the ones actively and supportively involved in the walking cycle. The calves and hamstrings are active in the walking cycle, while the back and neck muscles would be considered supportive. Ideally, you can start with the basic three or four stretching exercises and then follow up with exercises that stretch supportive muscles and that can be done while actually walking—much like going through the gears on a car, you gradually get warmed up and ready for your exercisewalking workout.

Calisthenics Done While Walking

My experience shows that the following calisthenics can be done while walking slowly. They should be performed in the following order:

Head Rolls—Head rolls can help cure a stiff neck and relax your neck so it will not get stiff from intense exercisewalking sessions. There are three variations:

1. Roll your head to the right all around the head and then roll to the left all around. Repeat 3−5 times.
2. Rotate your head to the right three times and then to the left three times. This not only stretches but strengthens the neck muscles.
3. Move your head down three times and back three times. You should watch where you're going before doing this one.

Do all three variations. Remember to do these before the end of your exercisewalking session as a cool-down exercise.

Shoulder Shrug—A number of variations also exist for shoulder shrugs. You can do 8−10 counts to the beat of your walking steps—simply lift your shoulders up, keeping your back and neck straight. Do five of these at first and build up to ten. Then do another five, rotating the shoulders in the shrugging motion. You can also alternate shoulders, shrugging one at a time, but this is more difficult to do while keeping your balance.

Windmills and Other Arm-Shoulder Rotations—Instead of swinging your arms back and forth as you walk, use a straight-arm swing and bring it up and around the shoulder. Alternate arms. By timing your swings properly, you'll find they will counterbalance your forward-moving leg. Keeping the elbows straight, repeat the rotations for 16−30 paces, or 8−15 paces per arm.

Almost anything goes when doing these upper body rotations. Here are a few suggestions for additional stretching once you have mastered the basic one just described:

- Stretch your arms upward, grabbing for the sky as you walk.
- Do some shadowboxing using arms and bending at the waist and neck.
- Circle your arms, flap your arms, and so on.

Trunk Rotations—Start by grasping your left hand with your right hand. Your clasped hands should form a cradle. As you step off with the right foot, swing your cradled arm in the direction of your right foot. As the left foot advances, swing the arms in the direction of the advancing foot. Continue these side rotations with each advancing step. As you become more comfortable and stretched, you can rotate your body farther backward with each swing by rotating the head with your arms.

These stretching and limbering techniques can be completed in a smooth series in about 5–10 minutes while walking at a relatively slow pace. There's nothing preventing you from doing a little stretching or rotating anytime you walk, especially when you are tense or sore. This can keep you going and exercise your upper body more than what can be done with just the arm-swing techniques given in Chapter 3.

With enough practice and an uncrowded walking path, almost all the calisthenic routines that can be done standing can be done while walking. It's efficient, fun, and sometimes challenging. These basic warm-up exercises will also prepare you for advanced techniques and exercises using weights, which will be discussed in Chapter 12.

Upper-Body Strengthening

Walking by itself will not provide sufficient upper-body strength. None of the other aerobic exercises will do so either, except possibly, swimming. Therefore, you have to supplement any aerobic or endurance exercise regimen with upper-body calisthenics to maintain or improve overall physical fitness.

We have already covered some upper-body exercises that can be done while walking. The exercises described in this section cannot be done in that way and should probably be done after you are finished exercisewalking. You may decide to perform weight training or some other form of progressive resistance regimen, but for the purposes of this book I intend merely to supply rudimentary exercises that can be done almost anywhere and require no special equipment—just the natural weight of your body and limbs.

Again, I suggest that you must decide on the kind of exercise program you wish to follow and choose which exercises will be a part of it. Just remember to keep a balance among the muscle groups for which each exercise is suited. If you exercise one muscle group more than another, you risk creating an imbalance in strength and tone that could lead to injury.

The major muscle groups of the upper body are found in the arms, chest, back, abdomen, and neck. The exercises I have chosen to highlight are very basic and conveniently involve more than one of these muscle groups.

Push-Ups

This well-known exercise stresses the chest, the shoulders, and the triceps muscles of the arms. It can be done a number of ways, and some variations change the angles of stress on the muscles. Thus, this exercise can provide some body shaping along with strengthening and toning. The basic movement for those who are out of shape (men as well as women) is to start with arms straight and hands shoulder width apart, on the ground or floor supporting the torso on your knees, back straight. For those in better shape (men *and* women), support the torso on the toes.

Basic Push-Up—From one of the starting positions just described, lower your torso by bending your arms directly out from your sides. Keep your back, hips, and legs straight throughout this movement. When your chest lightly touches the ground or floor, push yourself back up. Repeat until you can do no more. As you get into shape—get stronger, lose weight—this basic exercise will become easier to do, but it is a high-repetition exercise and to be able to do 40–60 *in a minute* is not an unrealistic (albeit in most cases long-range) goal. Some of the variations described next are easier, some harder, and some, as mentioned before, produce slightly different effects.

Push-Up Variations—*Standing Push-Ups* can be done leaning against walls or with hands braced on the sides of an open doorway. These are somewhat easy and should definitely be repeated until you can do no more. *Bench Push-Ups* can be done outside using a park bench or indoors using a chair. There are two ways to use the bench: place your hands on it or place your feet on it. You can imagine which is the more difficult! *Weighted Push-Ups* involve using weight to increase the effect of gravity on your arms and shoulders while doing push-ups in any of the already mentioned ways. All these variations are done in the same strict style as the basic Push-Up: arms lowering and raising the torso; elbows moving out from the sides; and neck, back, hips, and legs straight.

Sit-Ups

While not perfect, the variations of the basic sit-up exercise are probably the best waist or abdominal exercise that can be done without a lot of special equipment. In certain cases that depend on where you are or if you are alone, you may not be able to perform the basic sit-up, which requires that you anchor your legs for perfect strictness. Therefore, some of the variations will be preferred by the lone exercisewalker in the wilderness.

Basic Sit-Up—To anchor your legs, either have a training partner hold your ankles down or hook your feet under a park bench, the living room couch, or the straps of a sit-up bench at the local gym. Bend your knees to relieve unnecessary stress on the lower back. Most experts are tending toward recommending that you keep your arms to your sides or at least have your hands across your chest rather than have hands behind your head—again, to relieve stress on the lower back. From this starting position raise your head and shoulders until your chest touches your knees, hold for a breathe, and then lower. Don't jerk yourself around; make the motion smooth and even. As with Push-Ups, do as many as you can without blowing yourself away.

Sit-Up Variations—*Crunches* have you resting your legs across a chair or bench with knees bent. With hands clasped over your stomach, bring your head and shoulders up as close to your knees as possible. This is a tough but effective abdominal exercise.

When using a Sit-Up bench found in most gyms or health clubs, Sit-Ups can be made much more difficult by changing the incline, raising the legs higher, and causing the movement to fight gravity harder. These are called *Incline Sit-Ups*. Along running paths you may be able to come across such sit-up benches; otherwise this variation is strictly for the indoor crowd **unless** you can find a hill and a friend to hold down your ankles on the upward side of the slope.

Finally, there is the *Bent-Leg Sit-Up* that is deceivingly simple to perform anywhere by oneself and causes the least amount of strain on the back when done correctly. Lie on your back with your hands (not clasped) over your head. Bend your knees and bring your arms forward in an attempt to touch knees to elbows. Keep your spine and lower back flat on the ground, raising only your head and shoulders.

Putting It All Together

As mentioned in the introduction to Part II, the structure of my exercise clinic for walkers follows a certain order. Combining all of the information from Chapters 3 and 4, that structure, in outline form, would look like this:

1. Warm-Up
   - Stationary exercises: The basic four stretches (Achilles and Calf, Hamstring, Quadriceps, and Flying Lunge)
   - Push-Ups, Sit-Ups, and other optional stretching exercises
   - Walking calisthenics: Head Rolls, Shoulder Shrugs, Shoulder-Arm Rotations, and Trunk Rotations
2. Techniques Instruction
   - Proper posture
   - Synchronized movements
   - Heel strike and placement
   - Leg pull/heel–toe/roll–push
   - Stride stretch
   - Arm swing and breathing
   - Straight-arm swing
   - Walk climbing (brake step, rest step)
3. Practice of Techniques and Exercises
   - Technique exercises: Arm Pump, Goose Step, Heel and Toe Walks, and Leg Lift
   - Special problems: Slouch Walking, Duck-Footed and Pigeon-Toed Walking, Favored-Leg Walking, Lifting, and Shuffling and Scraping
4. Upper-Body Strengthening
   - Push-Ups and Sit-Ups
   - Other strengthening exercises
5. Cool-Down
   - Stretching exercises from head to toe
   - The basic four stretches, the minimum finish

Of course, as the students in my clinics advance in knowledge of and proficiency in the exercises and techniques, we move on to matters that are really less complicated but nevertheless build on the basics learned in the opening weeks of the clinic. Thus, the techniques become secondary to enjoying walking for its own sake. You don't need an exercise class setting to use the techniques or calisthenics. You should attempt to incorporate them into your daily walking activities.

In the next three parts of this book we will explore these areas, focusing on how you can convert your individual walking preferences into exercise, how you can design an exercisewalking program for your own needs, and how to choose the proper equipment for the kinds of walking you wish to do.

PART III

EXERCISE AND WALKING

Hippocrates is generally acknowledged as the first to have said, "Walking is man's best medicine." Through the ages doctors have prescribed walking as a preventative and a cure for a variety of maladies. Most of these prescriptions for walking were not based on any scientific tests but rather on centuries of medical observation that the healthiest people are those who make walking a major activity in their lives.

Walking is probably the best and most time-tested element of folk medicine. It was Leonardo da Vinci who made the first biomechanical studies of human walking in connection with his efforts to design cities and buildings for pedestrians. He carried out few tests that would meet with the approval of modern scientific method, but his observations were highly regarded in his time.

Signor Borelli published his *De Moto Animalum*, the first definitive book on the aspects of walking, in 1680. Nearly 200 years later Frenchman E. J. Marey was the first to identify and study the walking cycle, in *The Animal Machine* (1873). These studies marked the beginning of the biomechanical approach to walking studies as done today.

Marey studied the human gait by wiring feet for sound and using still photography techniques to chronologically record the various segments of the walking cycle. He did this by photographing the walker against a black background. The walker then covered and exposed selected parts of his anatomy while being photographed by a camera mounted on a vehicle that moved along a track with the walker. These photographs were shown in rapid sequence to create a moving picture that isolated the components of the walking cycle. Marey's was the most comprehensive walking study of his era.

The next great leap in the study of walking came after World War II, when studies of the lower walking action were made in connection with amputees. The culmination of those three years (1944–47) of prolific research was the two-volume report, *Fundamental Studies* (1947), that summarized all the technical information produced, and all research done, on walking since early times.

While much of this research did not concentrate on the exercise value of walking, it did produce important testing and measuring techniques that were brought to bear on exercise beginning in the mid-1950s. The real boom in research began in the 1970s in conjunction with the rise of jogging and the whole health-and-fitness scene, especially as a control for comparison with other exercises. Since 1971 more than 1,000 separate physical and medical tests have been conducted in regard to walking. By the end of that decade physical education researchers conclusively established the exercise values of different types of walking.

Although more studies could be done—and are being done, particularly with regard to comparing walking with other exercises and sports—we do now have a body of scientific and medical literature from which to fashion (for the first time) a comprehensive approach to walking as an exercise. This book synthesizes all the relevant walking studies into seven basic principles of exercisewalking. These principles, added to the techniques and exercises described in the exercise clinic for walkers, open to you the possibility of creating an exercise program custom-fitted to your needs and goals, a program centered on the walking action.

In this part, I intend to introduce the seven basic principles of exercisewalking (Chapter 5). In Chapter 6 we will look at various methods for determining the value of an exercise. These methods can be used to determine your present level of fitness and the value of exercise you would like to put together in a personal walking exercise routine—possibilities that will be discussed in Chapter 7. These chapters are the heart of this book. From the time of Hippocrates to the present, the prescription for walking has too often been vague and unspecific. Now we can formulate prescriptions for walking that fit the lifestyle and specific fitness needs of each individual.

5

THE PRINCIPLES OF EXERCISEWALKING

Walking technique is not enough to make walking into an exercise. As we noted in Chapter 3, walking has a limited effect on upper-body strength and needs to be supplemented with stretching and strengthening exercises. Nevertheless, in this chapter and those that follow we will examine how walking can be converted into exercise. This conversion involves seven principles applied to six basic walking styles that we will discuss later. First, let us look at the meaning of *exercise* and the various components that make an activity an exercise.

Exercise is a physical activity that conditions the body through regular and continuous repetition of body movements over a specific time period, at a specific speed, or for a particular effort. An important component of this definition of exercise is the *conditioning effect* that takes place. For example, if you walk five miles every other day for a week, keeping a constant pace and other variables the same, you will find that walking five miles becomes progressively easier. The body adapts to stress that is repeated often enough for conditioning to take place. In fact, it is an important principle of all exercise that work loads, speed, or frequency of body movements be increased so that the body will adapt by becoming stronger and by functioning more efficiently.

The conditioning effect, also called the *training effect*, has been observed in countless tests in physiology to be a phenomenon correlated to levels of fitness. That is, there is a significant difference in the training effect associated with a three-mile-a-day exercise and a seven-mile-a-day exercise. The body must build up gradually to different levels of fitness, or it will be strained rather than trained. When the body is subjected to increased work loads its organs respond by growing larger and stronger and more capable of performing additional work.

The Purpose of Exercise

There are two major reasons or purposes for performing exercises: to maintain your health and to improve your level of physical fitness. The minimum goal of exercise could be stated as maintaining physical activity at a level that keeps the body healthy. The ideal goal of exercise would be to become and remain physically fit. Both goals contain relative components that bear closer examination.

It is the "activity" part of exercise that contributes directly to a person's long-term health. Of the seven causes cited by the Framingham Heart Study (1955), inactivity was determined to be a contributing factor of cardiovascular disease. It is more likely that regular physical activity throughout life offers better protection in terms of health and longevity than vigorous training activity (e.g., sports, dance, exercise classes) according to studies by McArdle, Katch, and Katch (1981). Thus, even our minimal goal for exercise is well served by learning exercisewalking techniques and finding ways of converting everyday walking activities into effective exercise routines.

Yes, for the purpose of maintaining cardiovascular fitness and keeping the body healthy, *it's better to do a little bit of activity* (not necessarily exercise in a strict sense) *here and there than to remain inactive while planning someday to begin a comprehensive exercise program.* All the little bits add up to a higher cumulative level of physical activity that contributes to the long-term health of the individual.

The "relative" component of our ideal goal of exercise is the matter of what "physically fit" means to each individual. Actually it is a matter of what fitness means to you. Most doctors accept this definition: the state of body efficiency that enables a person to work actively for a sustained time without fatigue and to respond to sudden physical and emotional demands with an economy of heartbeats and only a modest rise in blood pressure. For the male tennis player this definition means that he should be able to play whatever amount of the game allows him to win (or at least to lose without exhaustion causing a forfeit) without being carried off the court. The sedentary office worker, while not needing the energy and strength reserves of the tennis player, must still be fit enough to meet the sudden, unexpected demands that life has to offer, such as the company picnic softball game, a night of dancing, or the emotional strain of meeting a deadline related to work—not to mention the unwanted chance that he or she may need to escape a burning building or chase a thief.

You will be the one to define ultimately what you consider physical fitness for yourself. But as an ideal goal for exercise, I suggest that becoming "physically fit" means an average state of fitness that will best carry a person through a long and emotionally satisfying life. It may fluctuate from day to day and week to week (and so on), but your physical fitness will be dependent on a combination of keeping active and exercising all body parts in a comprehensive and balanced manner. Therefore, while just keeping active without any concerted, planned effort can ensure health, exercising builds a reserve for the body to meet unexpected demands without hazard.

The Exercisewalking Principles

Every exercise, routine, and body action has certain physiological principles that can be used to determine or to predict its training effect. In the case of exercisewalking we must really discuss six different exercise styles. These styles are related to the manner in which we walk: at a natural pace; at a forced, brisk pace; with a load, such as ankle weights or a backpack; up or down a slope; and over rugged terrain; or some combination of these styles. To understand how each of these styles affects an exercise or training value you must understand a basic principle concerning that style of walking. Once you have an understanding of these principles you will be able to analyze the hundreds of

activities that involve walking and determine the training value of an activity. (Chapter 6 will provide mathematical methods for further analysis of exercise value in terms of heart rate, calories, oxygen intake, and so on.)

The seven basic principles of exercisewalking are derived from the hundreds of tests conducted by doctors, physiologists, and fitness experts during the last 70 years. But the major research I will be referring to in describing the principles was done in the last two decades, when researchers looked specifically at walking as an exercise.

Exercisewalking Principle #1
The Energy Conservation Principle

The human body will integrate the motions of the various segments and control the activity of the muscles so that the metabolic energy required for any distance walked at a self-chosen walking speed, will be the minimal energy expenditure needed to move the body over that distance. (Ralston, 1958)

The basic principle of walking, the Energy Conservation Principle applies to the broad base of exercisewalkers—those who walk for the sake of walking and set no particular pace but the one that is most comfortable. Most often this pace is chosen subconsciously and is based on a subjective feeling of "what feels right, good, or comfortable" (Murray et al., 1966, 1970). This comfortable walking pace varies with the individual according to sex (females naturally walk more slowly than males), body build (e.g., longer legs walk faster), environment (city walkers move faster than country walkers), and purpose (e.g., rushing to an appointment calls for a particular, balanced pace). This last category is of interest because both purposeful and nonpurposeful walkers choose their natural speeds subconsciously. The purposeful walker is close to becoming a dynamic walker—subconsciously bringing to bear certain techniques of exercisewalking.

The significance of this first principle of exercisewalking is that the natural pace that your body seems to choose is the most efficient form of pedestrian transportation but not the most effective walking style you may wish to use for exercise. The natural pace involves a minimum level of energy expenditure; it is used to *conserve* energy. If you walk ever increasing distances at a natural pace, you *can* eliminate or change this tendency toward conservation and raise the amount of caloric expenditure significantly (see The Long Distance Principle, pages 93–94).

What this first principle does signify, however, is that walking does not tax the body; it is an excellent activity to maintain health. But it does not improve fitness. To convert everyday walking into dynamic walking you must apply any one of the next six principles.

Exercisewalking Principle #2
The Speed Principle

There is a linear and constant relationship between step length and step rate if one factors in the differences of body height according to the following formula:

$$\frac{\text{stride length/body height}}{\text{step frequency/minute}} = 0.008 \text{ (Dean, 1965)}$$

Most people do their everyday walking within a certain speed range—100 steps per minute (2.5–3 mph) give or take 10 percent when walking on a flat, even surface. City walkers are usually on the high side of this range. Changes in walking speed can be achieved by increasing one's stride length, one's step rate, or both. The natural way to increase walking speed is through a combination of both stride length and step rate increases according to the formula just presented.

We don't have to think about this ratio; our bodies choose it naturally as we increase our walking speed. Further, this natural ratio of step length to step rate is one that minimizes the energy required by the body to move at that speed. In other words, if a walker consciously chooses shorter or longer strides than his natural strides, the energy required for the distance walked will be increased (Zarrugh, 1975; Molen et al., 1972; and Atzler and Herbst, 1927). Thus, walking fast while applying exercisewalking techniques will increase the metabolic expenditure over what fast walking can do without techniques at the same speed.

This supports our claim that applying exercisewalking techniques to your everyday walking will make it more dynamic and provide you with a greater exercise value. As an example, walking with a purposely increased stride length, as in Technique #5 (the stride stretch), represents an unnaturally longer stride length and requires a higher metabolic expenditure. Therefore, purposefully trying to increase the number of steps per minute as in a walk sprint routine (see page 164), while at the same time taking longer strides, will again positively increase the metabolic expenditure.

Eventually the length–rate relationship does become constant, however, as the exercisewalker adapts to maintaining walking speeds outside the normal range of walkers (i.e., 5–10 mph like racewalkers do). Walkers at these higher ranges achieve a new harmony of step length to step rate that is the most efficient ratio given those extraordinarily high speeds.

However, at least one test of racewalkers has shown that the caloric expenditure of walking rises dramatically at speeds greater than 4.97 mph (Menier, 1968). In fact, at speeds above this mark, racewalkers burn more calories than runners who are traveling at the same speed! This difference is attributable to the increased upper body motion—the arm pumping motion and the rolling of the hips—the racewalker effects to walk fast. It is difficult to walk fast continuously in the 7–10 mph range without adopting some version of the racewalker's technique, so one can assume that fast walking will burn more calories per mile than fast running will.

Another explanation for this difference—found even in the lower 5–7 mph range—is that the fast walker must take more steps per mile than the runner does when going at the same pace. That's because the walker's stride length is limited since he cannot extend his stride by jumping forward like the runner. The efficiency of walking faster than 4.97 mph is half that of running at the same speed (Menier), while running at speeds less than 4.97 mph is less efficient than walking at those same speeds.

This factor suggests a modification to the Energy Conservation Principle in the case of fast walkers and racewalkers. Namely, the metabolic expenditure increases at walking speeds over 4.97 mph so that while maintaining the linear relationship of increases in speed and energy expenditure, the slope of the line is much steeper and the increases are greater.

The formula describing the relationship of walking speed to energy expenditure is $E_w = b + mv^2$ (the energy of walking equals a constant number plus mass or weight of the walking body times the walking speed squared). Thus, the constant (b) will change for different ranges of walking speeds; first in the range of below 1.5 mph, where the walker is moving almost in slow motion or is perhaps, shuffleing. The second range is the functional or everyday walking speed of 1.5–3.5 mph. The third range is the brisk walking speed of 3.5–4.96 mph. The speed range of 4.96–10 mph is the fourth one used by racewalkers and walk-sprinters. In reaching this final speed range, most racewalkers must adapt exaggerated body movements—particularly for the upper body—to maintain these speeds.

The change from one range of speed to another is analogous to shifting gears in an automobile. Charted on a graph, the slope of the speed/energy expenditure line becomes steeper, but remains a straight line all the same.

Another interesting study has revealed significant differences between men and women in how they accelerate their walking speed. Women seem to rely on a higher step rate over a longer stride length to increase and maintain their walking speed than men do. Of course, this becomes even more pronounced when women walk in high-heeled shoes. (Murray *et al., op. cit.*). But regardless of acceleration possibilities, studies of city walkers' comparable gait/speed patterns for men are in the range of 75–140 steps per minute and 80–150 steps per minute for women.

Exercisewalking Principle #3
The Weight-Loading Principle

Loading weight on the body increases the metabolic cost of walking. Loading the limbs has a greater effect than loading the trunk of the body. (Inman, et. al., 1981; Wyndham, C.H., 1971)

Backpackers have long known and practiced this exercise-walker principle—but in reverse. To make their backpacking treks *less energy consuming,* they have taken the load away from the limbs and placed it close to the trunk of the body. By using a pack designed to place the load on the shoulders and hips, the backpacker has eliminated the constant acceleration and deceleration of arms swinging with the weight of suitcases. The arms are free to swing and sustain the body's balance while the larger muscles of back, shoulders, and legs more efficiently carry the load.

The advent of lighter hiking and climbing boots also heeds the reverse of this principle. One pound of reduced shoe weight is equal to seven pounds taken away from the back. The difference in metabolic expenditure results from placing weight on moving limbs, which requires more energy to overcome the wider arc of movement involved in propelling the body forward.

Another interesting result of weight-loading the walking foot is the tendency of such a foot to take a longer stride. Again the body in its weight-loaded condition strives to minimize its energy expenditure by taking longer, slower steps. This tendency minimizes the number of times the weight-loaded foot has to be accelerated and decelerated. However, the increase in step length results in greater vertical oscillation with a resultant increase in the amount of gravitational work the leg has to do.

Of course, the backpacker works the Weight-Loading Principle in reverse because his interest is carrying up to a third of his weight in equipment and food to live in the wilderness. For walking in the city, a weight of 14 pounds or so is sufficient to create a training effect. Another style of walking that uses this principle in a straightforward manner is weighted-limb walking. By putting weights on the ankles and wrists, the weighted-limb walker purposefully increases the metabolic expenditure of his walking.

With either style of walking you have a dynamic body movement that has excellent exercise value.

Exercisewalking Principle #4
The Slope-Walking Principle

The metabolic expenditure increases rapidly with increases in the grade of slope, walking both up and down the graded slope, except on the negative slope of lower grades (i.e., 0°–20° is less than level walking). (McDonald, 1961; Margaria, 1938; Zohman, 1978, 1981; and Effort Physiology Institute, 1977).

As you can quickly see from the accompanying chart, the metabolic expenditure of walking rises dramatically with the increases in the percentage of the slope one is walking up. Sur-

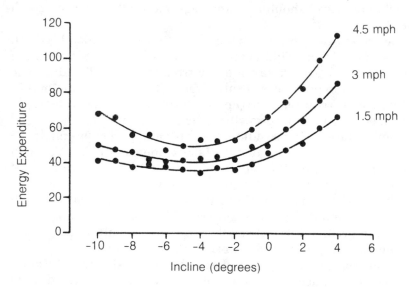

At three speeds, the effect of slope on energy expenditure while walking.

Caloric Expenditure at Various Speeds and Grades

Grade		Speed (mph)				
Percent	**Degrees**	**1.5**	**2.25**	**3.00**	**3.75**	**4.50**
40	21.8	12.1				
35	19.3	11.2				
30	16.7	9.7	18.1			
25	14.0	8.3	15.1			
20	11.3	7.1	12.4	12.9		
15	8.5	5.9	10.1	10.5	14.5	
10	5.7	4.9	8.2	8.5	12.0	15.1
5	2.9	4.2	6.5	6.7	11.0	13.1
0	0	2.9	4.3	5.7	7.1	8.6
− 5	− 2.9	2.3	3.3	4.4	5.3	6.4
− 10	5.7	2.2	3.0	3.9	4.7	5.5
− 15	− 8.5	2.4	3.2	4.0	4.7	5.4
− 20	− 11.3	3.0	4.0	4.8	5.5	6.0
− 25	− 14.0	3.3	4.6	5.7	6.5	6.8
− 30	− 16.7	3.4	4.9	6.1	6.8	7.0
− 35	− 19.3	3.5	5.2	6.6	7.2	7.2
− 40	− 21.8	4.0	6.1	7.8	8.4	8.2

Energy expenditure is measured in calories per minute (cpm) for a subject weighing 157 pounds. Note how cpm goes down then gradually increases again as downhill grade grows steeper. This is due to the need for braking against the momentum of going down too fast.

prisingly it also increases going down grades except for low level (0°−.2°) grades. Given a routine of walk climbing up and down the same grade, however, the net increase is still there when compared to the some distance of level walking. The braking action needed to walk down steeper grades at an even pace accounts for a large portion of the metabolic increase in that category. This principle applies to all types of slopes, whether tilted treadmills, hills, or stairs. (The table on page 91 shows the caloric expenditures for different grades of slope walking at different walking speeds.)

Exercisewalking Principle #5
The Leg-Lifting Principle

Walking on uneven and rugged terrain increases the metabolic expenditure in relation to the ruggedness of the terrain. (Passmore and Durin, 1955)

A walker must lift his leg higher, adding the work effort of overcoming the gravitational force of lifting the leg higher as well as the inertial force of stopping and starting it during the walking cycle. However, mere unevenness (such as bumps on an asphalt or dirt road) may not increase the metabolic expenditure by more than 10 percent. The surface must be rugged to yield large metabolic increases. For example, Passmore and Durin rated a plowed field at 30 percent. Strydom (*et al.,* 1966) determined an 80 percent effort for loose sand when carrying a weight load. In both tests the walking was done at a fairly brisk pace.

The leg-lifting principle of walking plays a role in a number of natural walking styles such as ice walking (e.g., glacier hikes with spikes (crampons) or snow hiking with lug soles). The need to hold the foot in place and to keep it from slipping requires greater muscle effort with each step. In deep snow, requiring the use of snowshoes or skis, the legs must be lifted as high as 12 inches—nearly 5–8 inches higher than in normal walking. When bushwhacking (i.e., hiking through brush, over rocks, and around fallen trees) legs are lifted higher and in different directions to accommodate changes in terrain. The exercisewalker can benefit from charting his course over rough terrain not only for the adventure but also for the increased exercise value.

Exercisewalking Principle #6
The Long-Distance Principle

A mile of walking is worth more exercise if it is part of a series of miles walked in succession than if it is walked discretely with longer than 10-minute rest intervals in between. (Cooper, 1982)

In other words, walking, say, five miles all at once has more exercise value, particularly aerobic value, than walking five miles one at a time with intermittent rest periods in between. Exercise experts have long known that the duration of a particular exercise works in conjunction with the frequency with which it is done. That's why, for example, a minimum of 15–20 minutes per aerobic exercise session is recommended to achieve a training effect rather than a shorter period of 5–10 minutes. This duration-of-exercise principle, applied to walking, becomes a long-distance-walked principle, since the walkers' exercise is done at a variety of intensity and speed levels, making time or duration less important than the number of miles walked. For example, the birdwatching walker stops and starts walking slowly for two to four hours and may walk only two miles. That walker has undertaken a two-mile workout, not a two- or four-hour workout.

The Long-Distance Principle is derived from my own experience and can be verified by measuring your heart rate at 10-minute intervals during an ever increasing series of miles walked. You will find that the average rate goes up with each mile walked. Dr. Kenneth Cooper, in his book *The Aerobics Program for Total Well Being* (Evans, 1982), has also demonstrated this effect in his aerobic tests of runners and walkers, deriving from these equations that give higher exercise values for walking or running more than a mile per session than for walking less than a mile at a range of speeds. This exercise principle also corresponds to Cooper's "endurance points." These are aerobic points that must be added for exercises that continue over longer periods. Cooper found that you use more energy if you run three miles continuously than if you run them with rest stops in between.

While more testing is needed, we know from experience that there is a trade-off between walking speed and distance walked during an exercise. The Long-Distance Principle implies that self-paced walkers can substitute a certain amount of miles walked for miles walked with a certain speed or intensity. The ultimate test of this effect is measuring the heart rate while exercising and determining the specific effect in each exercise.

We know that in a long-distance walking program miles walked can be balanced against maintaining a higher walking speed. In a 5–10-mile-a-day walking program, if those miles are walked in succession, an aerobic training effect will result. Since this training effect is individualized, each person will have to determine the exact distance for himself.

Exercisewalking Principle #7
The Exercise Multiplier Principle

Given any walking routine, the exercisewalker can increase the exercise value of it by increasing the walking speed, the level of incline, the amount of weight load, or the height of the leg lift with multiple rather than linear increases in the metabolic expenditure.

We have now come full circle, from the basic Energy Conservation Principle of the natural, self-paced walking speed to one enhanced multifold by applying walking techniques and combining walking styles. With the dramatic walking approach revealed in this book the exercisewalker has the potential of raising the caloric expenditure of a three-mile or one-hour, natural-paced walk of 300 calories to as high as 2,700 calories per hour (or 900 calories per mile walked). For example, walking 1 mph up a 40° incline with a 60-pound weight load will produce a 2,700-calorie expenditure in one hour. Stated otherwise, the walker has the choice of limiting or extending the time for his walking exercises by applying the previous exercise principles for all walking styles.

The vast majority of people who walk will remain self-paced walkers capable of some brisk walking. We are not trying to make anyone a macho/gung-ho walker but to give you a few options for a compressed, more intense walking routine that could supplement your regular, self-paced routine and thereby round out your walking program and convert it into a reliable exercise.

By presenting you with the knowledge of the scientific aspects of walking, I hope you will be able to design your own walking routines as well as have a rule-of-thumb knowledge of what kind of walking is valuable for an exercise. Above all walking should remain fun and the art of the individual walker. It should not become routinized like other forms of exercise. If this happens, walking's potential for being the lifelong exercise will be greatly reduced.

6

THE EXERCISE VALUES
OF WALKING

To make your walking activity an exercise, you must be able to measure it to determine your progress. These measurements do not need to be precise, but they must represent reasonable estimates of your activity. Each walking exercise must have a starting point, where the level of physical fitness is measured and a goal of fitness to be reached is established. You must measure your initial physical fitness to determine at what level you should start your walking exercises. Thereafter, you should check your progress until you have reached your final exercise goals.

Physical Fitness Levels

Physical fitness has many components but most exercise experts agree on three basics: cardiovascular endurance, muscular strength and endurance, and flexibility. Other ways of measuring health and fitness are often put under the general headings of health or well-being. These include sleep, digestion, stress control, weight control, and muscle tone or definition.

While the test for overall health is generally that of being free from disease, physical fitness is subject to different levels of measurement, usually a grading from poor to excellent. Levels of fitness are really levels of performance for the different body segments or functions—heart, muscles, and joints. There are physical tests to measure each segment and see how well it performs. These tests usually measure the number of repetitions of exercises that a body segment can perform. For example, you can measure your stomach muscles' level of physical fitness by doing as many sit-ups as you can in a specified period or until exhaustion.

In the exercise literature, fitness is usually divided into 4–7 levels depending on how the testers break down their data. Performance levels of the exercises are computed for the population-at-large and against highly trained athletes, then rated as to *poor, fair, good,* etc. The excellent or highest level usually represents the trained athletes' level of achievement.

Fitness levels for individual body parts can be averaged on a fitness profile to come up with an overall average of fitness for an individual exerciser. It's good to keep in mind that fitness has components, each with separate levels of performance. And it's difficult to keep these components equally fit. Many of our most highly trained athletes like runners have excellent ratings in one or two components like cardiovascular conditioning and flexibility. Often they are disproportionately weak in the other component, upper-body muscle strength. Some are high in just one category and weak in the others. For instance, many weightlifters have great skeletal muscle strength but lack flexibility and aerobic fitness. For overall health and well-being all the fitness components should be balanced at a minimum average acceptable level.

Fitness levels of individuals can also be correlated to intensity level of an exercise. For this book, I use five levels of fitness: I—poor, II—fair, III—good, IV—very good, and V—excellent. This multipurpose five-tiered rating system is all you will need to rate your starting fitness and to measure your progress. The charts and tables in this chapter will help you get an idea of what your level of fitness is.

As a walker, determine your level of intensity of a particular walking activity or exercise, then monitor your progress through

Part III: Exercise and Walking

Fitness Ratings Based on Body Fat Percentage

Males

Age	I (Poor)	II (Fair)	III (Good)	IV (Very Good)	V (Excellent)
20–29	28.6–32.8	22.3–28.5	18.0–22.2	13.9–17.9	7.2–13.8
30–39	28.0–32.3	23.6–27.9	20.1–23.5	16.2–20.0	7.1–15.1
40–49	28.5–32.2	24.6–28.9	21.5–24.4	17.7–21.4	9.2–17.6
50–59	28.5–32.2	24.6–28.4	21.5–24.5	17.7–21.4	9.2–17.6
60 and over	28.9–32.5	24.4–28.8	20.8–24.3	17.2–20.7	10.5–17.1

Females

Age	I (Poor)	II (Fair)	III (Good)	IV (Very Good)	V (Excellent)
20–29	33.3–38.5	26.2–33.2	23.2–26.1	15.1–23.1	4.8–15.1
30–39	31.3–38.1	25.5–31.2	21.5–25.4	16.7–21.4	5.1–16.6
40–49	31.4–37.4	25.5–31.2	21.5–25.4	16.7–21.4	5.1–16.6
50–59	34.7–39.7	30.4–34.6	27.0–30.1	22.7–26.9	10.8–22.6
60 and over	34.7–36.3	30.8–34.6	27.1–30.7	22.2–27.0	16.8–22.1

different levels (also monitor regression if you stopped exercising). The five-level system can also refer to the intensity level of a particular walking activity or any action to determine if it is intense enough as an exercise. Finally, the five levels can be applied to your total walking program to help you plot your beginning and conditioning programs to reach and maintain your desired level of physical fitness.

Most people should shoot for level III and maintain themselves at that level throughout their lives. This is the level of the moderate exerciser who doesn't want to give his or her whole life to exercise. By walking every day and including conditioning walks and the strengthening exercises described in this book, you should be able to achieve and maintain that level.

The measuring methods described in this chapter are intended to help you reach your exercise goals. Once you learn to measure the various benefits of a particular exercisewalking activity you can apply that knowledge to an understanding of your own fitness level in order to improve your fitness. On the following

A Quick Test for Fitness Level of Aerobic Walking

Fitness Levels	Walking Speed (mph)	Time Heart Rate Takes to Reach Training Zone (minutes)
Excellent (V)	5–9	3 or less
Very Good (IV)	4.5	3–3.2
Good (III)	4–4.5	3:20–3:45
Fair (II)	3.5–4.0	3:45–5
Poor (I)	3	Over 5

Choose your approximate fitness category and walk 440 yards (quarter mile) at the prescribed speed. Measure your heart rate right after walking so you get as close as possible to your actual heart-rate training zone while exercising. You may have to do this more than once. Knowing your aerobic fitness category, you can then choose an aerobic training program to fit your level and work from there.

---

pages you will learn to measure the intensity of your exercise-walking; the aerobic or cardiovascular effect; muscular strength, endurance, and flexibility; walking speed, distance, and inclines.

Before jumping into the methods of measurement, it might be a good idea to debunk an overly scientific approach to exercise. It *is* important that walkers develop a fundamental understanding of how to measure the effects of their work, but some fitness seekers tend to become so preoccupied by counting calories, heartbeats, and miles that they find themselves bogged down in decimal points and charts to the point at which they are spending more time on calculations than on exercise. And to what end? Exercisewalkers must realize that most of the measuring tools at their disposal are indirect methods that provide only estimates, not precise measurements. Therefore, it's best to get a handle on the theories behind the measurement methods so that you can use a rule-of-thumb approach to your own measurements. This approach is discussed at the end of the chapter.

To illustrate the necessity of learning to work with estimates, let's consider what is probably the most important measurement in any exercise: the amount of energy a particular activity forces the exerciser to expend. This indicates how much the activity is worth as an exercise and can be measured in terms of caloric rate and value.

An exercise's value can be determined through indirect and direct methods. The direct method, the only way to produce precise, accurate measurements, involves using the "human calorimeter." This piece of equipment is an airtight, thermally insulated chamber that measures the heat production of the human body. The athlete exercises in this chamber, and the heat that his body produces is removed by a stream of cold water flowing through tubes or coils through the chamber at a constant rate. The temperature of the water that leaves the insulated chamber will be raised or heated up by the exercising body. The air temperature and humidity in the chamber are kept constant. Oxygen is added to the air before it enters the calorimeter while carbon dioxide is absorbed through special chemical absorbants.

Obviously, the human calorimeter is not available to most walkers. Therefore, you must turn to less precise, indirect methods. Nevertheless, the estimates these methods produce are important for they offer a reliable guideline for behavior.

It's good to strive for the best estimate possible; however, the process used should not be too cumbersome or time consuming. Thus, for every formula and table of values, there is usually a rule-of-thumb approach that will serve just as well, particularly if you are out on the trail and don't want to stop and take measurements every five minutes. So I will try to give good estimates, tables, and the means to compute them as well as a rougher rule-of-thumb approach. The last one will make it possible to avoid complicated calculations and use range estimates when evaluating the exercise you have done or want to do.

Computing Work Intensity and Energy Expenditure: Caloric Burn Rate

There are several ways to compute the rate of caloric expenditure for an individual type of activity. Most of them are too complicated for practical, everyday use, especially while on the go, but these methods can be discussed to give you an understanding of the principles that come into play in energy expenditure during walking.

Metabolic Rate

Tests have shown how much energy (in calories) individuals use for certain activities, based on the person's weight.

The basal metabolic rate (BMR) is the rate of energy expenditure while lying awake in a relaxed position; it represents the energy needed to maintain an individual's vital functions while he is at rest. The BMR for a 110-pound person is one calorie per minute. *At rest,* that energy expenditure increases in direct proportion with the person's weight. For example, a 220-pound person burns two calories per minute at rest. A 110-pound person, walking at the normal pace, will burn approximately four calories per minute; his 220-pound counterpart burns eight calories per minute.

METs

Another unit of measurement that may come in handy is the MET, a term derived from the word *metabolism,* and used to

Weight (pounds)	Calories/MET
85	.68
95	.75
105	.84
115	.92
125	1.00
135	1.07
145	1.16
155	1.24
165	1.32
175	1.40
185	1.48
195	1.55
205	1.63
215	1.71
225	1.79
235	1.87
245	1.95

Activity	METs
Sleep	1
Walking (2 mph)	3
Mowing grass	4
Walking (3 mph)	4.5
Tennis	6
Shoveling snow	7
Racquetball	8
Cycling (15 mph)	10
Running (7 mph)	12
Walking upstairs	15

describe the intensity of a work load. The MET value was determined by measuring the amount of oxygen used by a 154-pound man each minute while at rest and assigning it a value of 1 MET. It coincides with our calories-per-minute rates when discussing a 126-pound person, for example, who runs a 10-minute mile. That person would be working at 10 METS and losing 10 calories per minute.

Therefore, you can use this rule-of-thumb equivalence to determine caloric or MET values for your own weight since the numbers change proportionately. By using the tables on pages 101–102, you can determine the caloric burn rate by determining the MET value of the activities listed.

Principles of Energy Expenditure

Before any walker can begin to adopt the measuring methods—scientific and rule-of-thumb—it is important to know certain facts about human energy expenditure.

1. When you are *not* at rest, the calories expended during an activity do *not* increase proportionally with increases in weight. For example, doubling a person's weight produces only 1.7 times the calories burned, not a full 2 times.
2. On the other hand, speed *does* increase the caloric burn rate proportionately at high speeds (especially above 5 mph). Between one and three mph, the same total number of calories is expended to walk one mile. But the calories are

Number of Calories Expended by Walking (per hour)

Walking Speed in mph	Weight in Pounds						
	100	120	140	160	180	200	220
2	130	160	185	210	240	265	290
2½	155	185	220	250	280	310	345
3	180	215	250	285	325	360	395
3½	205	248	290	330	375	415	455
4	235	280	325	375	420	470	515
4½	310	370	435	495	550	620	680
5	385	460	540	615	690	770	845

burned at a different rate: 4–5 cal/min at 2 mph, 5–6 cal/min at 3 mph, and 6–7 cal/min at 4 mph. So, if you walk a mile at 1 mph or 3 mph, for that single mile you will burn the same amount of calories. Likewise, if you run a 26.2-mile marathon in 4 hours, you will burn the same amount of calories as the person who set the world record doing it in 2 hours and 8 minutes.

3. Different activities burn calories at different rates, even when the speed and distance applied are the same. If you run a mile at 3 mph and compare this with walking the same distance at 3 mph, the caloric burn rate will generally be higher for running because the higher leg lifts of the jogger burn more calories over the same distance. On the other hand, at speeds of 5, 6, and 7 mph the walker burns more calories than the jogger or runner because the nature of the body action or movement has changed. Namely, it is now the walker who is making exaggerated movements to keep moving forward. The runner is moving at his natural pace given speeds or 5–7 mph, so there is no change in body action or movement. This difference is due to the fast walker's exaggerated upper-body and trunk movements. Also, the walker takes as many as 500 more steps per mile as the runner because his stride length is necessarily shorter than the runner's.

As an example, arm swinging would add calories. Walking up an incline would also involve increases in caloric expenditure because of increases in work load or the grade walked. Essentially the calories are increased with the need for more energy to lift the body higher. Adding a weight load while walking adds caloric expenditure proportional to the increased weight load as a percentage of total body weight. Walking over rugged terrain adds calories due to the higher leg-lifting action and the increased muscular action to keep the body stable or to push aside any obstructions. Thus there is a different caloric expenditure rate for the different styles of walking. You can use tables in this book to determine that rate or you can compute the intensity of the walking work effort by using the methods described in this part of the chapter. Unfortunately, most calorie tables on walking speeds published elsewhere are computed on the basis of natural walking styles rather than dynamic ones.

Each walking style or activity has a natural intensity level associated with it. This intensity level can be increased by increasing the speed at which that activity or style is performed (work rate) or increasing the load carried or the incline or distance the body is lifted. It can also be increased by changing the amount of activity of the body parts involved—especially use of additional muscles in the upper body but also the range of motion of the legs as they swing or the height to which they have to be lifted.

Oxygen Pulse and Heart Rate

A good way to measure the intensity or value of any walking activity is to use your heart rate. This is done by determining your heart rate for an activity for which you already know the MET value and comparing it to the heart rate you get during the new activity.

1. First, measure your heart during a specific activity for which you know the MET. Say your heart beats 120 times per minute while you were walking at 3 mph, which is a 4.5-MET activity.
2. Measure your heart rate for the new activity. Say you get 170 beats per minute.
3. Figure the MET value for the new activity by using a proportion:

$$\frac{4.5 \text{ METS}}{120} = \frac{\text{X METS}}{170}$$

$$120(X) = 4.5 \ (170)$$

$$X = \frac{765}{120}$$

$$X = 6.375$$

Note that you are really measuring your response to the MET value or given intensity value of an exercise to measure how efficiently your body performs it. The more efficiently, the less fatigue and the more and longer your body can perform. This assumes that your heart will work at the same rate in proportion to different exercise intensities. As you grow more fit, the proportion will, of course, change; but it will remain the same against a wide range of intensities.

Once you know the MET value or level of intensity of any exercise, you will be able to use this to determine your caloric burn rate for any other exercise merely by deriving it from the steady heartbeat during that exercise.

You can calculate the exact number of calories burned per minute or hour by applying a more complicated formula through which your oxygen pulse (the amount of oxygen consumed during any exercise in one minute divided by the number of heartbeats it took to deliver that oxygen during the minute) is calculated. Or you can consult the MET tables in this book.

Measuring Aerobic Effect: Heart Rate

Aerobic walking is really any style of walking done with a speed, duration, or effort to exercise the heart. Your heart is a muscle that requires rapid repetition so that it can function economically with the least amount of fatigue and stress. Heart/lung exercise consists of sustained rapid breathing while moving your arms and legs for at least 15 minutes and ideally as many as

30 minutes, three time a week. Your training goal is to raise your heartbeat to 70–85 percent of its maximum.

Strolling will probably not suffice to train the heart: at best, it will help improve circulation. Most other forms of walking can, however, be converted to aerobic walking by maintaining a brisk pace, climbing an incline or mountain, or walking with a pack.

Aerobic walking may or may not produce sweat. It depends on the walker's body temperature and the temperature of the air. Sweating should not necessarily be associated with walking. The key indicator is the heartbeat rate.

Depending on your level of conditioning, different walking styles and speeds and different walking periods (durations) will help you train aerobically. When you are in poor physical condition a speed of 3 mph for 15–30 minutes may bring your heart into the training target zone. A walker in excellent condition may require a speed of 4–5 mph for 30–60 minutes to reach his training target zone.

On page 106 is a chart of target heart-rate ranges for men and women according to age. Each range represents the heartbeats per minute that will produce a training effect for the heart in

Heart Rate Target Ranges by Age

Age	Your Maximum Heart Rate (beats per minute)	Your Target Heart Rate Range (beats per minute)
20	200	140 to 170
25	195	137 to 166
30	190	133 to 162
35	185	130 to 157
40	180	126 to 153
45	175	123 to 149
50	170	119 to 145
55	165	116 to 140
60	160	112 to 136
65	155	109 to 132
70	150	105 to 128

each age group if maintained for at least 15 minutes during any exercise period. It may be maintained for shorter periods of three to five minutes if done more frequently during the period. You can raise the level of your heartbeat by walking faster, climbing, or walking longer. Keeping your heartbeat in the training zone is an individual matter, not subject to easy formulation. Reaching the training zone will depend on current level of fitness, age, level of exertion, speed and duration, and frequency of the exercise. To keep yourself in the training zone, you will have to learn how to monitor your heart rate while training:

1. Compute your maximum heart rate. This roughly equals 220 minus your age. For example, if you are 40 years old, 220 − 40 = 180 beats per minute, your maximum rate.
2. Figure 70−85 percent of your maximum rate. This will be your training zone. Pick a percentage in this range, depending on the level of physical fitness you want to maintain: 70 percent x 180 = 126 heartbeats per minute (minimum) or 85 percent x 180 = 153 heartbeats per minute (maximum).
3. Measure your heart rate while walking, or, if you can't measure your pulse while moving, stop in the middle of your walking period and take your pulse measurement. However, walk around for about 10 minutes before attempting to take your pulse. Measure your pulse rate for 6−10 seconds, either at your wrist or behind your ear, and multiply the number of pulse beats by 6 or 10 to obtain the number of heartbeats per minute.

This method will enable you to monitor your heartbeat anywhere and at anytime. If you discover that your heartbeat is below the training zone, you can speed up or extend your walking period until you reach the training zone.

With practice, you will gain insight into which walking speed and duration will bring your heartbeat into the training zone. As you become more physically fit, the speed and duration must be increased to continue making progress. Otherwise, you would merely maintain the level of fitness you have achieved.

If you want a measurement of how your heart is doing or if you want to avoid taking continual measurements, you can measure the physical fitness of your heart by taking the three-minute step test, which measures your heart recovery rate.

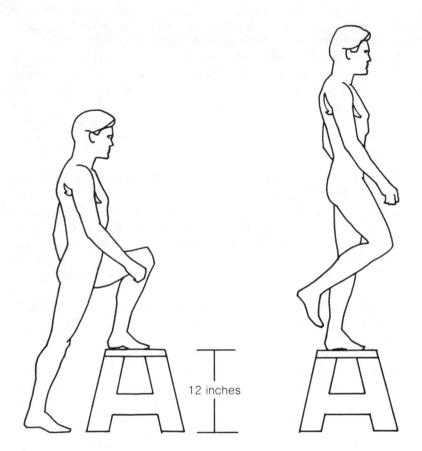

12 inches

Step Test

1. Step up onto a stair approximately 7–12 inches high. Take two steps up and two steps down in a five-second period, or 24 times in 60 seconds.
2. Do this for three minutes.
3. Stop the activity and then time your heartbeat for 30 seconds. Wait another 30 seconds.
4. The number of heartbeats in this second 30-second period is your heart recovery rate score.

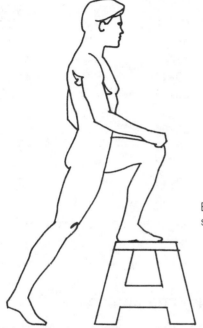

Each group of up-and-down steps takes five seconds.

There are, of course, a variety of other methods for measuring the heart's fitness, such as running in place, doing sit-ups, etc. All consist of doing strenuous physical activity to raise the heart rate to its maximum and then measuring the time the heart takes to return to its resting rate. You can set up your own schedule of improvement in this area. Compare your recovery rate with rates on page 110 for your level of cardiovascular fitness.

Note again that your heart rate will go down for a given-intensity exercise as your fitness improves.

Step Test Classifications
(based on 30-second recovery heart rates)

Level of Performance	Age			
	20–29	30–39	40–49	50 & up
Men		Number of Beats		
Poor (I)	50–59	50–59	52–60	52–62
Fair (II)	43–49	44–49	45–51	46–51
Good (III)	41–42	42–43	43–44	44–45
Very Good (IV)	37–40	39–41	40–42	41–43
Excellent (V)	34–36	35–38	37–39	37–40
Women				
Poor (I)	55–66	56–66	57–67	58–66
Fair (II)	47–54	48–55	48–56	50–57
Good (III)	45–46	46–47	46–47	48–49
Very Good (IV)	43–44	43–45	44–45	45–47
Excellent (V)	39–42	39–42	41–43	41–44

Thirty-second heart rate is counted beginning 30 seconds after exercise stops.

Measuring Muscular Strength and Endurance

A variety of methods by which to measure your muscles can be considered, including the common one of measuring the muscles width around. Observations of muscle tone (definition) will also give you some results. Perhaps the most significant measurement is that of muscle performance. You can measure this by doing a series of push-ups, sit-ups, or leg lifts, before starting and after completing your walking exercise program. With sit-ups, see how many you can do in 30 seconds. With push-ups, chin-ups, or leg lifts, see how many you can do overall. Leg lifts should be done using a series of increasing weights to measure the maximum number of repetitions you can do at each weight level. (The chart on page 111 gives you the averages that represent levels of physical fitness.)

You should observe definite improvements in muscle strength

Physical Fitness Tests

Push-ups for Males, No Time Limit

Age	Poor (I)	Fair (II)	Good (III)	Very Good (IV)	Excellent (V)
20–29	0–19	20–34	35–44	45–54	55 & up
30–39	0–14	15–24	25–34	35–44	45 & up
40–49	0–11	12–19	20–29	30–39	40 & up
50–59	0–7	8–14	15–24	25–34	35 & up
60–69	0–5	6–9	10–19	20–29	30 & up

Modified Pushups for Females, No Time Limit

20–29	0–5	6–16	17–33	34–48	49 & up
30–39	0–3	4–11	12–24	25–39	40 & up
40–49	0–2	3–7	8–19	20–34	35 & up
50–59	0–1	2–5	6–14	15–29	30 & up
60–69	0	1–2	3–4	5–19	20 & up

Sit-ups for Males, Per Minute

20–29	0–32	33–36	37–42	43–47	48 & up
30–39	0–24	25–28	29–34	35–39	40 & up
40–49	0–19	20–23	24–29	30–34	35 & up
50–59	0–14	15–18	19–24	25–29	30 & up
60–69	0–9	10–13	14–19	20–24	25 & up

Sit-ups for Females, Per Minute

20–29	0–28	29–32	33–38	39–43	44 & up
30–39	0–20	21–24	25–30	31–35	36 & up
40–49	0–15	16–18	19–25	26–30	31 & up
50–59	0–10	11–14	15–20	21–25	26 & up
60–69	0–5	6–9	10–15	16–20	21 & up

and endurance from any walking exercise program. Walking longer, walk climbing, or backpacking will further enhance muscular strength. This applies the theory of overload in which muscles develop by increasing the frequency, intensity, and duration of the exercise.

Measuring Walking Speed and Distance

To determine the exercise value of a particular walking activity we can also measure its aerobic intensity in relation to the speed in which it is undertaken and to the distance traveled. By using the guidelines and tables on page 000, you should be able to compute approximate intensity ranges that are broken down into five levels of fitness. By determining the intensity level for yourself, you can also rate yourself on what level of fitness you are at and what fitness goals you would choose.

Measuring Speed

You can measure your walking speed either by measuring the number of steps per minute or timing yourself over a known distance. Walking speed is expressed in steps per minute, in minutes per mile, or in miles per hour. I found the steps-per-minute approach to be the best because it helps you monitor and control your walking speed while walking. You can speed up or slow down if you are going too slowly or too fast.

To use the steps-per-minute approach, know the length of your stride or step. Do this by marking off a distance of 25 feet and count the number of steps required to walk this distance. Mark your last step before completing the measured distance and subtract that distance from the total and divide it by the number of steps. This will give you your average step length (see below).

It's a good idea to measure your step length from time to time because your steps grow longer from practicing your walking exercise techniques.

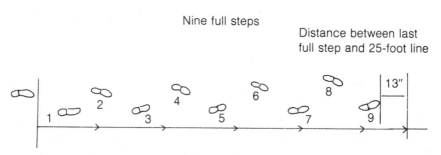

Measuring Steps Per Minute.

Once you know the length of your step, you will be able to measure your steps per minute by counting as you walk. If you multiply the number of steps by 60, you'll have your steps per hour. If you divide that amount by 5,280 you'll have your miles per hour speed. Once you've done this calculation a few times, you'll be able to do it in your head. (The chart below gives you a conversion table for converting steps per minute into mph.)

Walking Speed Conversion Table

Miles per Hour	Steps per Minute	Minutes per Mile
1.00	30	60.0
1.50	40	40.0
2.00	45	30.0
2.50	60	24.0
3.00	90	20.0
3.50	100	17.0
3.75	110	16.0
4.00	120	15.0
4.25	125	14.0
4.50	130	13.0
4.75	135	12.6
5.00	140	12.0
5.50	150	10.9
6.00	160	10.0
7.00	160–180	8.6
8.00	180–190	7.5
9.00	190–200	6.7
10.00	200+	6.0

NOTE: The mile-per-hour-to-steps-per-minute rate conversion will vary from individual to individual depending on stride lengths for both the natural and dynamic or exercise walking. For speeds in excess of 5.50 mph, the tendency will be to increase speed more by lengthening the stride than by increasing the number of steps. You will be able to compute your own steps per minute (spm) rate by timing yourself and counting your steps over a measured distance under a range of walking speeds from slow to fast.

Measuring Distance Walked

If you know your walking speed and you maintain a steady pace, just multiply speed by time spent walking and you'll have the distance. However, most walkers will vary their pace over long distances, which makes this method impractical. When you cannot easily compute the distance you walked from a map, the best measuring device is the pedometer. You can set many pedometers for your step or stride length, and they will convert the number of steps you take into miles. Some pedometers merely count the steps, and you'll have to do the arithmetic on your own. Pedometers are useful because they eliminate much of the counting and computation from the walking and can help you compute your speed. Chapter 17 goes into more detail about the use of the pedometer.

Measuring Flexibility

Flexibility is one of the four aspects of an exercise. Many activities tend to tighten the muscles, developing some muscles so that they become stronger than their opposite pair. Inactivity or lack of exercise also robs the muscles of flexibility due to disuse. This in turn restricts the range of motion and the skill, dexterity, quickness, and grace of your actions. When you lack muscle flexibility you are unable to move as fast. Lack of flexibility slows you down in general and can contribute to your overall decline in physical movement.

The stretching exercises and calisthenics in Chapter 4 will contribute to improving flexibility if you are inactive or to maintaining flexibility while strengthening your muscles. You will be able to measure your progress by testing the range of motion for the individual body joints and body parts. You should concentrate first on keeping the major joints and muscles—neck, shoulders, hips, lower back, knees, and the back and front of your leg muscles—flexible.

Here is a series of tests to monitor your flexibility:

1. *Trunk Flexion Test.* Try to touch your toes while keeping your knees locked.
2. *Neck Stretch.* Try touching your shoulder with your head without shrugging your shoulders.

3. *Hamstring and Lower Back Stretch.* Sit with your legs extended and close together and try to press your head down to your knees. You may grab the back of your calves to help pull yourself down.
4. *Spread Eagle Stretch.* Sit with your legs straight and spread apart on the floor. Without bending, stretch them as far apart as they will go. Measure the angle.
5. *Hurdler's Stretch.* Sit with one leg extended straight out in front and the other bent back behind you. Try touching your head to your knee. Reverse legs and try with the other side.
6. *Wrist Extension and Flexion.* Push your hand back against wrist.
7. *Shoulder Flexion.* Raise each of your arms one at a time and push the elbow of the raised arm back.
8. *Lower Back Stretch.* Lie face down and lift your upper body up, bending it as far back as you can.

Measuring Inclines for Slope Walking

Before taking to the hills or stairs you should estimate the grade of the incline you want to walk climb. For hills you can do this by using a topographical map and locating the elevation of your starting and finishing points, then measuring the distance in between, usually via the route you will travel. With these figures you can construct a simulated elevation triangle (see top figure, page 116) with the height equal to the change in elevation, the base equal to the straight-line distance between your lowest and highest elevation. The resulting angle on your simulated drawing, which rises from the base line to the diagonal line, is the average grade of ascent of your slope walk. (If it's in the 6°–11.3° range it's easy; the 13°–20° range; medium; and the 21°–45° range, hard. These ranges will correspond to the III to V levels of fitness exercises in Chapter 11. In other words, you should not begin such a routine until you have progressed through the first two levels of level walking.

Climbing stairs is a little different from hill climbing but not much. You should know that, like hills, stairs vary in the degree of incline, but it's usually around 27.5° (unless, of course, it's a set of stairs built in the Middle Ages or by unsophisticated architects who did not account for the degree of human effort to get up them or wanted to save money and use fewer steps). Since

Measuring Incline Using Information
from a Contour Map

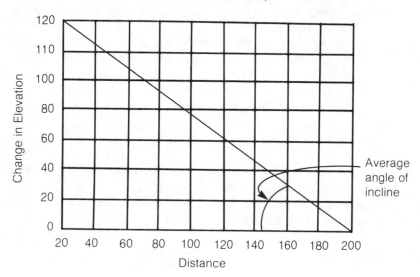

In this example, the change in elevation is 120 feet and the distance between the highest point and the lowest point is 200 feet. Using regular graph paper, you can create a similar chart keeping in mind that the distances must be plotted in equal proportions—in the example, one box equals 20 feet.

Measuring Incline of a Stair

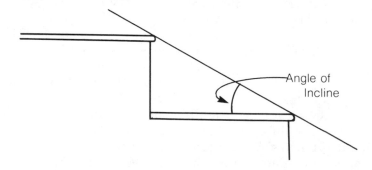

you can't easily compute the incline of stairs with elevation maps, I suggest you measure a sample of the individual stairs themselves with a ruler or, even better, a protractor. The height of the riser is your vertical side of the triangle, the distance from the edge of one riser to the edge of the next is the diagonal, and the width of the riser (i.e., the step) is your baseline. Then use the elevation-triangle method just described. If you have a protractor, measure the angle from the step to the diagonal, which you can form by placing the ruler or even a straight stick spanning the edges of the two risers (see bottom figure, page 116). The protractor will then indicate the angle.

The Rule-of-Thumb Approach to Measuring and Evaluating Exercise

As mentioned earlier in this chapter, there are convenient rule-of-thumb measuring methods that can be substituted for the methods discussed so far. But first, here are some pointers on methods that should be used in measuring exercisewalking activities.

When measuring normal or **self-paced walking** the best method is to measure the distance walked. You can get your own calories-per-mile work rate by looking under your weight column to find the caloric value for each mile walked in the second table in the Appendix, pages 258–259. If you are using walking as a basic conditioning exercise, you can measure your heart rate before, during, and after walking. However, once you notice no improvement in your basic heart rate, you'll have to move on to more advanced fitness level conditioning exercises.

When computing the exercise value of **fast-walking styles** the best method is to measure your heart rate because you are mainly interested in the intensity of your work effort. Of course, you can increase the intensity of the exercise by increasing the speed so once you have been able to correlate a specific heart rate with a given speed you will know you have reached that heart rate if you have reached the speed. However, this is only good for a specific conditioning range. As you improve, these correlations will change.

You increase your brisk or fast walking styles for 3–5 mph

while at the same time increasing your heart rate while exercising. You should measure your progress by using the step test and by measuring your heart rate while at rest. Your resting rate should decline as you get comfortable doing more exercise. You should also measure your heart rate while exercising. It, too, should be lower. In other words, there should be fewer beats per minute for the same amount of exercise. The more you exercise, the more conditioned you become.

By increasing your walking speed you can reduce your walking time. Thus, you get more out of every minute of brisk walking than you would get out of normal walking. The caloric value for the distance you walk is about the same; you merely achieve the same burn rate in less time. For example, walking 10 minutes at 1 mph is worth one-third of walking 10 minutes at 3 mph, mainly because you walked a longer distance and had more leg repetitions. And that's the simplest arithmetic an exercisewalker needs to bother with!

Weight-loaded walking revolves around the amount of extra weight you add to your body while walking. In effect you are exercising at the rate of a person who would have your new combined rate. Thus, the work effort expended when weight loading is proportional to the work effort of heavier persons. The effect of adding weight will vary depending on where it is added and your capacity to carry that weight. Both weight-loaded walking and fast-walking styles contribute to the amount of overall work effort while walking. As an example, a person of 150 pounds will need a smaller work effort if he's at fitness level III than a person at the same weight but only at fitness Level II. With each physical fitness component you have a level associated with it which is, in effect, your starting level in an exercise program. But it's also your work effort efficiency level for any particular work effort.

Based on normal walking, you raise your caloric burn rate per minute 0.2 calories for every 7 pounds of additional weight you add to your trunk or *for every pound to your legs*. That means that, if you add a 35-pound backpack to a 110-pound body, the number of calories you burn while walking at a normal pace in one hour will go from 240 K to about 312–315 K. In other words, you will be burning calories not at the rate of a 110-pound person but a 145-pound person. If you added again as much as your weight (30–80), you would double your calories. Of course walking with double your weight is very strenuous. But in terms of percentages you can safely and gradually go up to carrying one-third of your body weight. This means that you can increase your caloric burn rate per hour by up to one-third by adding additional weight to your trunk.

Rules-of-Thumb for Use on the Trail

The following rule-of-thumb approaches come in handy for determining exercisewalking values while you're on the trail.

The Walking Distance

The basic exercisewalking measurements are time and distance walked. You should really be interested in distance here. However, if you are not sure of the distance, you can guestimate from the time you spent walking the average walking speed you used over that distance. Each mile walked at any speed has a basic caloric value. Of course, if you add more upper body action or a weight load, that mile will have a greater caloric value. But assuming normal or free walking within a certain speed range, the caloric value of the distance walked remains constant.

The Walking Work Effort

You can increase the caloric expenditure for each mile walked by increasing the work effort you must apply over that mile. You increase it by adding weight to the body, which means that your new caloric burn rate is that of somebody who weighs as much as you do with your additional weight load. By using the caloric tables based on body weight you can compute the increase in calories per mile. It usually increases by a factor of one with each pound added to the trunk and a factor of five or seven with each pound added to a moving limb leg or arm. You can also increase the caloric effort if the incline is steeper or the terrain is more rugged.

Walking Intensity

The harder you work while walking, (the more intense your exercisewalk) the greater the caloric output. To work harder the body must have a greater amount of oxygen to increase the output of its energy within a limited time. This, in turn, taxes the cardiovascular system, raising the heart rate. Work Rates that raise the heart rate into the training zone of 70%–85% of its maximum rate also train the heart and the skeletal muscles.

Conclusion

Many of the measuring methods described in this chapter are simple enough that they can be used while you're walking without interrupting your exercise. Measuring your heart rate and steps-per-minute, for example, become as natural as breathing for practiced exercisewalkers. Veteran walkers, however, may even take the rule-of-thumb approach a step further. Exercisewalkers at a high level of fitness may intuitively know when their work intensity or energy expenditure rate is changing. This does not necessarily mean however, that they should stop monitoring their heart rate. Basic signals such as extra sweating and heavier-than-normal breathing may warn the exercisewalker of existent changes, but the walker should follow up on these signs with more reliable measurements, as described in this chapter.

7

CONVERTING WALKING ACTIVITIES INTO EXERCISES

Walking for exercise can be done like any other exercise for which you set aside a specific training time and perform according to a schedule or routine, or you can give the walking you already do an exercise purpose and monitor it accordingly. You can make the walking you do more exercise oriented by applying the walking techniques described in Chapter 3 and by using one or more of the exercisewalking principles from Chapter 5. By making the walking you presently do more dynamic, you are actually exercising without having to set aside extra time for "exercising." Walking has that distinct advantage over any other form of exercise activity because it readily blends in with your daily activities, making it easier to stick to as well as to start.

Before making your walking activities more exercise oriented, you should determine what your level of fitness is. The tests in Chapter 6 can help you determine which of the following five levels of fitness best describes you: I (Poor), II (Fair), III (Good), IV (Very Good), V (Excellent). Again, physical fitness is relative to the individual's needs and age. These levels have been established by various research studies with reference to the fitness and performance of the general population divided into age groups (and often by gender).

Most people who are sedentary for periods of six weeks or more fall into the lowest category, regardless of previous physical conditioning efforts. Studies show that if you stop exercising it will be only a matter of time before your fitness level drops into the lower range. If regular walking at a slow to moderate pace is practiced without any further, more vigorous exercise, you should expect no change in a poor or fair fitness level. On the other hand, regular exercisewalking as described so far in this book—involving brisk walking, hill climbing, leg lifting (hiking), long-distance walking, or weight-loaded walking—is capable of raising your overall fitness level into the good to excellent range.

Walking Activities

Walking is something you already do. To convert your walking activities to exercisewalking you need to identify the exercise style of walking being performed and then analyze what can be done to it to provide a greater training effect.

Let's look at some walking activities and analyze them in relation to the exercisewalking principles so the most can be gained from each movement.

Strolling

Strolling is perhaps the slowest form of walking. Any slower and our feet would merely scrape along the ground without being lifted. By definition strolling would not qualify as aerobic walking, but it still counts in a walking-for-miles program (see page 213). Strolling time should be rated as one mile for every hour spent strolling. This amount should not be sneezed at since strolling hours and miles can add up to significant work. An after-dinner stroll could stretch to two hours or two miles while a Sunday morning or afternoon stroll could stretch to three or four hours. Even walking the dog for 20 minutes a day can add another mile or so a week.

If 30 miles of additional walking is your exercisewalking goal, strolling could make up to one-third of this goal. However, you shouldn't base your whole exercise program on strolling. It's not vigorous; so it has the effect of a limbering-up exercise rather than the effect of training. Strolling is particularly effective if it is done in conjunction with more vigorous walking. Strolling is valuable as an exercise because repetitious movements of the body's walking muscle groups each hour aids circulation and burns off calories, albeit at a slow rate.

Everyday Walking

This is the most common form of walking—it's the kind we do to get from place to place on relatively smooth and flat ground, city pavement, country roads, and park paths. It can be called *walking with a purpose*. It is characterized by an average speed of 3 mph but some people may walk only 1–2 mph. The caloric value of everyday walking is about 300–400 calories an hour, depending on how much you weigh and on your speed. Everyday walking also raises the heart rate to the 50–75 percent training level. If you are in poor physical condition, the heart rate may go even higher.

Walking for Exercise at Your Normal Pace. The walking techniques learned in Chapter 3 can easily be practiced during everyday walking periods. Applying techniques is a more defined and conscious form of walking, which can be done in business clothes or in any type of loose-fitting clothing. The heel-toe motion and application of a wider stride will result in a brisker pace, converting much of your everyday walking into brisk walking. One can also allow the arms to swing in a moderate arc. Rhythmic breathing exercises can also be practiced during this activity. Concentrate on the proper placement of the heel and parallel leg movements while maintaining a properly erect posture. You can do your foot-rolling motion even in dress shoes if they are flexible enough.

Walking Tours. Taking walking tours of cities or even countries is another opportunity to use the everyday walking pace. These tours are becoming an increasingly popular form of sightseeing while traveling and are the city equivalent of hiking in the wilderness. However, architecture, rather than nature, is their

The Six Basic Styles of Walking and Related Activities
(including measurements of exercise value)

Walking Styles	Average Speed (mph)	Average Duration (minutes)	Average Distance (miles)	Calories (per mile)	Heart Rate (% of max)
1. Self-paced slow walking, strolling, ambling, birdwatching, shuffling, beach-combing, golfing	1–2	15–60	1–2	100	0–50
Functional walk-to-work, walk touring, "beat" walking, appointments, shopping, walkathoning	2–3	60–150	4.6	100	50–70
2. Hiking dayhiking, bushwhacking, trekking, rambling, orienteering	1–3	60–600	5–50	100–300	50–70

The Six Basic Styles of Walking and Related Activities
(including measurements of exercise value) (continued)

Walking Styles	Average Speed (mph)	Average Duration (minutes)	Average Distance (miles)	Calories (per mile)	Heart Rate (% of max)
3. **Long-distance walking** trail, beach, or road walking, cross-country	2–5	300–600	20–50	100–300	60–85
4. **Walk climbing** stair climbing, hill walking, peakbagging, snowshoeing, mountain trekking	1–2	120–360	12–15	200–600	50–90
5. **Brisk walking** aerobic walking, marching, rushing, Swedish exercise, speed walking	3–5	15–60	2–5	100–130	70–85

The Six Basic Styles of Walking and Related Activities
(including measurements of exercise value) (continued)

Walking Styles	Average Speed (mph)	Average Duration (minutes)	Average Distance (miles)	Calories (per mile)	Heart Rate (% of max)
(Fast) Racewalking Olympic race-walking, jogging, cross-country skiing, roller skating, walk sprinting	5–10	15–120	2.5–20	106–192	70–85
6. **Weight-loaded walking** backpacking, heavy-limbed walking, portaging	1–3	60–360	.67–3	300–900	70–90

main focus of study. Guidebooks of major tourist areas not only show the walking route but give the amount of time it takes to cover it. If no book exists, tourist bureaus usually have pamphlets or guides available for this purpose. If you have the time, and you should try to make it your goal, walking is the best way to get to know an area. It's just the right speed for exploring, learning, getting impressions, and even meeting people. Walking usually offers the proper perspective from which to view older buildings because these sights were built by people who moved about on foot. In those times, life's tempo was a walking pace. Walking influenced their vision and was perhaps the source of their inspiration.

Walking tours usually range in duration from an hour to half a day. Each city or sightseeing area has walking tours to meet your time requirements, so you can get in a good day's walk while traveling. Even if no guidebook is available, an improvised tour or even a morning or evening walking workout can be fashioned with a sightseeing purpose in mind. This is particularly appropriate for walkers on business trips with little time for sightseeing. Use a city map or your own sense of direction and walk a circle or an arc around your hotel.

The pace of a walking tour is usually 3 mph or less. It is usually faster than strolling because it has a functional purpose with a self-imposed time limit and intermediate stopping points.

Walking tours help you maintain your physical fitness while traveling. Because of the amount of time spent sitting on planes, buses, cars, and trains, your body can get out of shape during vacation periods. Walking will also help relieve the stress of a hectic vacation or business trip. Some people make their whole vacation a walking tour of a country or region.

Walk touring also is an excellent antidote to the overeating that often results from sampling the food, drink, and desserts in foreign countries or U.S. cities you are visiting. An hour's tour is worth the calories of an extra breakfast roll with butter and marmalade. Three hours of walking will help eradicate the effects of a full lunch with dessert. A full day's walking (six to eight hours) will make a sizable dent in the calories consumed at a multiple-course meal with wine.

Hiking and Backpacking

This is perhaps the most enjoyable form of walking. Unfortunately, many of us do little of it, and still others have not yet discovered its joy. It's amazing how many enthusiastic hikers are not even conscious of the health-giving effects of their sport or pastime. When asked about such benefits many do not care to know about them. Some feel that hiking and exercise are contradictory terms—one is for freedom, the other discipline. But, it doesn't have to be that way.

The world is filled with places that are perfect for hiking. In fact, there are so many that it would be impossible to list all of them. In the United States there are mountain and hill areas in the great Northwest, the Colorado Rockies, Arizona's Grand Canyon, the Sierra Nevada Mountains, along the Appalachian Trail, and the White Mountains of New Hampshire. Europe, too, has many hiking sites, including the Black Forest and Bavaria in Germany, the Swiss and Austrian Alps, the fjords in Norway, and the mountains eastward toward the Swedish border. In addition, England, Scotland, Wales, and Ireland have rugged hill country for hiking and walk climbing. People in these areas make walking a way of life, and you can often see it in their physiques. To help you understand the health-giving benefits of hiking, here are some suggestions for exercise hiking.

Speed. Although hikers' speed has traditionally been a slow 2–3 mph, there are a number of ways to prepare yourself for hiking faster. Three mph is by no means a speed barrier. Many hikers and even backpackers are certainly capable of going faster, to four, five, and even six mph, depending on the roughness of the terrain and the hiker's current physical condition. This kind of walking becomes more like marching, however, and it may contradict your personal goals for wilderness wandering. Often hiking involves a route in and a route out. If these are the same paths, a hiker might consider covering one of them at an increased speed. Another device for increasing your hiking speed is to mix hiking with running for at least one hour of the hiking period. Walk 25 paces, run 25 paces; or walk 50, run 50. This will give you the opportunity to train your heart during a hiking day and can give you the ability to move more rapidly. A one-hour

Backpacking in the mountains combines several walking styles: leg lifting, weight loading, and long distance.

hike/run can be placed strategically during the day when you want to get to a place fast.

Stiff hiking boots often hinder the ability to walk faster while hiking because they impede the reflex action of the feet by working against the natural walking motion. (See Chapter 16 for more information on good walking shoe design.) Most people who walk in high stiff hiking boots are not able to walk more than five miles a day without experiencing discomfort, even after the boots are broken in. Unless the terrain is particularly rocky, you might consider going to a lower-cut boot or a lighter-weight hiking boot with a more flexible sole.

Distance. A hiker averages 5–10 miles a day over a 5–7-hour period. This is a relatively slow pace, but with a little effort, hikers can increase their hiking distances to meet an exercise purpose. Hike-walking distances of 10 miles or more are possible in a day. If you are ambitious, a 20-mile hike can be achieved after a series of 10-mile hikes have been completed. (In general, 20 miles as a single-day hike is not recommended because it will leave the unprepared body sore and tired.) Don't plan for more than 10–17 miles, unless the one-day hike is preceded by a training period of increasingly longer walks amounting to at least a medium level of physical exertion.

Many hikers already count their miles and keep charts. An experienced hiker starts with a map and compass and knows where and how far he's going. Without a map distance, a pedometer can help if you can determine how the terrain will affect your normal walking stride. A pedometer is also a useful measuring device for locating or finding your position while hiking. Again, if measurements are not desirable, use your watch to estimate your distance. For difficult terrain, pace your speed at 1–3 mph. Having practiced your brisk walking speeds, you'll be able to use them during hiking and adjust your hourly mileage. If you're just starting out, use the simple device of "equal time in" and "equal time out." A two-hour hike is one hour in and one hour back. However, if your trail goes down in elevation for most of the hike, you should figure the uphill return to be less than twice the time going down (e.g., 1 hour down, 1½ hours up). Know where you're going beforehand so you don't get lost.

Hiking more than three days will give you a full opportunity to turn your hiking/backpacking trip into a complete exercise workout. On such a trip you should start slowly and build up your miles, avoiding, if possible, the onset of blisters.

One excellent way to carry out an extended trek (four or more days) is to hike to a location close to where several trails meet and to set up a base camp. From there you can plan a couple of day hikes that won't require a heavy pack or heavy boots. Base camping allows you to explore a wider area more thoroughly and—if you are in mountains over 8,000 feet—to acclimatize more gradually to high altitude without the added stress of a heavy pack. You can cover more distance on such day hikes and take on steep trails that would be difficult with a heavy pack. After a couple of day hikes you should be in good shape to move your base camp to another location and explore a new area in a similar manner. This technique allows you to work yourself into shape gradually, while still adding mileage to your exercisewalking program as well as covering more ground and seeing more sights.

A good mileage regimen over an eight-day period would be the following.

First Day: 6 miles	Fifth Day: 12 miles
Second Day: 8 miles	Sixth Day: 15 miles
Third Day: 12 miles	Seventh Day: 12 miles
Fourth Day: 10 miles	Eighth Day: 15 miles

Advanced hikers can increase each day's distance by five miles.

Increasing Duration and Frequency. When speed and distance goals have been set at low levels one can still achieve a training effect with hiking by extending the frequency and distance. Weekend hiking can be one or two weeks of walking packed into a two- or three-day period. Weekly hiking of less than two days can be combined with everyday walking of one or two days. For most people, however, hiking tends to be a seasonal activity that is often limited to once or twice a month during the warmer times of the year. Thus, as a regular walking exercise, hiking is usually placed in the seasonal walking category. If it is your favorite sport, you might be able to make it a monthly exercise. A few lucky persons like forest rangers can make it a weekly exercise.

Most people have only seasonal opportunities for hiking, and when it is combined with camping and sightseeing, hiking mileage drops to about five miles a day. Hiking, if performed on a more regular basis, would be a perfect exercise. Hiking can become an acceptable weekly exercise if done in three days with one day of rest in between. The hiking should last at least one hour each day, and the speed should be at least 3 mph. Many hikers limit their actual hiking time to less than five hours. Instead of speeding up your hiking pace, extend your hiking time to 8–10 hours to get more exercise value from it. (See section on long-distance hiking, Chapter 12.)

Body Composition and Heart Rate. The exercise value of hiking will depend on the terrain. Hilly or mountainous terrain will have greater value than flatlands. Hiking over rugged terrain has a similar caloric burn rate to running, particularly when it includes some hills and other obstacles. Hiking with a pack will also enhance the exercise value. It makes the heart work harder, thereby raising the heart rate very quickly into the training zone.

When computing the caloric burn rate, you should add the weight of your pack to your own weight and use the caloric tables in the Appendix. Thus, if you weigh 180 pounds and carry a 30-pound pack, your weight is really 210 pounds. When computing total weight, don't forget to add the weight of your boots and clothing. The best method is to stand on the scale wearing all of your hiking gear. (Remember, however, that the weight of your boots have a 7/1 poundage factor.)

Improving Techniques. When hiking up hills or carrying a backpack, you should lean forward slightly. Your stride will naturally shorten uphill, and it will lengthen downhill. If your arms are free, let them swing naturally. You can pump them more vigorously going uphill to help propel you forward. Backpacking is really like working out with weights: your muscles are training harder because you are lifting your legs higher and applying a greater work effort.

Colin Fletcher, in his book, *The New Complete Walker* (Knopf, 2nd ed., 1968, 1974), recommends resting three to five minutes every hour or so during a long and heavily loaded hike. You can use this time to make adjustments to your pack, take a picture, or just contemplate the scenery. Change socks if the pair you are wearing is wet. Pamper your feet just as you would care for your car on a trip through Death Valley. Don't rest for too long, however, or your leg muscles will cool off and stiffen. Again, rest stops of 3–5 minutes can be taken every hour. I recommend doing 10 minutes of stretching exercises before and after a long rest stop to help get your muscles going.

Hiking is a vast subject requiring its own book to deal with route selection, equipment preparation, wilderness survival, nature study, and other topics. If you are not already hiking, there are a number of good books on this subject. I recommend Colin Fletcher's *The New Complete Walker* as the best book on the subject.

Walking Hills

Hill walking is probably the most vigorous form of walking, whether it's walking up mountains or stairs. Unlike technical mountain climbing, you don't need ropes and pitons to do walk-climbing, but you might want to use a walking stick or staff. (See Chapter 18 for effective uses of the walking stick and staff.)

The pace required for ascents up mountains on foot is too variable to be subject to time measurement. A conservative rule of thumb is one hour for every two miles plus 30 minutes for every 1,000 feet climbed. Experienced walk climbers will take less than this rule-of-thumb formula, but if heavy packs are used, they may not do much better. While the time down the mountain is often faster than the time up, steep and rough descents often take as much time as ascents over the same area. Plan a half-day walk climb to be six miles and a full day to be 10–15 miles. Set the pace on your pedometer at about half your normal step length for such climbs.

Walk climbing is a good example of the trade-off of speed and exertion to raise your heart rate to the training level. Climbing stairs and climbing mountains have a similar aerobic effect. Fifteen minutes of climbing stairs will convince you that it easily makes your heartbeat reach the training zone.

Making Your Walk Climbing More Exercise Oriented. The key to benefiting from walk climbing is to make it a weekly part of your walking program. We have many opportunities for walk climbing that we miss. Once you realize the heart training rate and caloric burn rate you can reach with walk climbing, you'll stop avoiding climbing stairs and hills. Because of the higher leg lift, walk climbing better develops your stomach muscles than normal walking, so you should try to make it part of your walking exercise program. Schedule at least two walk climbs of 10 minutes each week into your walking routine.

Finding inclines in cities may take some searching. Some will consider walking up and down stairs sufficient; while others will take to the hilly parts of their environs. Choose a route to work that goes from lowest to highest and time your ascent to see if it lasts at least 10 minutes. Find a mountain or hill nearest your house. Make this your training ground if it's convenient to reach. Plan your vacation time in the mountains and organize walk climbing outings from your hotel at least every other day.

Even if your climb lasts only a few minutes or seconds, you can get the most from it by doing the following. Lean forward into the climb and take as wide a stride as possible. At home, you can skip steps on a stairway to practice. Hold on to the handrail to avoid falling. The wider your stride, the higher your lift and the more exertion is expanded.

For walks longer than an hour, you should take a more natural, shorter stride to pace yourself and preserve your energy for the total effort. Rest stops on walk climbs can be three to five minutes long every half-hour or a minute every 15 minutes. When climbing mountains you'll have an opportunity to vary your pace as the terrain becomes flatter at various points. Speed up here and get a running start for the next incline. Arm swinging is very useful with walk climbing. The arc is shorter than with everyday walking and is more a pistonlike action than a pendulum swing. Using a walking stick or staff and setting it at proper intervals while pushing forward will produce a similar effect. Swing the free arm, too. If there is no established path up the mountain, your climbing may become more erratic, and you'll have to abandon the rythmic pace.

Most people manage to take their walk climbs on a seasonal basis as part of a hike or vacation in the mountains, but try to convert your walk climbing from a seasonal into a weekly activity. If you use walk climbing as an aerobic exercise, you must do it at least twice a week for two nonconsecutive 10 minute periods. Otherwise, any walk climbing you do should be added to your walking-for-miles program and be counted at the speed you actually do it or at the estimated speed of 1 mph.

Barefoot Walking

Barefoot walking is almost synonymous with beach walking unless you're a poor country boy and have an opportunity to clock most of your walking time barefoot. Beach walking is also seasonal walking unless you live near a sandy shoreline in a warm climate. Practice barefoot walking as much as you can because it exercises your feet, strengthens the arches, and toughens the bottom of the feet. Walk barefoot around the house and in the garden during the warm months. If you're concerned about stepping on something sharp, exercise sandals with arch support are the next best thing. Try to avoid flat sandals. Their flat surface works against the natural arch of your feet and tends to impede the natural walking movement.

Beach walking is perhaps the most reliable form of barefoot walking. Walking through loose sand is a great walking exercise for the feet and the arches. Many athletes purposely train in sand to make them work harder. Sand, more than any other surface, enables the feet to go through their full flexing motion while also stretching the leg muscles, and next to walk climbing, barefoot sand walking is the best walking exercise. Plan some of your walking as barefoot sand walking. It can involve walking the perimeter of a large body of water such as a bay or walking the circumference of the island paradise you're vacationing on. If your route is more than 10 miles around, split it up into a series of half-day or all-day hikes. If getting back to your home base on foot is a problem, arrange to be picked up at the end of each day. If this is not possible, bring a pair of shoes along and walk the shorter distance back to your home base. Start the next day where you left off. Use transportation creatively as part of a dynamic walking method discussed in the next chapter.

Normal walking speed for beach walkers is about 2 mph. With effort you can speed up, but you'll see that maintaining high speeds for more than one hour at a time will be difficult. You should try to work out daily by walking briskly or doing walking sprints in the sand. One way to maintain a rapid pace for a longer period of time is to walk near the water on the wet sand. Despite the workout, barefoot walking can be done for long periods without foot fatigue and blistering because there is no sock or shoe friction.

Walking in Snow

Heavy snow can have the same training effect as walking in heavy sand. Using waterproof boots, you can hike in packed snow or snow that isn't too deep. There are various ways to walk through the snow, three of which require special equipment: snowshoeing, downhill (Alpine) skiing, and cross-country (Nordic) skiing. Without snowshoes or skis, however, walking through snow can be difficult but can help you enormously in intensifying the work effort of your walking. Yet, when most of the United States experiences snow for at least three or four months out of the year, getting outside in the fresh air to walk during those months is going to require special equipment.

Snowshoeing is the winter equivalent of hiking. Snowshoes allow the walker to stay on top of the snow and, with practice, "shuffle" across flatlands and climb up or down hills. Although the snowshoes greatly reduce the resistance that deep snow creates for the walker, snowshoeing still requires a great deal of energy and effort while making travel over long distances acceptable. Of course, the resistance is what enhances the exercise benefits of walking in snow.

Nordic skiing has become very popular in recent years, partly because it makes travel in snow-covered wilderness areas possible and provides excellent aerobic exercise even when performed on a track in a municipal park. Great distances can be covered with ease by experienced Nordic skiers, and the whole body receives an excellent workout.

While most Alpine skiing requires skill in handling downhill navigation, it can become exercisewalking when applied to walking on snow on the flat or walking uphill. Next time you go

downhill skiing, avoid the jammed lift lines and walk up the hill, either using a side-step technique or walking in V-step fashion. Both ways provide good leg-strength exercise, which is vital for keeping skis together and providing the ability for the legs to pump up and down when skiing back down the hill.

Brisk Walking/Speed Walking

Brisk walking is walking at 3.5–4.96 mph or faster. It is really any fast walking speed that can be done in business clothes. Researchers have determined this to be the speed at which the heart rate for most people will rise to its training rate. We have all experienced brisk walking in the normal course of our lives. Hurrying to an appointment and too tired to run, we still move our feet at a rapid pace. Many people can brisk walk for a 5- to 10-minute period, but for a walking exercise, you must learn to brisk walk for at least 10 minutes each exercise period or 30–60 minutes a week. This will be a new experience for the beginning exercisewalker.

Walking fast is a rapid leg movement of 120 steps a minute instead of 60 steps per minute, the everyday walking pace. The walking programs in Chapter 8 will show you how to increase your speed gradually. If you've never experienced the sensation of speedwalking or have forgotten it, see Chapter 10 on advanced walking techniques (Walk Sprinting).

As a brisk walker you can hope to raise your walking speed to 5–6 mph without using any special walking techniques. You can practice brisk walking exercises by applying the walking techniques learned in Chapter 3 and later in Chapter 10. It will help if you swing your arms rhythmically, synchronizing the swing with your leg motions and with your breathing. An even faster form of walking, racewalking, is described in Chapter 12.

Perhaps the easiest way to sustain a period of brisk walking is to walk using a four-second rhythmic counting method—"one and, two and, three and, four and." After you have practiced this rhythmic pacing method, it will become second nature to "feel" your walking speed. Rhythmic walking not only helps you determine your speed; it also teaches you to maintain it by speeding up and slowing down to meet your training purposes. Once you've learned to determine and control your walking speed, you can speed up many of your everyday walking activities by turning them into exercises rather than just movements for getting from place to place.

The Next Step

Now that you have considered the advantages of making your everyday walking activities more exercise oriented, the next step is to develop actual exercisewalking routines. The next part of this book will suggest how you can design your own personal routines as well as focus on particular walking styles and explain how they can be adapted into exercise routines.

PART IV

EXERCISEWALKING ROUTINES

I recently started weight training at a health club in New York as an experiment to improve my upper body strength. The results have been satisfactory so far, but in the weeks I've been training I have seen how many men drop out of the club's training classes. In speaking with some of them, I discovered that after sticking to one weight training routine for more than a year, they "burned out." Working out at a health club seemed to cut the trainers off from the rest of their world.

The routinization and high intensity of many exercise programs can be self-defeating—you may advance a level or more in fitness and then "plateau," at which point the exercise routine no longer works or you become utterly bored. The better approach to a long-term program of fitness would seem to suggest varying exercise routines and incorporating them more into your life. Exercisewalking routines, as you will see, have a great deal to offer in this approach: variety both in the exercises and in the environment where the exercises can be done.

Part IV of this book shows how to convert walking exercise activities into routines. That is, it shows how the different styles of walking incorporate the various exercisewalking principles discussed in Chapter 5 and how they can be used as part of walking routines, either on their own or as part of the recreational or functional walking that you already do.

Exercisewalking routines are specific exercises involving either a walking style or a walking activity. There are only six basic styles but perhaps 100 walking activities using these styles. There are basic and advanced routines as well as maintenance routines and you should start with the routine that best corresponds to your current level of physical fitness. Some routines are done by setting aside a time and place for exercising. Others are accomplished by blending the walking routine into your everyday walking.

The routines in chapters 8–12 help you increase walking distance, enhance speed, apply technique, and use other pointers to make walking more exercise oriented. Chapter 8 discusses designing personal exercisewalking routines and suggests some rudimentary approaches to progression in fitness as well as to maintaining a particular fitness level. In Chapter 9 you will learn self-paced walking routines; in Chapter 10, aerobic walking routines; and in Chapter 11, special leg-strengthening routines. Chapter 12 focuses on advanced routines for those at high levels of fitness. All routines are described in terms of the exercisewalking principles that are applied.

Exercisewalking is a method of physical development using walking styles and activities to train and maintain the body's health and physical condition. The exercise part of walking is distinguishable from walking as recreation, function, sport, or art because it is a more systematic and comprehensive training program.

Walking can be a conditioning exercise medium only when it is repeated regularly and not just undertaken on a one-shot basis. This is not as prohibitive a qualification as it might seem. Many people actually do get regular exercise through walking but don't consider the activity's orientation as an exercise before—or after—the fact. Upon closer examination of their daily habits, however, they often realize that their walking is regular, continuous, and systematic and therefore may qualify as exercise.

Walking is an efficient exercise because you needn't set aside massive amounts of special time to participate in it. Instead, you can use existing walking time or convert some transportation time into exercise time. Even if you are, or have become, totally sedentary, you can find time to do your walking exercises.

Making walking more exercise oriented means increasing the distance walked on a daily and weekly basis. It means applying walking techniques to all walking styles and activities. It means being conscious of the different exercise values of walking and how they add up to the daily exercise requirements you set for yourself. It also means making use of a variety of walking styles to enhance the exercise value and to keep walking interesting.

The exercise routines that follow, based on different walking styles and activities, must be learned as separate techniques or approaches. But after you understand them you will be able to keep them in mind when you do your regular walking activities, or, if you prefer and you have the time, you can set up exercise periods just for walking.

8

DESIGNING PERSONAL WALKING ROUTINES

Many different walking exercise routines and activities can provide varying levels of physical fitness, depending on what your personal goals are for level and type of fitness. You might only want to achieve a comfortable fitness that gets you through the workday without great fatigue and lets you participate in moderately active sports, or you might want to improve your strength, endurance, and cardiovascular capacity significantly to participate in vigorously competitive sports like soccer or running. Walking exercises can fulfill any of these goals.

Three Exercisewalking Routines

All walking exercise programs have a number of common characteristics. Each is based on exercise schedules which progressively increase walking time (minutes), distance (miles), speed (steps per minute, mph), frequency (number of times practiced) each week. A full schedule of walking exercises consists of a starter program, a progressive exercise program, and a maintenance program. Knowing the ranges and target goals of these exercise programs will help you fashion your own program.

A Starter Routine for Out-of-Shape Walkers

A starter routine usually lasts from 4–6 weeks and begins with as few as 10 minutes of daily or every-other-day walking and progresses to 45 minutes daily in the fourth to sixth week. The weekly walking hours increase 1–3 hours. You can vary the walking frequency from 3–6 times a week, depending on the amount of time spent on each walking session. When you have only 10 minutes your frequency should be six times a week. If your sessions are 30–45 minutes long, your frequency could be three times a week. (In the latter case, walking every other day is preferable.) The average distances walked in starter programs increase from one to three miles daily or from about 3–6 miles weekly.

The walking speed in a starter routine ranges from 2–4 mph or

---

Sample Walking Program for Beginners

For those people who find that as they walk their heart rate is below their target zone.

Week 1: Walk 20 minutes a day 3 times a week, or 15 minutes a day 5 times a week.

Week 2: Walk 25 minutes a day 3 times a week, or 18 minutes a day 5 times a week.

Week 3: Walk 30 minutes a day 3 times a week, or 20 minutes a day 5 times a week.

Week 4: Walk 35 minutes a day 3 times a week, or 22 minutes a day 5 times a week.

Week 5: Walk 40 minutes a day 3 times a week, or 25 minutes a day 5 times a week.

Week 6: Walk 45 minutes a day 3 times a week, or 30 minutes a day 5 times a week.

---

from 60–120 steps per minute, depending on the level of conditioning. If you prefer to maintain a low or moderate speed, you should increase the duration of your walk until you've reached your heart target training rate. Start with a total of 1½ hours and build to three hours and increase your frequency to six times a week.

Once you've completed your starter routine, you should either go on to a more progressive routine or a maintenance routine. You will be at a comfortable but acceptable level of fitness. If you stop now, your conditioning results will reverse themselves in 5–10 weeks.

A Progressive Walking Routine

This routine should be followed for an additional 15–18 weeks and gradually raise your level of fitness from moderate to excellent. It begins where the starter program left off and progresses from three hours of weekly walking to eight. This involves a per-day or per-workout session of about 45 minutes and in some programs as many as 75 minutes. The steps per minute increase from 120–176 at a speed of 4–6 mph. The daily mileage usually stays in the 3–4-mile range, though some programs advocate as many as eight miles per day for slow walkers who walk at 2 mph. Weekly mileage will range from 9–26 miles. Racewalkers often train at a weekly walking mileage of 125 miles, and long-distance walkers go even higher, up to 200 miles per week. This is full-time training and produces a conditioning effect equivalent to that of an Olympic athlete.

A Basic Maintenance Routine

A maintenance program is usually related to your last practiced weekly walking exercise level. If you reached three hours of walking or about eight miles a week, you can maintain that level by continuing that level at a normal speed. This is also true for higher physical fitness levels. Three hours of weekly walking will amount to a 10–25-pound caloric burn rate annually. If you were that many pounds overweight when you started, you would be able to lose that weight in a 6–12-month period by maintaining this level of activity.

Walking Program for Progressive Development

Week	Pace (mph)	Distance	Repetitions per Session	Total Time (minutes)	Caloric Expense	Total Distance (miles)
1	4.5	220 yds	11	34	255	2.75
2	5.0	220 yds	11	34	255	2.75
3	4.5	220 yds	8	37	290	3.50
4	5.0	440 yds	8	37	290	3.50
5	4.5	440 yds	4	37	340	3.50
6	5.5	880 yds	4	37	340	3.50
7	4.5	550 yds	4	38	345	3.25
8	5.5	880 yds	4	38	345	3.25
9	4.75	550 yds	4	37	365	3.25
10	5.5	880 yds	4	37	365	3.25
11	5.0	1.0 mile	2	40	370	3.50
12	5.5	.75 mile	2	40	370	3.50
13	5.0	1.0 mile	2	40	390	3.50
14	5.75	.75 mile	2	40	390	3.50
15	5.25	.75 mile	2	38	455	3.50
16	5.75	1.0 mile	2	38	455	3.50
17	5.5	.50 mile	2	42	470	4.00
18	5.75	1.5 miles	2	42	470	4.00
19	5.5	.50 mile	2	41	470	4.00
20	6.0	1.5 miles	2	41	470	4.00

An Advanced Maintenance Routine

At the higher levels of training you do not have to train as hard to maintain your conditioning unless you are a competitive walker. To maintain good to excellent condition, a well-conditioned walker should set his weekly target goals of exercising four times a week (four to six hours) at a speed of 4–5 mph. At this pace you should be able to walk 9–16 miles a week. This is a good base from which to go higher if you wish.

In the four chapters that follow, you will see examples of these three types of routines. You can use the routines in this chapter as designed or modify them using the exercisewalking principles expanded upon in the rest of Part IV. A routine is something you will need to stick to, so design it in such a way that it never gets dull and always meets your fitness goals.

9

SELF-PACED WALKING

Self-paced walking is the walking you do without thinking about it. This style of walking can be slow (60 steps per minute or 1–2 mph), giving you enough time to stop and look around, or normal speed (2–3 mph). The exact pace you adopt usually is governed by your mood: when you are relaxed you are likely to walk slowly; when you are hurried you walk at the normal pace. The pace is also influenced by your environment. A country road or city park will make you want to walk more slowly whereas the pavement and concrete covering your route to work or to the local supermarket will tend to make you increase your speed.

In this chapter we will describe walking routines that incorporate self-paced walking styles: slow walking and functional (normal) walking.

Slow Walking

Slow walking takes many forms. The old *art* of walking, for example, is a self-paced walking style. One term used to describe slow walking is *to saunter*, which means to walk leisurely or stroll. This is a slow, aimless type of walking, an idle stroll, and its origins can be traced to the time of the pilgrimmages to the Holy Land during the Middle Ages. Those who were on their way to the Holy Land were walking or going "à la *Sainte Terre*," and the derivative *saunter* came to refer to the rambling style of walkers who walked like Holy Landers. Other sources say that *saunter* actually came from the French phrase *sans terre*, referring to those without land or home.

In addition to *sauntering*, slow walking can be described as *strolling*, *wandering*, or *rambling*. The terms cover walking that falls within a range of 1–2.5 mph, with fewer than 100 steps taken per minute (though the average is 1–2 mph, or 60 steps per minute, as stated above). This is known as the *comfortable* walking speed. Remember that walking under 1 mph (e.g., *shuffling*) can be both uncomfortable and inefficient.

Strolling is the term used most often to refer to this type of walking in the United States. Note that this is not to be confused with *hiking*, which is really reserved for walking over rugged terrain (see Chapter 11).

Wandering is the term favored by Germans, and it is truly an art in that country. *Wandern* is the German national pastime. It is a manner of moving about or traveling without destination or purpose, though to qualify as *wandern* (on foot), it must be done in a natural environment away from paved streets. For some Germans the pastime is a serious spiritual activity in which they commune with nature.

Rambling is used to refer to slow walking by the British, and it is basically the same as the American *strolling*.

As mentioned earlier, even slow walking has exercise value: it improves circulation, tones leg muscles, and provides a means of weight control. It does not, however, provide improvements in aerobic or cardiovascular fitness unless the walker is completely out of shape to begin with. In such cases slow walking can help you reach the first level of fitness. Slow walking can help anyone *maintain* a basic level of fitness, but for most, it must be supplemented with other, more vigorous types of walking.

In order to make walking more exercise oriented in the case of slow walking, or strolling, you must essentially do more of it. Because the pace is slow, it can be combined with other activities without detracting from either the walking or the recreational activity you are pursuing. Try birdwatching, catching up on news with an old friend, or even holding casual meetings while strolling. You can listen to your favorite music while walking with today's prevalent portable equipment or, with practice, even read a newspaper.

The advanced exercisewalker may take long walks to stretch a self-paced walking routine to a distance of 50 miles or more (see Chapter 12).

Below are some examples of how to add to your regular strolling time and distance. (Refer back to Chapter 7 for more complete discussions of this style of walking.)

- Take after-dinner strolls (may add up to two hours, or two miles).
- Take weekend-afternoon or -morning strolls (may add up to three or four hours, or three or four miles).
- Take walking tours on visits/vacations to other cities or countries (may add up to more exercise than strolling because it is often done a little faster).
- Get to know your own community/area by walking around it.
- Art galleries, street fairs, and museums provide plenty to see and random routes to stroll.
- Walking your dog 20 minutes a day can add over two hours of walking a week.
- Play extra rounds of golf.

Normal Walking: Functional/Occupational Walking

The second type of self-paced walking activity is the kind you do daily to get from place to place. It's a purposeful kind of walking. Unlike strolling, where there is no distance goal or destination, normal walking or functional walking is very practical and usually faster than strolling. The most common forms are walking to work and running errands. Normal walking is the walking you do without being conscious of your speed. It's not walking for its own sake but walking for a practical purpose.

City walkers who walk in the 2½–3½ mph range set the pace for normal walking. Although it feels comfortable, it is done at 10 steps per minute more than country walking or rambling. The country stoller takes what is called the minimum-energy walk, at the rate of 100 steps per minute; this pace feels most comfortable because it conserves the body's energy. The mean pace of 110 steps per minute for the city walker comes from a range of 75–140 steps per minute for men and 80–150 for women. The caloric value of this type of walking is 300–400 calories an hour, depending on your precise weight and walking speed.

The exercise benefits of normal walking can be enhanced by practicing any of the walking techniques described in Chapter 3 that are possible to do while wearing standard business clothing, as long as the apparel is loose-fitting.

Applying these techniques—heel-toe motion, wider stride, arm swing, rhythmic breathing, even the foot-rolling motion, if your dress shoes are flexible enough—often makes normal walking brisk walking, with the accompanying exercise benefits. Like strolling, normal walking can be enhanced as an exercise simply by doing more of it. One of the best and most common ways to accomplish this is to walk to work.

How to Integrate Self-Paced Walking into Your Daily Routine

Once you've developed a craving for walking, you'll easily find twenty minutes (for one mile a day) somewhere in your day. Walking opportunities arise when just sitting around waiting for somebody or for something to happen. How about the television program that's too boring to finish watching? Those twenty minutes are easy. You can also find twenty minutes by walking away from an argument—it's a no-win situation anyway. If you find yourself just sitting, drinking too much, or eating too many snacks, just walk away from it. Think of all the other boring and time-consuming things you do in a given day.

You can divide the work day into walking segments.

Before Breakfast (6–8 A.M.) Before Dinner (4–7 P.M.)
Coffee Breaks (9–11 A.M.)   After Dinner (7–9 P.M.)
Lunchtime (12–3 P.M.)   Midnight Stroll (10–11 P.M.)
During Work (9 A.M.–5 P.M.) Weekends and Vacations

There is a walking opportunity hidden in each of these segments. Here are some suggestions:

Before Breakfast Walk

This one is for the early birds, a 1-2 hour walk before breakfast. Everybody else is asleep, and you don't want to disturb them. What a way to start the day and burn off your breakfast calories before you've even consumed them. A walk may even wake you up so you won't need an extra cup of coffee.

During Work

Yes, even here there are opportunities to walk. Take the stairs instead of waiting for the elevator, even if it's only walking down the stairs of your office building. Use the stairs instead of the escalator. Take a walk to visit your office workers instead of summoning them to your office. During your coffee break, take a walk and stretch your legs. The walk may supply you with the same stimulation as a cup of coffee. An appointment across town can usually be reached on foot quicker than by taxi, bus, or subway. During the work day, traffic jams slow down most vehicles going across town. You can beat the traffic without working up a sweat on most days.

To and From Work

Based on recent U.S. Census Bureau statistics, more than 5 million Americans, or about 5.6 percent of the working population, walk to and from work without relying on any other form of transportation. In the metropolitan New York area, for instance, the figures represent a dramatic increase of 13 percent since the 1970 census figures. In New York, Boston, Philadelphia, and Chicago the number of walkers falls between 100,000 and 405,000, a figure illustrated by the many businesspeople who can be seen in standard, business clothing plus colorful jogging shoes. The hundreds of miles of sidewalks and pedestrian walkways in these four cities often make it easier for residents to get where they are going on foot rather than by car, bus, subway, or taxi. A series of transit strikes in the late 1970s brought everyone

Top 12 U.S. Walk-to-Work Cities
as a Percentage of Working Population

Cities	% of Walking Workers	Number Who Walk	Total Number of Workers
1. New York Metro	10.76	405,146	3,763,970
2. San Diego, CA	10.69	92,500	864,926
3. Boston, MA	8.51	109,417	1,285,696
4. Pittsburgh, PA	6.52	60,128	921,995
5. Philadelphia, PA/NJ	6.43	124,437	1,934,293
6. Buffalo, NY	5.76	28,852	500,523
7. Chicago, IL	5.68	176,810	3,113,944
8. Minneapolis/ St. Paul, MN	5.57	58,419	1,047,979
9. Milwaukee, WI	5.35	34,203	638,946
10. San Francisco/ Oakland, CA	5.32	82,350	1,549,220
11. Newark, NJ	5.31	45,837	863,074
12. Washington, DC	5.13	80,099	1,562,495

in New York to their feet and has kept them there ever since. Traffic jams, parking space limitations, hefty bridge and tunnel tolls, and crowded busses and subways also provide strong incentives for walking. Other factors that have motivated people to walk to work include the scenic beauty of cities like San Francisco and Washington, DC, energy conservation efforts, and simple convenience because many people live within a mile or two of their workplaces.

Commuting time including time spent waiting for buses, trains, and planes can be valuable walking time. You can often get to your destination faster by walking than by taking mass transportation if your usual traveling time is 30 minutes or less. Waiting can often take 5–15 minutes, and if you have connections to make, waiting and transferring time could double or triple this time. Walking to work also saves you the stress of crowded subways, buses, and traffic jams. Remember those delays when you've waited 20, 30, and even 60 minutes or more or got stuck when transportation broke down? Even if you come up short after you've compared walking time with riding time, you must remember that this is your exercise time. Take a few more minutes to complete your exercise time properly.

When commuting time is greater than 30 minutes, you don't have to give up on the idea of walking to work. Take the bus or train to a station which is a 20-minute walk to work and walk from there. If you're driving, you can do the same by parking your car within walking distance to work and returning to it at night on foot. Parking places are often easier to find outside the center of the city, and you might be able to save on parking fees. By parking at different locations, you can vary your route.

While walking, you can route yourself away from heavy traffic and do a little sightseeing or bird watching (if it's through a park) on your way to and from work. Many like a walk in the rain, but if that's not your cup of tea, take a rest day and ride the bus or take your car to work on a rainy day. Remember, a walking for miles exercise program can be relaxed. You should enjoy it, so don't push too hard and spoil it for yourself. Shape a walking for miles program around your existing schedule.

Mealtime

Walks are also recommended before and after meals; even if it's only 15 minutes, it will do you some good. Before a meal, it can even depress your appetite. Mealtime is a good reminder of the trade-off between calories and walked miles to help you keep your calories in/calories out balance sheet balanced. If you have errands where you have to carry a package or two, lunchtime is a perfect time to do them. A walk after dinner can help you cut down on extra portions of dessert. For many, the walk itself will become the treat. When company comes over, don't let that cramp your walking style. Take your guests for a stroll around the neighborhood while discussing the same things you would while sipping your cognac or apertif. Depending on the quality and subject matter of your conversation, you may be out for hours.

Walking While Waiting

No matter how busy or hectic your schedule is, you often find yourself hurrying up just so you can wait again. Walk while you wait. If you arrive early for an appointment, don't occupy some-body's waiting room for 15–60 minutes. If you are in unfamiliar territory, make a mental note of where you've been walking. Walk blocks around the neighborhood in ever increasing circles. If you have 30 minutes to spare, go 15 in one direction and 15 back. If you arrive early at airports or bus and train stations, or your departure has been delayed, check your baggage and take to the road. Airports have a lot of space for walking. If you're not alone, bring your friend with you so you can have a conversation along the way. Bus and train stations are usually centrally located, so you'll be able to do some sightseeing or run a quick errand. Double-check your departure time before you start walking and allow 15–20 minutes for boarding and finding a seat.

Pacing the floor can also be a walking exercise, and it's not only for nervous people. If you don't have much waiting time, you can still pace the floor, train platform, or waiting room. In 15 minutes of pacing, you can often cover a half-mile and keep your baggage in sight the whole time you're pacing.

Vacations

More and more people prefer to take an active vacation. They hate to go away to eat, drink, sleep, and come back fatter than when they left. Tennis, golf, skiing have been the focus of many vacations, now walking and hiking tours have also become popu-lar. Even if there is no central sports focus to your vacation, you can still make walking a daily integral part of it. There is always temptation to take a car in a resort area despite the fact that finding a parking place is so time-consuming. Once parked at the resort, you should try to use your car as little as possible and walk to the beach, restaurants, or supermarket. Make a mental note to study a map of the resort area before or at the time you first arrive and plot places to visit that are within walking distance. This will get you out of the "take your car everywhere" rut and will make you feel much more athletic when you com-plete your vacation stay.

Much time at the beach, lake, or swimming pool is spent lying motionless in the sun. While nothing should deprive you of your well-earned rest, a substantial portion of your tanning time is overkill. Therefore, instead of a sunbath, take a sunwalk. Oil and cream your body as usual, then walk 30 minutes down the beach and 30 back. You will be able to do both sides of your body in one exercise walk. If you are really ambitious, walk for an hour or walk until you can't go any further. That's how my United States cross-country coastal walk started: I just kept following the beaches from New York to Florida. Your beach-walking route can be extended to sunrise and sunset walks of 1–2 hours each. What a way to burn off all or some of the calories of the meal you had or are about to have! Walking the perimeter of a land mass near the place where you're vacationing can also be an interesting walking exercise project. Walking gives you the opportunity to understand an area much better than if you merely stay in one spot.

Winter vacations provide similar opportunities for squeezing in walks. Even if you're already skiing all day, consider a day without a ski lift ticket and walk up every slope you ski down. It's not only good training for your legs, but you will find that your skiing will improve because walking up gives you time to reflect on your technique and makes you appreciate your ski run more. You might choose a day when the lift lines are particularly long and slow-moving. Cross-country skiing is also a good alternative to downhill and gives you a break from lift lines.

Except during romantic strolls, you might try using a pedometer to measure the week or two of creative walking that you squeezed into your schedule. If you feel uncomfortable with this, use your car, a map, or even odometer to measure some of the distances or use your watch and average walking speed to measure miles.

Students

Philosophical discussions and even some group study reviews can be discussed while strolling. The ancient philosophers, called "peripatetic" or walking philosophers, did it, so why can't you? Walking helps make you alert while stimulating the thinking processes.

For Couples

When planning a romantic outing, scout out the walking possibilities beforehand. Taking a walk after dinner or after the theater, movie, opera, concert, or play is a way to relax and will help you get into a romantic mood while getting some exercise. In an age when couples are looking for romantic interludes, you may score more points for cementing your relationship than with any other single activity, save one. Next to lovemaking, a stroll and a relaxed conversation creates the most intimate moment between a loving couple. Do me a favor, though; while taking a romantic walk, avoid the subject of exercise. You can count your miles along with your blessings the next day.

Some Words on Golf

The benefits of walking from golf playing were studied in 1965 by Leroy Getschell as part of his doctoral dissertation at the University of Illinois. He studied the metabolic, cardiovascular, muscular, and motor fitness benefits of golf playing in 20 middle-aged men who played 12 hours of golf a week during the normal season from April 15 to September 30. He compared the golfers to two groups: one that did no regular exercise and one that did vigorous calisthenics and running for a seven-month period, all under supervision.

The results of the Getschell study showed that golf provides a lower exercise benefit than vigorous calisthenics and jogging do. What is significant for the exercisewalker is that there are positive physiological benefits from golf including weight control, overall body strength and leg strength, and strength increases per body weight when measured by the dynametric strength test. However, no significant results for individual muscle strength were shown nor were there any significant flexibility improvements. But, the golfers did show significant improvements in pulmonary ventilation during the last minute of a treadmill walking test at 4 mph on a 8.6 grade and also showed lower respiratory quotients from the second minute on in the treadmill test and lowered their mean heart rate.

Time motion studies of golf players show that for the average player 37 percent of the playing time is spent walking, 34 percent standing and 29 percent hitting and putting. So while walking at a moderate pace may burn 334 calories an hour, playing golf for an hour will burn only 223. Still, an 18-hole golf game can burn over 1,000 calories or more, so twice through in a day can be a significant amount of activity that can be further enhanced by carrying the weight of the golf bags instead of using a cart.

My friend Helen, in St. James, Missouri, has converted her golf playing into a walking routine. She does it by playing a couple of rounds of 18-hole golf in a row, thereby spending up to half a day on the golf course, twice a week in the warm months. And she maintains this routine throughout the year, except when it's wet or snowing. She's estimated that she will do up to two miles of walking for every 18 holes. And she'll add to the exercise effect by carrying her own golf bag.

To compute the caloric expenditure of carrying your golf bag, merely add the weight of the bag to your own weight and check the weight table in the Appendix, page 256. Remember that in an hour of golf you will have only spent 22 minutes walking.

10

AEROBIC WALKING

Many people have come to associate speed with aerobic exercise. They think that if an activity is not a fast routine it can't raise the heart rate into the training zone. Well, in fact, aerobics can be slow, too. A walker properly weight-loaded with 25 pounds or more, or a stair climber moving at 1–2 mph, can get the same training effect as a runner training with seven-minute miles. Walking with a work load (weights or climbing) and walking for speed are both valid approaches to aerobic conditioning as you will see in this chapter.

The routines contained in this chapter are more vigorous or dynamic. The exercisewalking activities here are used for higher caloric burn rates, greater muscle toning and strengthening, and, most important, effective aerobic or cardiovascular endurance training. The routines that follow can best be called *dynamic exercisewalking,* and they do more than just maintain the basic level of activity or health. Rather, they are conditioning exercises, but they are not so advanced that they should be viewed only as a medium for fitness. Dynamic walking requires more action, work effort, and energy expenditure. It is the walking associated with developing cardiovascular endurance or aerobic fitness, the walking we use to achieve physical fitness.

Aerobic walking is really any style of walking done with a speed, duration, or effort to exercise the heart. Your heart is a muscle that requires rapid repetition so that it can function economically with the least amount of fatigue and stress. Heart/lung exercise consists of sustained rapid breathing for at least 15 minutes and ideally as many as 30, three times a week. Your training goal is to raise your heartbeat to 70–85 percent of its maximum.

Aerobic walking may or may not produce sweat. It depends on the walker's body temperature and the temperature of the air. Sweating should not necessarily be associated with walking. The key indicator is the heartbeat rate.

Depending on your level of conditioning, different walking styles and speeds and different walking periods (durations) will help you train aerobically. When you are in poor physical condition a speed of 3 mph for 15–30 minutes may bring your heart into the training target zone. A walker in excellent condition may require a speed of 4–5 mph for 30–60 minutes to reach his training target zone. Walk climbing or walking with a backpack often brings the heartbeat into the training zone, even at 1–3 mph. But climbing is not as easy as or accessible as walking with a weight load.

Measuring your pulse rate during or immediately after your walking exercise will tell you your heart rate level. If you notice that your heart continuously does not reach the training target zone, you have reached a physical fitness plateau. To reach the next level of fitness, increase your speed and workout time. (Walk climbing, walk sprinting, walk/running, racewalking, and long-distance walking may produce further improvement.) These can all be valid walking exercises as long as you measure your activities and monitor your progress.

As stated previously, strolling will probably not suffice to train the heart: at best, it will help improve circulation. Most other forms of walking can be converted to aerobic walking, at least during aerobic training periods. Thus, one can do aerobic exercises by maintaining a brisk pace, climbing an incline or moun-

tain, or walking with a pack. But fast walking and weight-load walking are the most reliable aerobic walking styles.

If you increase your walking speed or increase the weight you carry while walking progressively, you will put just the right amount of stress on the heart to cause a training effect. The leg-lifting and walk climbing routines in Chapter 11 also contribute to cardiovascular fitness, but that's not their primary function. Rather, it's muscle-strengthening function because more use of the skeletal muscles is made, particularly of the leg muscles. Further, these later walking styles are generally of a more strenuous nature and assume an already high level of cardiovascular fitness. Finally, the climbing and leg-lifting routines are ones that are less accessible because they are dependent on geography, weather, and the availability of equipment. In other words, they cannot be done regularly. Aerobic training must be a regular activity and should involve walking styles that easily can be done on a regular schedule. Fast walking and weight-load walking, as you will see, can easily be adopted for aerobic fitness.

Long distance walking can also constitute aerobic walking particularly if done at a moderate to brisk pace and without long rest intervals. The aerobic effect may not be as consistent as with brisk and weight-loaded walking, but over a long enough time (and therefore, distance) a conditioning effect can be achieved.

Fast Walking

All of us have experienced what it is to walk fast. Perhaps you are late for an appointment and there are 10 blocks between you and your destination. You take off walking fast. You don't run (you might muss your appearance or bump into someone); so you try to get there as fast as you can while walking fast. Most people can go between three and five mph using this method by simply making their legs move faster. However, walking fast for longer periods of time must be learned through practice. And while practicing you will also be training your heart and walking aerobically. Walking faster is also a method that you can use for enhancing almost every other walking routine or activity— walking to work, backpacking, climbing, bushwhacking. Increasing your speed multiples the effect of other routines by a squared factor (V^2).

Fast walking is walking at 3.5–4.96 mph. It is really any fast walking speed that can be done in business clothes. Researchers have determined this to be the speed at which the heart rate for most people will rise to its training rate. Although sustained speeds over 5 mph are difficult to achieve without learning race-walking, the fast walking range is probably the range most people will use. To achieve higher fitness levels they will add fast walking to weight-load and leg-lifting rather than adopt a race-walker's style.

Even everyday walking routines like those mentioned in the last chapter and in the next two chapters can be enhanced by gradually increasing the speed to 3–5 mph. This is what we mean by a dynamic walking exercise.

The pumping arm motion plays an important role in helping you increase your speed. You can do it with straight or bent arms (see techniques in Chapter 3). While bent arms will enable you to walk even faster, straight-arm swinging is more appropriate to use on the street and when you are walking to work so that you don't have to telegraph to people that you are exercising. It's up to you.

To monitor your walking speed you can use the steps-per-minute method or a pedometer (see Chapter 6).

Various routines are associated with fast walking. The basic prescription for learning to walk faster is simply to walk faster. This requires an effort and also breaking the psychological barrier that makes one wait for a bus or a cab, instead of walking.

The following walk sprinting routine is both a technique and a routine because it will help you increase your overall walking speed by practicing speeding up in short bursts.

Walk Sprinting

The walk sprint is one of the most useful techniques for increasing your walking speed and endurance. Sprints are quick bursts of speed (as fast as you can walk) for short distances. As a training device, walk sprints can be repeated 5–10 times during a one-hour walking period. Include 30–60 seconds of sprinting each 6–12 minutes of normal or brisk walking. Walk sprints are not only a form of training to increase your speed; they are also good cardiovascular conditioning if done at regular intervals during your walking workout. Increasing your walking speed is one of the important ways of making your walking exercises into an effective aerobic training method.

Sprints indicate your fastest walking speed and help you set a goal in your regular walking exercises. They also give you the needed practice of walking faster and faster. Start by trying to walk 100 yards at 120 steps per minute. Do 8–20 repetitions, two or three times a week, and increase the distance in 100-yard increments on a weekly or biweekly basis until you reach 880 yards without stopping. Increase your steps per minute in increments of two to six steps each week or two weeks. Whenever the training becomes difficult at the increased speed, decrease the distance and work your way back up again.

Sprinting is an advanced walking technique, so don't attempt it until you have reached at least a medium level of physical fitness. Assuming you are at Level III or higher, here is a table for working out a walking sprint routine.

Sprint Walking Routine

	Week	Duration (seconds)	Training Period 20 minutes	30 minutes	60 minutes
Level 1	1	5	10 sprints	10 sprints	10 sprints
	2	10	10 sprints	10 sprints	10 sprints
Level 2	3	15	5 sprints	5 sprints	5 sprints
	4	20	5 sprints	5 sprints	5 sprints
Level 3	5	30	5 sprints	5 sprints	5 sprints
	6	60	5 sprints	5 sprints	5 sprints

The approximate intervals between sprints are as follows: 20-minute period, 2 minutes; 30-minute period, 3 minutes; and 60-minute period, 6 minutes.

As you build up your endurance, you'll be able to sprint faster and longer. You can work sprint training of Level 1 into every workout. Level 2 should be every second workout, and Level 3 every third workout.

Weight-Loaded Walking Style

This is really any kind of walking done while carrying an additional load attached to any part of the body. The most common weight load is that carried by the backpacker. Carrying your own golf clubs, or portaging your canoe overland will also qualify. Later we'll see how walk training with weights added to the arms and legs is an increasingly popular weight-training routine for developing the skeletal muscles. In this section we'll give you the basic weight-loading routines that really apply to

Weight-Loaded Walking Program
Basic Six-Week Training Course

| Fitness Level | Week | | | | | | Distance |
(initial–final poundage)	1st	2nd	3rd	4th	5th	6th	(in miles)
I (0–12)	0	0	1–2	3–7	8–12	12	.5–1.5
II (0–15)	0	0	1–5	6–10	11–15	15	.75–1.75
III (0–20)	0	1–5	1–10	11–15	16–20	20	1.25–2.00

Accelerated Four-Week Training Course

IV (1–25)	1–5	7–15	16–25	25	(at 3.5–4.5 mph)		1.75–2.25
V (2–30)	2–10	11–20	21–30	30	(at 3.5–4.5 mph)		1.75–2.25

Four-Week Progressive Training Course

I (7–17)	7	8–12	13–17	17	(at 3–3.5 + mph)		1.5–1.75 +
II (10–20)	10	11–15	16–20	20	(at 3.5–4 + mph)		1.75–2.25 +

Pounds should be added to the initial weight indicated at the rate of one pound every exercise day—note that for the accelerated Four-Week Training Course you may start the first week with more than one pound (1–5) for Level IV and more than two pounds (2–10) for Level V—until you reach interim weekly and final weights for the program.

---

increasing the work effort and therefore cardiovascular endurance of the walker while also providing overall muscle strength and endurance. For this, the loaded backpack is the best device because it keeps the weight at the trunk of the body.

If you are already a backpacker, you will be able to compute the exercise value of the backpacking you do for fun by keeping track of the weight you carry. With this information you can then use the weight calorie tables in the Appendix to determine the exercise value of your backpacking activity. Also remember to evaluate the weight of your hiking boots by multiplying this weight by five when adding it to your total body weight.

The backpacking walker is really exercising with the intensity of a person who is heavier, i.e., equal to the total extra weight plus your own. Most overweight persons are already weight-loaded walkers. They will add the overweight portion of their body as their backpack weight. Now that the backpack has become fashionable even for city dwellers, you can really wear your backpack everywhere. As a result, it has become an important training tool for the exercisewalker because it is probably the safest and most comfortable way to carry weight on the trunk of the body.

Many of the same exercise principles that apply to hiking also apply to backpacking (see Chapter 7).

The Backpacking Worker

Walking to work is a great way to start your day off right, getting good exercise and avoiding the annoyances of traffic snarls and delayed mass transit. Your daily walk to and from work can be excellent training for developing aerobic fitness as well. While it's true that the average walking speed of 2–3 mph per hour (60–90 steps per minute) is not sufficient to raise your heart rate into the training zone of 60–85 percent of maximum capacity, there are ways to overcome this. One way, of course, is to increase your pace (more than 3.5 mph). Others include walk climbing or stair climbing; we will review these methods in Chapter 11. But perhaps the most clever walk-to-work training routine is walking with a weight-loaded backpack. Tests conducted at Israel's Heller Institute show that this method of aerobic walking may be more efficient than brisk or fast walking because it can reduce the amount of training time from 12–6 or even 4 weeks in which to achieve basic fitness levels.

In cities such as New York women seem to have thought through the walk-to-work clothing problem better than men. Time and again, you see a woman dressed in business clothes and colorful running shoes, gliding gracefully along Fifth Avenue with a light backpack or canvas bag containing her dress shoes. Nobody ever constructed women's dress shoes for comfort, so the female executive doesn't even try to keep the same shoes on the street and in the office if she's a walker or jogger.

Backpacks have also become common, even chic, apparel for the modern pedestrian. Even workers in business suits can be seen carrying them instead of their briefcases. The packs are either slung over one shoulder or worn in standard backpacking fashion. While pack sizes can vary, the "day hiker" like that shown in the illustration, appears to be the most popular one. If you don't own a dayhiker, they cost from $9 to $60 and are sold in sporting goods stores.

Now that you have your backpack, let's put it to use. Wear a weight-loaded backpack for about 30 minutes every working day. You may want to start off by carrying the papers and reports, etc., that you would normally carry in your briefcase. As you grow accustomed to that, you should set a weight goal for yourself ranging from 12–20 pounds and build up to carrying that amount of weight over a six-week period by adding a pound a day starting in the second or third week according to the chart on page 165. With this routine you should keep your walking speed at constant, normal levels throughout the walk. As you increase your weight load, you may need to supplement the load with small barbell weights or your own homemade containers filled with sand or dirt. A sandwich baggie (5½" x 6½") or a ½-pint milk container or a 12-ounce aluminum soft drink can is equal to one pound when filled almost full of sand. To weigh the pack, just step on the bathroom scales without the pack, then weigh yourself again with the backpack on. The difference in the two weights will be the weight of the pack.

You should monitor your heart rate during training and at rest to chart your progress, and of course you should check your physical health with a doctor before undertaking this kind of an exercise routine. Your weight-load goal depends on your initial fitness. Once you have achieved your basic fitness goals you can maintain your particular level of conditioning by keeping your weight load and walking time constant.

The chart on page 165 shows only one of many weight-load routines. You can devise a routine for yourself through experimentation with greater distances and a more rigorous pace. If you decide you want to achieve even higher levels of physical fitness, you may increase the weight to 20, 25, or 30 pounds. If you do this, however, I strongly recommend getting a backpack with a frame so that the weight will be transferred from your shoulders to your waist. It might also be a good idea to save your advanced routines for after-work workouts and weekend backpacking outings to vary your exercise program.

11

LEG-LIFTING AND CLIMBING ROUTINES

This chapter covers two walking styles in which the emphasis is on exercising the legs. The stomach and buttocks are also stressed, but generally leg lifting and climbing are leg work—intensive walking styles. If activities using these styles are practiced regularly, they can also be used for aerobic training. In fact, this would constitute a higher intensity of aerobic training than that achieved through fast or weight-load walking and can be used for those at the IV or V fitness levels. Of course, those at level II or III can use moderate leg-lifting and climbing activities.

In effect, leg lifting and climbing represent a further intensity progression over self-paced and fast-paced walking styles, though there is an overlap. The two leg-lifting styles described in this chapter have the potential for being more vigorously applied. Fast walking, for most people, has the natural 5 mph limit. And weight-loaded walking is also limited, for most people, to 30 percent of their body weight. Walk climbing, on the other hand, if grades are steep, and trekking (the most vigorous leg-lifting form) can involve even higher exercise intensity values than those achieved by carrying a loaded pack. Of course, weight-loaded walking can be combined with leg lifting and climbing to further enhance their exercise value. But in this chapter we will examine the latter exercise routines in their own right.

After the self-paced walkers, the leg lifters and climbers represent the most common types of walkers in America. Both walking styles involve lifting the legs higher than normal while walking. In most cases the higher leg lifts are a function of the character of the terrain being walked on.

Leg-Lifting Routines

Many natural walking styles use a higher leg lift than that of normal walking. This greater range of leg motion means the leg is not only swinging forward but also lifting higher and therefore working that much harder against the forces of gravity. The most common example of a leg-lifting walking style is marching, particularly marching in place.

Leg Lifting in Place

Soldiers, drum majorettes, and bands march, but that would seem to be the extent of public participation. Boy scouts and military reservists may also already be getting their marching exercises. Marching is, however, a bona fide leg-lifting activity. As we said, it is equivalent to running in place. You can march in place for a period of minutes and achieve the same benefit as running without the potential for injury from the jolting effect of jogging. When marching, you should try to lift your knees as high as your waist. Beginners may start by lifting one-half to three-quarters of the distance to their knees. Advanced marchers can lift higher than waist level, 100 steps a minute. Beginners can start with 100 marching steps in five minutes and then add 50 steps on each second or third day, raising the total to 1,000 in 10 minutes. It is recommended that you march to march music or other music in 2/2 or 4/4 time.

A variation of marching in place is the *stork walk*. You lift your legs, knees touching chin and toes pointing down, while walking around just like a stork. The technique is used for exercise, but also aids circulation and digestion. It was developed for people confined to small spaces like prison cells, monastery rooms, and hotel suites.

Hiking

Perhaps the most common and natural leg-lifting activity is hiking. As mentioned in Chapter 7, hiking may be considered the American counterpart of rambling and wandering but really represents a different walking style. Even though all three of these walking styles are usually done in a natural outdoor environment, hiking is done in a more rugged terrain where trails are not as well groomed or in many cases don't even exist. Perhaps it is the North American wilderness that spawned this more rigorous leg-lifting activity and its even more vigorous variations: trekking and bushwhacking. Hiking is walking for a considerable distance through relatively rugged terrain. It is the rugged terrain that necessitates the higher leg lifts. To clear rocks and mounds, to span gaps and crevasses, the hike walker generally has to lift his leg higher. Unlike marching, hiking is not done to a rhythmic cadence. Rather, the leg-lifting rhythm is determined by the degree of ruggedness of the terrain. It is, of course, difficult to achieve a leg-lifting (hiking) style if the countryside or trails are groomed, as they are in much of Europe. Unlike America, northern Europe has very little wilderness. There are, however, exceptions, such as Lapland, Scandinavia, Iceland, and Greenland.

Trekking

Trekking comes from the Dutch *trekken* (to draw or travel). A trek is an arduous, slow journey and in the past was used especially to refer to an organized migration to found a new colony. Today trekking refers to hiking trips taken in mountainous country like the Himalayas. It's not necessarily mountain climbing, but involves the kind of difficult terrain found mainly in mountainous regions. In the Himalayas trekking takes place in the foothills or about the base of the mountains. Since it is over the most rugged and rocky terrain, a large amount of leg lifting is done to span crevasses and to lift the feet over rocks and boulders.

Bushwhacking

Bushwhacking originated with rugged terrain and walking activities off the beaten path or through the bush. A bush is, of course, any low treelike or thickly branching shrub; *the bush* refers to any wild or uncleared land such as a wilderness area. Areas of Australia and Africa are still called *bush country*. Those who worked in the bush are called *bushwhackers,* such as the Confederate soldier guerrillas of American history and the current Australians who live in the bush.

As a walking activity, *bushwhacking* means leaving the trail or beaten path and heading out cross-country. This involves a lot of leg lifting, much bending from side to side, and some stooping under obstacles. If you actually combine your hiking with trail building or maintenance, you will also be doing a lot of work with your arms, swinging a machete or wielding pruning shears.

You can always make your hiking more vigorous by leaving the trail and heading into the bush. But be sure you have mastered the use of map and compass or are in the company of someone who has. (Orienteering, a similar sport, is another leg-lifting activity that can be done by hikers.)

Walk Climbing

Walk climbing in many ways is similar to the leg-lifting walking style. Climbing actually contains a leg-lifting portion, when you raise your leg up to place it onto the next level of elevation on the hill, mountain, or stair riser. But after lifting the leg you then place it down and lift the whole body up to where you placed the forward-lifting leg. Now the weight of the body is supported by the climbing (forward-stepping) leg, and it is left to that leg to lift the body's weight the distance the leg-lifting leg just traveled (see illustration). Depending on the angle or grade of ascent, the distance the body travels upward is increased. To do less work, of course, the walk climber usually shortens his step as the grade of ascent increases, to make each step's work easier. This suggests that, if you really want to work hard, you should stretch out each step of your walk climb. This will also increase the speed of your ascent and make it a more intense exercise. You can also try to get your legs moving faster through

the leg-swing and push-off phase of the walking cycle by stepping out faster.

Walk climbing while whacking through the bushes and having to navigate over rocks and boulders is perhaps the most strenuous of exercises. It certainly tops the list if it is also attempted while carrying a backpack.

Walk climbing or slope walking routines, like walk sprinting routines, consist of repetitive walks up measured distances of inclines. With hills you can measure your distance with a pedometer set for short steps. Or, knowing your approximate walking speed, you can measure it by the time it takes to get from bottom to top. I have a friend, Jerry, who lives near New York's Harriman State Park and therefore has a variety of hills available to him for his walking exercises. He has all the hills labeled on his map based on the time it takes him to walk up and down them. He has one-hour climbs and some two- and three-hour walk climbs. On the same hill he has also marked off intermediate points just in case he doesn't have time to go all the way to the top.

Of course we are all not as fortunate as Jerry to have mountains in our own backyard for a daily walk climb. Most of us have to settle for an occasional weekend or vacation period, when we can practice our walk climbing routines. But even if you are in the flat country of the Midwest, there are still some slope-climbing opportunities (e.g., climbing stairs).

Perhaps the most exciting development for walk climbers is the availability of many office buildings during and after work hours for stair-climbing workouts. The modern high-rise office building in big cities and suburban commercial parks is the mountain range of the future. You often need to get permission from the management of your office building to use it after hours.

This could be the sedentary office worker's perfect walking routine. If you work in a skyscraper, you can make creative use of the elevator. Let's say you work on the 100th floor but can only manage 25 flights at the beginning of your routine. Take the remaining 75 by elevator. Eventually, once you have reached the proper fitness level you may wish to climb all 100 as a test of your new fitness and, as mountaineers are fond of saying, "Because it's there."

Modern commercial buildings usually have about 8–10 steps per flight of stairs, and private homes may have as many as 13 per flight. But you can count them. If there are many flights, they usually have the same number of stairs. Depending on your level of fitness, you should start with about four to six flights per day and increase the number of flights by adding one to four to each week's session. The walk up is what really counts but the one down exercises the muscles of the front leg more, so do both if you can. I recommend a minimum of three sessions a week and a maximum of five if you are relying on slope walking as your primary exercise.

Walk-climbing sessions should progress by a combination of walking time and grade difficulty. Measure your time up and consider that time going down as your bonus or cool-down unless you are walking a 20-percent grade or more. Progress from easy to difficult grades over at least a six-week period if you are already at fitness level II. Otherwise stay with easy grades and increase your time walked in 15-minute increments over a four-week period.

It is important to view your slope-walking routines as supplements and not replacements for your level-walking routines. They not only help with aerobic training but also train muscles

Stair-Climbing Routines

Week	Flight Numbers by Fitness Levels per Session				
	I	II	III	IV	V
1	5	15	35	80	130
2	7	20	45	90	140
3	9	25	55	100	150
4	11	30	65	110	160
5	13	35	75	120	180
6	15	40	85	130	200

NOTES ON STAIR CLIMBING

Buildings. Floors and stairways contain long (24 steps) and short (13 steps) flights.

Residential. Apartment Building 2–4 flights with about 16 steps for each floor. Private homes generally have one flight per floor of 13–15 steps per flight. Angles of ascent vary.

Flights into Miles. You can measure your stair and hill climbing into miles walk climbed. They're worth 2–5 times the caloric expenditure of flat miles depending on the slope grade walked. Depending on riser height and step number there are 2,600 stair steps to the mile or approximately 160–200 flights per mile (13–16 steps per flight).

Slope. The angle of ascent for most stairs ranges from 20–30 degrees. If you use the same stairways repeatedly you can measure the angle of ascent by using a protractor or other angle-measuring device and measure the angle of tilt of the bottom side of the stairway where it meets the ground or by drawing an imaginary line between the edges of two consecutive risers and measuring the angle of that line using the steps' platform as your base. Then use the caloric tables for incline walking to get the caloric value of your climb.

Basic Rule: Try to walk down a stairway as many times as you walked up because it will balance muscle development in the front and back of the legs.

Combinations. You can combine stair or hill work with other exercise routines or use it as a substitute for speed work. Climbing stairs is generally slow walking so you can combine it with weight-loaded walking and move at 1–2 mph slower than with fast walking weight-loaded routines.

Stair climbing and walk climbing, if practiced 3–5 days a week, can serve as your sole aerobic conditioning routine and can also provide sufficient leg muscle development. It's more interesting to combine these walk-climbing routines with other walks, in which case stair climbing for either two 15-minute sessions or five five-minute sessions can serve as a supplementary exercise to self-paced, weight-loaded, or long-distance routines. You should determine the exact measure of each to make the proper combinations.

Number of Sessions. You can hill or stair climb every day or do it only two days a week (as a supplement to other walking routines). Whether you choose two or five sessions per week you can still progress at the weekly rate indicated for the various fitness levels.

Aerobic Workout. While stair climbing can be an effective aerobic walking routine you may wish to increase your walking speed rather than the number of flights. Monitor your heart rate and increase your climbing speed if you need more effort to reach the training zone. Some stair climbers skip steps—take two or three steps at a time—to make this exercise more dynamic.

---

that are not used in most flat-ground exercises. I remember when a friend and I climbed the Statue of Liberty—a climb of 171 steps, which we accomplished in about 60 minutes. She complained the next morning about stiffness and muscle pain in her legs; I experienced none. We were surprised since she had been running up to 50 miles a week for the past five weeks as training for the New York Marathon. I had been walking the same number of miles, training for a long-distance walk.

This was a graphic example of the difference between walking and running muscles and their relationship to climbing muscles. Still, on longer climbs even I, with my so-called walking muscles, will begin to experience soreness. So I'm convinced that, while similar, the muscles you use for walk climbing and level walking are different, and you should do both routines for all-around muscular development of the legs.

I will have more to say about the relationship between walking and climbing in Chapter 13.

12

ADVANCED ROUTINES

The walking exercises presented in this chapter are not only exercise routines but also involve some advanced walking techniques. However, they are really extensions of the routines from the previous three chapters, so they shouldn't pose any problems for advanced exercisewalkers.

As an example, long-distance walking is really an extension of self-paced walking routines. The walking style may be the same; only the distances become longer. Extending the distance and therefore the duration of a walking exercise workout doesn't merely result in a linear progression of added exercise benefits with added walking miles. Specifically, walking 10 miles at one time provides greater benefits than walking the sum of 10 individual miles with rest intervals in between. This phenomenon of "the distance sum being greater than the parts" is really the seventh exercisewalking principle. In other words, it is not only the increased frequency of a walking workout or intensity but also the duration that affects the exercise value.

The second group of advanced walking routines is racewalking, or Olympic walking. This is really an extension of the brisk and fast walking routines in Chapter 10, only racewalking is generally the fast walking technique needed to walk at speeds of 5–10 mph. As you will see, it involves exaggerated body movements developed for competitive walkers to help them move forward as fast as possible while still adhering to the walking action. Racewalking, however, is a walking technique and walking routine that is not limited to competitors. Racewalking can be practiced as a fitness walking exercise without ever having to compete. Racewalking is especially good for runners and other high-speed athletes. In fact, it's more difficult and vigorous than running at any speed. Racewalking clubs and clinics for fitness walkers are held on weekends in many American cities.

The third section of this chapter, weight training with walking, is probably the most advanced of all walking routines along with racewalking and should really be attempted only by walkers at fitness levels III–V. Lower-fitness-level walkers should start with the weight-loaded backpacking and trunk-loading routines outlined in Chapter 10. These latter routines are really the basic exercise versions of the weight-loaded-limb walking routines presented in this chapter. Weight-loaded-limb walking, besides being a vigorous aerobic training exercise, is perhaps the most effective way to use the walking action as a muscle-building activity. Using the bent-arm swinging motion and the leg-swinging motions that are natural to walking, you can take advantage of the total muscle flexion or total body flexion action of the natural walking movement. It's kind of the "ultimate biceps curl," one that uses almost all the body's muscles with one curling or flexing action.

Long-Distance Walking

There are many historical accounts of incredibly long distances walked as feats of human endurance. It is believed, for instance, that Marco Polo walked 25,000 miles on his round trip to the Far East through North Africa.

In 1801–1802 Johann Gottfried Seume walked from Germany to Sicily, Italy, and back. During 1806–1807 he walked to Russia, Finland, and Sweden. Each of his long-distance walks was described in books he wrote on the subject. During the 1890s American and British "Pedestrians" walked long distances against the

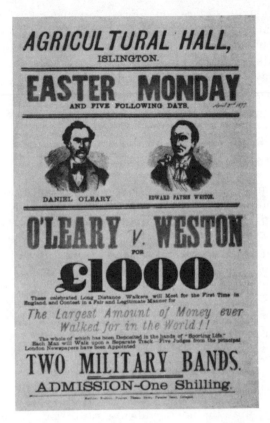

Poster announcing a long-distance walking match between Daniel O'Leary and Edward Payson Weston.

clock or against each other. In 1909, at age 70, Edward Payson Weston walked from New York to San Francisco in 105 days. This marked the longest walk in a 50-year career of long-distance walking. It was almost duplicated four years later when, at age 74, Weston walked 1,500 miles from New York to Minneapolis in 30 days. Weston died at age 90 in 1929. Weston was really the father of American walking, having introduced and publicized its health and fitness benefits with his crowd-pleasing long-distance walks starting in 1861, when he walked from Boston to Washington, DC, for the inauguration of Abraham Lincoln.

These *pedestrians* were considered America's first professional athletes because they earned as much as $50,000 in a single prize. Posters showing their competitions resembled those of prize fighters. Walkers trained for these events as rigorously as do many of today's athletes and were given comparable press attention and prestige. It is believed that pedestrians and long-distance walkers were the forerunners of today's long-distance marathon runners and long-distance walkers. Today's long-distance walkers, however, do not compete with each other but rather try to set distance and speed records or to fulfill personal goals.

In 1974 American David Kuntz completed walking around the world (14,500 miles) in about four years. The longest continuous walk (13,000 miles) will probably be completed in 1983 by Englishman George Meegan, who has walked nonstop for more than seven years. Walking politicians are not uncommon. Senator Lawton Chiles of Florida won election in 1976 by conducting his whole campaign on foot, and Presidents Jefferson, Lincoln, and Truman were also great walkers. West Germany's President, Karl Carstens, has walked the length of West Germany from north to south by completing his walk in installments on weekends or on special vacation days.

Picking a Route

Choosing a long-distance walking route can be a matter of historical as well as personal interest. There are now many long-distance routes mapped out and illustrated in guidebooks that mark continuous cross-country and cross-continent walks. You may also want to plot your own walking routes through towns and villages on special country roads. Highways are usually illegal to walk along and are also less interesting. In addition to health and fun, long-distance walking gives the walker a sense of history and an affinity for one's native land and forefathers. The more ambitious walkers pick routes that have never been walked before, while others use the walk to discover their roots.

If your forefathers came from Europe and landed in the colonies, you might start at a location like Jamestown and walk along the bank to where they finally settled. Later you might follow the Great Kentucky Road or the Appalachian Trail to where succeeding generations moved westward. If your forefathers were pioneers, you might follow the route of the Oregon Trail or the Sante Fe Trail to their home in the West. If you are a military buff, you might hike through Civil War battlefields such as Vicksburg or Bull Run. If you are young at heart, you might consider a walk that is also a physical challenge, such as walking the perimeter of a great body of water like the Great Salt Lake or Lake Erie.

Choosing Your Distance Goal

There's a bit of an overlap between hiking and long-distance walking. Generally any distance over 100 miles can be deemed a long-distance walk; less than 100 miles is a hike.

Before you prepare to make a long-distance walk you should do a few test walks to determine your pace, endurance, and equipment/supply requirements. If you've done little or no extensive hiking, I suggest you start with 50–100 miles in a four- to seven-day period along a route similar to the one you propose to do. If this is successful, you can build up your mileage in increments of 50 or 100 miles on subsequent outings. Depending on the time, 50–300 miles are manageable long-distance walks available to you. Because of their high daily mileage, such walks are clearly walking workouts of a more leisurely pace.

Planning the Intervals

Interval walking makes long-distance walking accessible to great numbers of people and a training exercise as well. Completing a long distance in intervals makes it possible to prolong the health-giving effects of walking over a number of months and even years. If you're a student or retired person, the job may be easier since you have larger blocks of free time. Some workers have arranged with their employers to take a year off. Since long-distance walks take months and even years for many walkers to complete, such an undertaking involves saving up money, quitting work, selling the home, and winding up personal affairs. If these can't be done, plan your long-distance walk for weekends, holidays, and vacation time.

Once you've set a definite goal for completing your walk, you can estimate the number of walking days you will need. In a walking day you can cover 5–50 miles, depending on personal tastes, terrain, hours walked, and walking speed. A good pace to sustain over a long period of time on an uneven surface is 12 miles per day.

Making Your Long-Distance Walking Exercise Oriented

Physical Conditioning. Depending on your training goals and initial physical conditioning, you may or may not wish to begin special training exercises to prepare for your long-distance walk. I have given you three approaches that change according to your level of conditioning. Long-distance walks can be conditioners in themselves, but if you are in poor condition, it will take a large portion of your walk to get you into the kind of condition that ensures fast and steady progress. If you plan to walk more than two weeks at a time, the walking will be your conditioning, and you can gradually build up your mileage. If you are completing the walk in intervals, you must also assess your present condition when planning your daily mileage. If there are more than two-week intervals between stopping and picking up your long-distance walk, your conditioning may decline unless you keep up your daily and weekly walking exercise. As a rule of thumb, you will lose your conditioning level within five weeks unless you institute a maintenance program (see Chapter 7). Each individual's maintenance requirement will vary. You can monitor your condition before, the night after ending your walking interval, and right before beginning your next interval.

Building Up Your Mileage. While long-distance walks can be used as a conditioner, you must be careful to build your mileage slowly. Blistering and general body fatigue at the beginning of a walk will make it difficult for you to finish. If you are in poor condition, you should start with 10 miles and build up your daily mileage in increments of two to three miles a day, every other day. Medium condition requires starting at 15 miles and adding five miles every other day. Those in excellent condition can start at 20 miles a day. I recommend that all long-distance walkers take a rest every six days of walking. There may also be days when reducing mileage 50 percent from the previous day will be necessary to combat fatigue and blisters. Warning: don't plan on doing more than five miles of walking in a given day until you've read Chapter 16 on foot care and blister prevention.

During your walking day, try to maintain a steady rhythmic pace. Don't be disappointed if your speed drops to a stroll or amble. To get through a full day of walking, you'll have to learn to vary your speed. Resting is useful if kept to a minimum of three to five minutes per hour. Any greater rest period requires that you do stretching exercises and start out slowly to warm up your body. I found that one long rest stop during the day at lunchtime was enough and required only one warm-up period rather than many.

If your long-distance walking is done at intervals greater than one month, it will probably count most toward your walking-for-miles program. If you set an annual goal of 1,500 long-distance miles, you will certainly meet your quota for miles.

Perhaps a more reasonable interval would be three days a month which will give you 360–900 miles a year, depending on your daily mileage. This kind of distance work will also contribute to your aerobic walking. My own test results show that long-distance training done in intervals will bring the heart into the 50–75 percent training range and will produce conditioning effects similar to those of more intense training for short periods. You can do your own testing using the heart rate evaluation method in Chapter 6.

Speed. Increase speed while trying to limit your walking to 8–10 hours a day. This will allow your body to recuperate and regain its strength and enthusiasm for the next day's walking. Begin the day with warm-up stretching exercises. Start walking slowly and build up your speed gradually. A well-conditioned walker, walking on smooth surfaces like country roads, can average 20–25 miles a day. A racewalker in good training can sustain a daily average of 40–50 miles per day. However, walking over rugged terrain can reduce the average to 5–10 miles a day. If you're using your long-distance walk on smooth surfaces to get into shape, you should estimate your average daily mileage to be about 12. If you're in medium physical condition, use 18; in good condition, use 24.

You should practice your speed exercises daily. Starting at one and work to two, three, then four hours of sustained speeds in excess of 3 mph. In the beginning, do these exercises when you are fresh, perhaps one hour after you have started walking, to warm up your muscles. Don't wait too long to do the exercises or you will be too tired to sustain them.

Fat Control. At first, the temptation during long-distance walks is to eat and drink as much as you wish of anything you like. Go ahead and do this for a few days if you'd like to get this food craving out of your system. But after awhile you will learn to bring your eating habits under control, and with a minimum of effort you'll find that you may begin to lose weight and body fat. For each mile you walk, count on burning off at least 100 calories or more depending on your speed and level of effort.

Muscle. Don't despair if in the beginning your weight stays the same or even goes up, particularly if you are an ectomorph. Your body is undergoing a transformation from fat to muscle. Since muscle is heavier than fat, the first few pounds of fat and water lost will be counterbalanced by muscle gain. On my Atlantic Coast walk I lost 13 pounds and reduced my body fat 5 percent.

Racewalking

Racewalking has the same relationship to exercisewalking as running does to jogging. The main differences between walking fast and racewalking are the requirements that the front foot must touch the ground before the rear foot is lifted and that the leg must be fully locked at the knee in the support phase of the stride. Racewalkers also pay more attention to their arm-swinging action than other fast walkers, but their hands do not reach higher or farther back than the chest. Finally, the race-walker tries to make his stride as long as possible by rotating his hip forward and down. This gives the impression that the hip is swinging from side to side while, in fact, it moves down and forward. By training and applying special walking techniques, the racewalker probably walks twice as fast as the average fast walker.

The racewalker begins each stride with a straight leg to achieve maximum pulling power and to avoid "creeping." Creep-

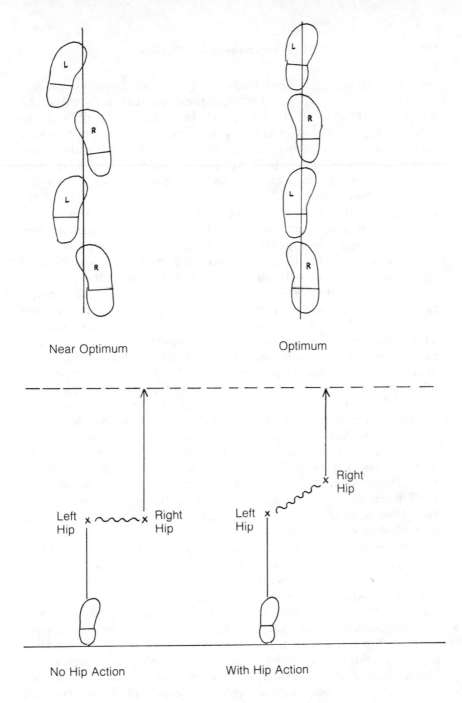

Near Optimum

Optimum

Left Hip   x ⌇⌇⌇ x   Right Hip

Left Hip   x ⌇⌇⌇ x   Right Hip

No Hip Action

With Hip Action

Competitive Racewalking Foot Placement.

ing is walking with bent knees, a little like Groucho Marx's famous film walk. To avoid creeping, do not lean forward at the waist or shoulders. If you bend forward, it is difficult to straighten your legs fully. Judges will disqualify competitors in a race if they creep. Lifting, another reason for disqualification, is a springing motion evidenced by high shoulders and high arm action. Placing the forward foot on the ground before raising the rear foot helps prevent lifting. Lifting can also be avoided by pulling with the leg to move yourself forward rather than pushing off with your rear foot. Judges look for lifting during any burst of speed when passing or at the finish line. Thus, racewalkers try to maintain a fast, even pace throughout the race.

The sport of racewalking, like walking, is growing by leaps and bounds. Walking marathons have been organized, and many racewalkers compete in them. Racewalking distances range from one mile to the annual 330-mile race from Paris to Strasbourg. This rapid growth of racewalking as a sport is even more amazing considering that it is perceived as funny by the public. Some of this perception comes from watching films of early competitors who used exaggerated hip-swinging motions in their walking styles. Today such movement is not noticeable because to achieve economy of motion racewalkers do not sway side to side. In any case, racewalking is new and unusual and will take time to achieve wide acceptability. Think of our initial perception of the martial arts (karate, judo, taikido). The short, quick movements and yelling seemed strange at first until we grew to understand their purpose. Many racewalkers are initially concerned about how they appear to others, but once they learn the movements, these feelings disappear.

If you want to prepare for racewalking, I suggest that you find a coach. There are also some textbooks on the subject that are worth reading. Racewalking training is so specialized it would require a separate book to do it justice. Racewalkers in top physical shape are some of the finest physical specimens, and many top-flight racewalkers successfully compete beyond the age of 40. They have been physically tested and often demonstrate levels of health many years younger than their chronological age. Many runners have turned to racewalking because it not only improves their chances to compete but also reduces the running

For Racewalkers/Advanced Walkers

This chart shows the gradual buildup of your mileage for the first eight weeks of preparation. Sunday, Tuesday, Thursday, and Saturday are the buildup days, while Monday, Wednesday, and Friday are for minimum mileage or rest. Consistency of effort and gradual buildup with lesser efforts or rest between is the best way to build stamina.

WEEK	1	2	3	4	5	6	7	8
Sun.	6	9	8	10	10	10	12	12
Mon.	R	R	5	R	5	R	7	R
Tues.	8	10	12	15	10	20	22	20
Wed.	5	5	5	5	8	9	10	10
Thurs.	8	9	10	15	15	15	15	25
Fri.	R	R	R	R	R	R	R	R
Sat.	12	10	12	15	20	20	18	30
TOTAL	39	43	52	60	68	74	84	97

R = Rest

injuries that often force them to give up running. The average athlete has a much better chance of making a racewalking team than a running team.

Once you study racewalking with a qualified coach, you will learn that the racewalking styles can vary and can be quite personalized. Racewalking techniques get walking as close as possible to running without leaving the ground. The racewalker's gait is like the runner's in that there is a slight overlap of the feet. It is believed that by passing the legs closer by one another and by eliminating excessive side-to-side body motions, a more efficient and faster forward motion is achieved. Training for racewalking competition is as grueling as, or more grueling than, running competitions. Racewalkers build up their weekly mileage from more than 40 to more than 120 miles in an eight-week period. Many of their workouts are done at a 5 mph pace or faster.

Racewalking may not be for every walker, but we have the racewalkers to thank for refined walking techniques. They have practiced every walking movement to determine which ones are best suited to economize on movement and speed. This is not to say that racewalkers have the last word on good walking techniques. Many of their techniques have grown out of the highly technical requirements and judging of racewalking competitions. The exercisewalker should not feel bound to accept all racewalking techniques, but he can certainly modify and adapt his own techniques to resemble those used in racewalking. As more attention is focused on the sport of walking, other techniques and improvements will evolve that can be applied to all styles of walking.

Walking and Weight Training

Basic weight training and walking involves loading weights onto the limbs for performing the walking action.

We have seen the effects of weight loading the trunk of a walker's body through the use of a weight-loaded backpack or weighted waistbelt. In this section we will deal with special routines involved in weight loading the walker's limbs. This is really an advanced walking technique, particularly when the load attached to each limb weighs more than one pound. Walking weight training should not be attempted by persons who are out of shape or in minimal shape.

In addition, any person who is overweight should get to within 5–10 pounds of normal weight by walking without weights before adding these to his body. In other words, the overweight portion of your body is all the extra weight you will need to begin performing these walking weight-training routines.

Weight training and walking is a relatively new concept, but a number of such programs have achieved widespread notice. The advantage is that it combines strength exercises with aerobic exercises. This cuts down on the time used for both routines. It also is a balanced exercise program of upper and lower body conditioning. For the exercise walker, it means he can use walking to achieve the highest levels of fitness without having to change to other high-intensity and high-injury-risk exercises. The walking action, because it is smooth and safe, is perhaps the best continuous aerobic activity to combine with weight training.

Other aerobic activities are not as well suited. Problems exist with other aerobic exercises and sports. The staccato movements of aerobic dancers are not suited to the smooth full-flexion action the weight trainer needs. Weights added to the roller skater or bicyclist would disturb his balance and cause some falls. They would sink a swimmer. And they would probably throw off the balance and rhythmic motion of the cross-country skier. Weights used for team sports would probably distort the actions of players, interfering with their timing and other sport skills.

On the other hand, walking is an action I like to compare to the bicep curl or any of the other curls of weight training. But walking is a multiple curl of almost all of the body's muscles in one continuous, rhythmic motion. I call it *total body flexing*. Each of the 1,500–2,500 steps and accompanying upper arm swings constitutes one enormous curl of almost all of the body's muscles. The high repetition with light to moderate weights will not produce bulky but longer, leaner muscles and create cardiovascular fitness, which regular bodybuilding usually does not provide. So using the walking action as a weight training adjunct not only makes sense to enhance the exercise value of the walking itself to its highest level but also can be an effective body-shaping regimen. It can particularly keep the upper body strong as aging begins to diminish the strength accumulated over the years.

While the safety record of adding heavy weights to limbs has not been established, the walking action seems to be the best one to use for this type of training. Certainly running, jumping, or roller skating with weight-loaded limbs would be dangerous. For example, the jolting effect of jogging with weights would be enhanced, causing great damage to the joints, back, and especially the lower knee. I have heard stories of many joggers who ran with ankle weights incurring injuries. However, carrying up to a pound of weight in each hand while jogging may be safe. Check with your trainer as well as your doctor before beginning any weight-training program involving the attachment of weights to moving limbs.

In addition, I would caution you not to allow the weights to hang from your arms without pumping them, or to wear them on arms and legs for long periods of inactivity. Such a procedure does not provide any exercise benefit and may unnecessarily stretch the ligaments and lead to serious injury. When not specifically doing your exercise routines you should give your body a

Weight-Loaded Walking Routine—
Six-Week Basic Progressive Training
(Fitness Levels III to V only)

	Walking Speed Arm/Leg Repetitions	Walking Distance (miles per session)		Hands			In Combination with hands and trunk			Count weight of boot or shoes		
				III	IV	V	III	IV	V	III	IV	V
Week #1	mph = 1-2 spm = 30-45	.5	Men	1	1	3						
			Women	½	½	1						
Week #2	mph = 1.5-2.5 spm = 40-60	.5-1	Men	1	2	3						
			Women	½	1	1						
Week #3	mph = 1.5-3 spm = 40-90	.75-1.25	Men	1	2	3	5	5	5	1	1	1
			Women	1	1	1	0	0	5	½	½	½
Week #4	mph = 2-3.5 spm = 45-100	1-2	Men	1	2	3	5	5	5	1	1	1½
			Women	1	1	1	5	5	5	½	¾	1
Week #5	mph = 2.5-3.0 spm = 60-90	1.5-2.5	Men	1	2	3	5	5	5	1	1½	2
			Women	1	1	1	5	5	5	¾	1	1¼
Week #6	mph = 2.5-3.0 spm = 60-90	2-3	Men	2	3	4	6	8	10	1¼	2	2½
			Women	2	3	3	5	6	7	¾	1	1½

Advanced Progressive Training

	Walking Speed Arm/Leg Repetitions	Walking Distance (miles per session)		Hands			In Combination with hands and trunk			Count weight of boot or shoes		
				III	IV	V	III	IV	V	III	IV	V
Week #1	mph = 2.5-3.0 spm = 60-90	2-3	Men	3	4	5	7	8	12	1½	2	2¾
			Women	2	3	3	5	6	7	¾	1	1½
Week #2	mph = 2.5-3.0 spm = 60-90	2.5-3.5	Men	4	5	6	8	9	15	1½	2	3¼
			Women	3	5	5	6	7	8	¾	1	1½
Week #3	mph = 2.5-4.0 spm = 60-120	2.5-3.5	Men	5	6	8	9	10	18	1½	2¼	3½
			Women	3	5	5	6	7	8	¾	1	1½

Walking Speed Arm/Leg Repetitions	Walking Distance (miles per session)		Hands			Trunk			Feet		
			III	IV	V	III	IV	V	III	IV	V
Week #4	mph = 2.5–4.0 spm = 60–120	3–4	Men	6	7	10	10	12	20	1¾	2½	4
			Women	4	6	7	7	8	12	1	1½	2
Week #5	mph = 3.0–4.0 spm = 90–120	3–4	Men	7	8	12	11	13	22	1¾	2½	4½
			Women	4	7	8	7	9	15	1½	1¾	2½
Week #6	mph = 3.5–5.0 spm = 100–140	4–5	Men	8	10	15	12	15	25	2	3	5
			Women	5	8	10	8	10	15	1½	2	3

Weight-Loading Limbs Routines

You can practice this routine by itself or in conjunction with other aerobic and muscle-building routines, such as fast walking, leg lifting, or climbing. If using these routines for muscle development and toning be sure to pay attention to the rule of specificity in skeletal muscle development. You have to train specific muscles in the same way you would do weight training in a gym.

Note that the weight tables assume a 180-pound man and a 130-pound woman. The age bracket in 30–50 years old. If you are younger or older, lighter or heavier, you should adjust the weight up or down. Remember not to exceed 30% of total body weight in the total poundage used. If a particular weight-load addition is too

heavy—you experience soreness the day after—drop back by half of that increase and work your way back up from there.

For muscle toning concentrate on hand and ankle weights. If you are interested in building your upper body, increase weights from 1–15 pounds on each hand. Use arm-pump swings with all hand weights over two pounds. Ankle weights should generally not go any higher than five pounds on each ankle (always count boot weight). Trunk loading in combination with hand and ankles should not exceed 25 pounds even for 200-pound persons. Remember that weight on swinging arms is worth five times what it is on the trunk and worth seven times the trunk weight for the legs.

chance to recover by removing the various weight straps and belts. Furthermore, you should not begin a heavy-limb walking weight-training routine until you have advanced to at least level III in your walking program. It is advisable to use other dynamic walking routines like slope walking, speed walking, and leglifting to build up your cardiovascular fitness and upper-body and leg strength before beginning such a weight-training routine, particularly if you use more than one pound on any limb.

The walking weight trainer's overall weight goal is to build up muscle strength while helping maintain cardiovascular fitness. Ultimately the walker will be able to carry 20–30 percent of his body weight without impairing his walking style and techniques. Of course, if too much weight is added prematurely, walking techniques may be impaired. In fact, this should be your general rule of thumb: Never add weight that will make you compromise your walking techniques (i.e., shorten stride, lose posture, lose speed, or interrupt your rhythmic breathing).

The weight-load walker can practically add weight to four areas of his body: ankles (or foot), waist, back, and hands (or wrists). Be sure to get ankle straps that tie or hook so they hold securely. You will probably experience soreness 24 hours after each weight-training exercise. Therefore, practice heavy-limb walking routines no more than every other day to allow for muscle recuperation.

You should not do all your exercisewalking as weight-load walking. Give your muscles a chance to relax and stretch. Give yourself a chance to walk without any stress. It's also good for your psychological well-being.

Always remember that there are certain practical limits for weight-load training. As an example, it is virtually impossible to carry 30 percent of your body weight in your hands or on your ankles for any significant distance and still call it walking. So most of the weight is carried by the trunk of the body in a backpack. I recommend limits of 30 pounds for the back with upper limits of 10 pounds each for the hands and three pounds for each ankle. (Keep in mind the weight-loading corollary regarding weights on the limbs producing greater energy cost than weights on the trunk. A pound on the foot is worth seven on the waist and back, and a pound on the hand is worth two or three times the same on the waist or back.)

To prevent stretching your arm ligaments when weight-training walking, keep your arms bent and pump them vigorously during the walking cycle.

Heavy-Limb Walking Calisthenics

The second part of the heavy-limbed routine involves the performance of upper-body calisthenics with hand-held weights during walking exercises. I have already shown how to do a number of calisthenic exercises for stretching and strengthening the upper body. To some of these you can now add weight training. There are also routines specifically designed for training while walking and for training muscles used in sports related to walking, such as roller skating and cross-country skiing.

Before starting to walk you should practice the routines while standing still (i.e., as you did in slow motion with the basic walking techniques themselves). As you become skilled in moving the weights in their proper arcs, start doing it while taking one complete walking cycle. Stop, analyze your movements and make any corrections or adjustments, and repeat.

Note that with these weight-training calisthenics you should hold the weights in your hand rather than having them strapped to your wrists. This will give you better control and will also do a better job of strengthening the muscles in the wrists and forearms.

PART V

BUILDING YOUR EXERCISE PROGRAM

There is no quick fix to achieving and maintaining optimum health and fitness. An exercise program is a long-term proposition—a lifetime proposition—and therefore, a program that evolves as you learn more about your body. I am not about to prescribe a set of numbers or exercises to be done over a 12-week period and coyly tell you to keep up the good work. That is a problem with certain exercise systems you may have read about in books or magazines. For 12 weeks, you can do some kind of super-intense routine, but try to keep going. You and anyone else will reach a point when you have burned out. What do you do then?

Thus, in building your own exercise program, take a long, hard look at which fitness level you will be able to stick with. All of those levels can be reached, but not all of them can be maintained. Being at Fitness Level V for a year or two and then dropping to I or II probably does more harm than good. Certainly maintaining one *active* level is more balanced and healthful. Keep "staying active" as your first goal, then "staying fit" as the second goal, so that if you must fail at one goal, fail at the second, far more difficult goal. (*Difficult* in the sense that staying fit becomes progressive.)

This part of the book will be an attempt to summarize and synthesize the techniques, principles, exercises, and routines of the previous parts into a comprehensive, yet adaptable and flexible, program. Chapter 13 discusses walking as the fundamental exercise for the human body and how it can be the core of any exercise program, even for the athlete who already excels in other sports. The next chapter carries on this theme but in light of what it takes to stay active and fit for a lifetime. Because walking is already part of daily activities throughout a person's life, it is the lifetime exercise. In Chapter 15, the approach to developing a lifetime walking program is explained in terms of cardiovascular training, walking for miles, and weight control.

13

WALKING AS THE CORE EXERCISE

Walking may be described as the "core exercise" for other sports and exercises. It is the perfect conditioning exercise, particularly for those sports involving leg strength and continuous rhythmic motion. Walking not only starts you out with a basic conditioning level; it can also become an integral part of your training in both the medium and advanced stages of physical fitness. Many sports are one-sided in the muscular development they produce. If walking is practiced in conjunction with a sport, it can fill in the muscle-development gaps of that sport.

The Basic Conditioner for Other Exercises

Other exercises have either a high threshold of entry like running or a threshold that is too low, like bowling. That is, an exercise with a high threshold of entry requires you to be already in good shape for vigorous activity—you have to walk before you can run! A low threshold requires too little in terms of fitness to ever create a conditioning effect. Walking seems to be just right for preparing muscles, lungs, and the circulatory system for the more strenuous and most enjoyable stages of other exercise programs. The relationship between running and walking is a good example.

Walking and Running

Walking is the perfect starter program for running and can be combined with running through the training period to improve performance, distance, and speed. It is a good example of how walking can be used as a conditioner for other exercises, particularly those that involve a higher intensity of effort. By first walking, those in poor physical condition can build sufficient body strength to run or can start by mixing jogging with walking. Walk/running is for people who want to use walking as a way to increase their running distance and endurance.

Many runners are embarrassed to start walking when they are tired; they would rather run on until they can go no farther. Walking enables runners to extend their running period and distance and allows them to make greater progress. When first trying to run, go as far as you can, then walk at a normal pace until you have recovered. Try each time to increase your time and distance while shortening the distance you walk.

Many runners who walk think they are cheating when, in fact, they are enhancing their training. The most painful part of long-distance running occurs in the first one to three miles, when the lungs experience an oxygen deficiency. Most joggers starting out tend to associate running with this pain. If they can progress beyond it, they will be more relaxed about their running.

Walking can help the runner smooth out the valleys of his training. The first long-distance marathoners did not run the entire distance; they often kept their pace by mixing walking and running. Walking between running stretches is infinitely better than stopping and starting up again. As heart/lung capacity grows stronger, you will find yourself doing less walking and more running. By stretching out your running with walking, you will also be able to do more running training. Many beginners will quit for the day once they become fatigued and breathless. Their whole training effort may be lost if they are not able to run each time for at least 20 minutes. By attempting to run less, they are straining rather than training themselves. Walking will help stretch the training period of running so that a training effect can take place and give the runner the necessary confidence to continue.

Walk/running is also an effective way to raise the heart rate in the shortest possible time. It shouldn't be viewed only as a means to better jogging but as an end in itself. You can choose to walk/run in any ratio—50 percent walking, 50 percent running; 75 percent walking, 25 percent running, for examples. You can do a kind of fartlek training that favors more walking than running (e.g., walking five minutes, running one minute).

My own experience with walk/running training convinced me that walking was a powerful training tool to extend nonstop running distance. In a three-week period I was able to build my running distance from 0–30 miles without stopping by using the following walking interval training. Every day I ran as far as I could and then started walking until I felt I could start running again. I did this type of training for two to six hours every other day. Anytime I misjudged my ability to run, I reverted to walking. By the third week I was able to extend my running training to a very high level of proficiency in a short time. I don't recommend this kind of training for everybody, but it dramatically demonstrates the case for walking as an integral training device.

I first experienced this ability to run long distances without stopping at the end of a three-day, 100-mile walk. After having walked about 20 miles for a good part of the day, my walking partner, a cross-country runner, suggested we run the remaining 20 miles to reach our destination more quickly. We did it without stopping and with no leg pain or sensation of being out of breath. The day's walk had so warmed us up that we were physically and psychologically ready to conquer any distance. Again, however, I want to do more testing on this "walking warm-up" phenomenon before recommending it to you as a training method.

As a conditioner, walking gradually warms up the muscles and even stretches them. Many athletes involved in team sports are advised to walk 5–10 minutes before hitting the practice field for soccer, football, baseball, or any other sport that requires the participant to spring into action. Likewise, a walking cool-down period after playing sports is also advisable. Many sports enthusiasts are guilty of immediately sitting, or lying down, or hopping into a car for the ride home after the game is over. If you stop abruptly after any physical activity, the blood stops circulating and tends to pool in one place and puts dangerous stress on your heart. Walking after sports activity serves as a decompression period to help your body revert to its normal prestress function.

The Bridge to Fitness in Other Sports

In addition to preparing you for more strenuous exercise programs, walking also seems to improve performance in other sports by building good breath control, body coordination, and endurance. With the strength gained from walking, you develop new confidence in your ability to participate in other sports activities. It acts as a booster, and since walking can be added to your daily schedule without taking extra time, your new walking strength can be an unexpected bonus in increasing your performance.

Walking exercises are particularly well suited for building muscles and enhancing performance in sports requiring leg strength, particularly those where continuous rhythmic motion is used. Roller skating, ice skating, Nordic and downhill skiing, mountain climbing, and, of course, running would be good examples. I will describe the relationship between these sports and walking, but this list is by no means exhaustive. I believe that future studies will prove that the overall muscular development from walking exercises correlates with muscular needs of more leg-strength sports than any other exercise. I have personally observed or heard how walking training helps improve the skills needed for karate, boxing, soccer, football, tennis, racquetball, hang gliding, golf, water skiing, wind surfing, surfing, bicycling, and roller skating.

Mountain Climbing and Walking

Mountain climbing requires technical skill, balance, and a great deal of bravery. Above all, mountaineers require health, physical fitness, and a capacity for enduring difficult weather conditions and sudden changes in temperature.

It's no secret that mountain climbers train by walking. To prepare for the mountain-climbing season, mountaineers develop their leg strength and overall endurance either gradually over several months of weekend outings or more quickly with one or two weeks of full-time walking. In the late 1970s one of the women on the Anapurna Woman's Climbing team walked from Poland to France as part of her training.

Hill climbing, or *walk climbing* as referred to in this book, has traditionally been the most prevalent training for mountain climbing. Some historians believed that this type of training originated in the "fells" of the English Lake District and was called *fell walking*. Edward Whymper and many of the members of the first successful Mt. Everest climb trained for their climbs by fell walking. A typical fell walk training day would be nine hours long and cover about 12 miles. Climbers allowed for six hours of walking, one hour of resting, and two hours of contingency time.

Mountaineers also do a lot of walking rather than rope climbing on many climbs, so they have developed their own special walking techniques. They generally walk much slower than the average hill climber or walk climber because they have to conserve their energy for the climb, particularly at high altitudes where the air is thin and oxygen is scarce. The lack of air, along with heavy lifting work done by the legs, requires slow steady movements. They constantly test their speed to see if it's too fast, and their speed fluctuates during the day. In the beginning of the day the pace is purposely slow to allow the body to warm up. When the pace finally accelerates, it sustains itself at full power only a few hours before it slows down again. Thereafter, the mountaineer awaits his second wind, which usually keeps the pace going for the rest of the day.

When air becomes extremely thin, the lungs rather than the legs slow down the climber. The legs need extra time to accumulate energy, so the rest step is used. Every step requires an alternating rest. One foot advances to a new position, and its leg rest while the body is supported by the rear leg. Then the rear foot advances.

At high altitudes rest stops are frequent in the beginning of the day, two or three minutes every 45 minutes. However, longer rest periods are made every two or three hours. The descent may be equally or even more strenuous since the legs often must act as brakes on the way down, requiring the body to turn sideways with bent ankles and contorted hips.

Skiing

Downhill skiing is a sport requiring substantial leg strength for endurance and performance. As a ski instructor I trained more than 300 beginning skiers with a walking program. My own skiing ability increased from intermediate to expert when I walked up every slope I skied down. Many skiers think that skiing provides all the leg strengthening they need. As a result they spend half the ski season getting into shape while skiing poorly and less aggressively. Edge control and the up–and–down leg-bending motion critical to good performance are linked as much to leg strength as to skill. Deep powder skiing and skiing long steep runs require good leg strength for a good, professional-like skiing performance. Like the mountaineer, the skier should start getting into shape for skiing with weekend walks at least two months before the season begins.

Nordic, or cross-country skiing, has an even greater affinity to walking than does downhill. Many say that cross-country skiing is like walking. This is certainly a useful guideline for the beginner, but the similarity will stop there if it's just normal walking. Cross-country skiing, like walking exercises, becomes more dynamic in intermediate and advanced stages.

In winter regions, when walking becomes difficult in the snow, you can replace your walking exercises with ski walking exercises. The two complement each other. The skier and the walker move their legs in parallel motions synchronized with their arm-swing movements and breathing. Like walking, Nordic skiing has

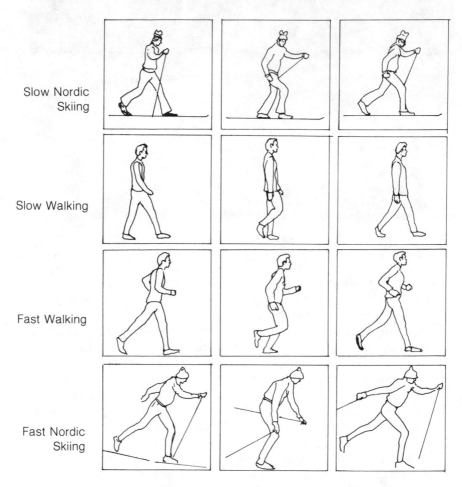

Slow Nordic Skiing

Slow Walking

Fast Walking

Fast Nordic Skiing

Slow and Fast Nordic Skiing Compared to Slow and Fast Walking.

a wide range of speeds and strides. Improving your walking techniques will help you improve your cross-country skiing techniques and provide you with a stronger kick, wider stride, and more vigorous action. Many skiers walk along on their skis, barely using their pole motion. They don't push for maximum leg extension, nor do they kick or push off with sufficient force. They merely shuffle along on their skis. Poling is like the vigorous arm motion of the walk sprinter. The ski poler reaches out, arm stretched forward and slightly bent, pulls the pole down, and pushes off straight back to propel himself forward.

The skier, unlike the walker, leans slightly forward. Like the walker, the skier always has one foot on the ground, but like the dynamic walker, he pushes forward with the rear foot and stretches his forward leg with a slightly bent knee so he can glide on impact. The glide, however, seldom exceeds one-quarter of the total stride length, or the skier would be overgliding or overstriding and allowing his skis to slow down the speed of his body. Then he would have to expend extra energy to get his momentum going again. Flexibility is as important to skiing as it is to walking for lengthening the stride. As with walking, the skier's speed will be determined by the length of the stride and the increased number of step repetitions per minute. Because of the gliding effect, however, the strides will be greater, A skier who wants to go 7.3 mph can accomplish this with an eight-foot stride and 160 steps. A walker taking that many steps could only do 5.5 mph.

Because of the winter temperature, greater speed, and upper body motion through poling, the cross-country skier burns more calories than the walker or runner. Some cross-country ski races are unique in that competitors eat during the competition to give them enough energy to finish. I do not want to mislead you as to the simplicity of cross-country skiing by comparing it to walking. There are further refinements and differences in the two sports. Further tests will be needed to properly correlate the muscles used by both the sports.

14

THE LIFETIME EXERCISE

All exercise programs and books recommend themselves in glowing terms and with long lists of benefits. This really is the part of any book or program that motivates the person to start and maintain the exercise program. So, before I give a list of various fitness benefits offered by walking as an exercise, consider the single most important reason for adopting walking as your primary exercise: walking is a lifetime exercise, one that you can do all your life, which will provide you with benefits throughout your life.

Most other exercise programs see life through 6–12-week cycles or training periods. They assume that you will be following their regimens day in and day out for the rest of your life. In fact, your physical fitness will rise and fall along with the other ups and downs of your life, and as time goes on your body will change with your age. You will not be able to stop or reverse this aging process, despite the ads that promise this effect. The best you should hope for is to slow down or retard this aging process and maximize your health at any age, but not be fanatical about "regaining your youth." You won't be able to look like Jack La

Lanne or Clint Eastwood at 50, 60 and 70 unless you want to spend four to eight hours a day exercising.

You have learned the daily and weekly workouts for walking in Part IV. This is where most exercise books and articles stop. They assume that you are going to go right on repeating the same series of routines over and over again. But exercisewalking is really a lifetime prescription that must change as your life changes.

Walking for exercise is a lifetime project because it fills all the gaps left by other fitness programs:

- It is a *total* fitness program. Unlike many athletic programs, exercisewalking is not based on specificity. Contrary to what many of us believe, many ex-athletes are in poorer physiological condition than those who never practiced or trained for sports but just pursued recreational sports activities. Further, many current world-class athletes do not have the high overall levels of fitness that average working people who exercise regularly have because they train regularly, paying attention to the endurance, strength, and flexibility aspects of their exercise programs. As an example, world-class weightlifters are notorious for neglecting their cardiovascular training. The current trend among athletes is to supplement their specific training activity with training in areas in which they are weak, and there is evidence that this also helps their overall performance. Most professional athletes, however, do not come to grips with the needs for a total approach or lifetime approach to health and fitness until they retire.
- Exercisewalking avoids the dogmatic approach to fitness. Many exercise programs of the past were presented without any word as to whether or how they could be varied. If variations existed, they were contained as part of a series of rigid prescriptions similar to the original exercise routine. These aspects contributed both to the routinization and to the monotony of the program. And these were also the seeds of the program's later failure. The reader was given very little or only selective information about the exercise principles underlying the author's programs. Most often there was not enough information from which to extrapolate further

variations. This is the "dogmatic" approach to exercise. Like religion, this approach is often necessary for those who do not have enough internal motivation or discipline and therefore need a cookbook approach. And actually, such imposed discipline is often essential, particularly for high-level conditioning exercises. But, as already mentioned, this approach usually lasts only a short time (sometimes less than six months) before the burnout, dropout, or boredom phase sets in. Exercisewalking, on the other hand, will keep you going for many years and could serve as the core of your lifetime program, being supplemented by other programs from time to time as your level of motivation and exercise enthusiasm grows for them.

- Exercisewalking helps you avoid the yo-yo effect. You've seen it with some of your friends who train for marathon runs and other competitive sporting events. They work really hard in the period before the competition. And afterward their level of activity drops off dramatically. They are really violating the lifetime exercise principle of moderation. This principle says it's better to do a moderate amount of exercise regularly than to do a lot with periods of inactivity in between. It's also better to do little moderate exercise than none at all if that little is at a low rather than an intense level.

Just like dieters, who yo-yo back and forth with their weight levels, many high-intensity exercisers yo-yo back and forth with the amount of time and effort they put into their exercise programs. So, when choosing your fitness level goal, try not to set it too high. There's much to be said for maintaining only a III level. It requires less time, less effort. You will probably be able to stick with this kind of program for most of your life. A higher fitness level will usually require a greater time investment to get there and a greater amount of willpower to stay there. Many people shoot too high to reach Fitness V and then fall down because they cannot maintain it over the long run.

Don't forget that most professional athletes and top competitors do their training 8–10 hours a day. For them it's a full-time job. Many exercise programs developed by superathletes are just too demanding and therefore unrealistic for the average person. So don't let those exercise gurus bowl you over with their macho talk and their high performance fitness levels. When they retire from competition they'll be in the same boat with you in trying to devise a program to fit basic fitness and health needs. Some of them will even falter in solving this problem because they never learned the principle of moderation. The death rate and low level of physical fitness of superathletes out of their prime throws suspicion on this type of training regimen. It's just too intense to be realistic.

- You can stick with exercisewalking for a lifetime because it's *fun*. When all else fails it is fun that makes anyone come back and stick with an exercise. Walking, as we have already seen, more than any other single exercise or recreational form, offers the most variety. Variety is also the spice of exercise; it is what will make it "taste" good to you over the long run. Discipline is good too, but most people can discipline themselves for short-term periods at best. Walking has six different exercise styles and hundreds of activities or variations on these styles. Walking can be done while socializing, and it has many related activities like exploration, nature study, and adventure, which take your mind off the work effort needed for the exercise part of walking.

Building a Lifetime Exercise Program

Many of you have already completed one-third (age 25) or one-half (age 37) or even four-fifths (age 65) of your natural life, so the lifetime maximum of walking 75, 150, or 210,000 miles may no longer be possible. It is claimed that the greatest walker of all time was Thoreau. With a full lifetime devoted to walking, he is said to have walked 250,000 miles. That's 10–12 miles or four hours of average walking per day. Wordsworth in his 80 years, walked 185,000 or, as has been reported, about 10 miles a day on the average. These goals may not be realistic for you, but you *can* leave a walking legacy for your children by teaching them the principles and techniques of this book. Above all, however, you can instill in them an understanding of the fun and variety walking has to offer as an exercise through all stages of life. And you can teach them that, more than any other exercise, it stands for an active lifestyle throughout one's life.

Many exercise books fail to tell you what to do after the 12-week fitness routine is finished. Can most 12-week exercise programs go on and on for the rest of your life? Could you afford to keep your membership and that of your spouse at the local health club for a lifetime? And would you want to, if you could? For all the reasons given so far, you probably wouldn't.

As you go through life, various events can influence your devotion to exercise and physical fitness. During the first two decades of your life your exercises are usually connected with game playing: Little League, baseball, football; sandlot games like stickball, hide and seek; adventure games like surfing and hiking. If you are active in those years, you certainly develop a knowledge of what it's like to be active. If you are sedentary, then it becomes a big problem later in life, for if you don't change, your physical fate—that of decline—is set, and it'll be a great challenge to make a turnaround.

From your 20s on up, you have various bouts with physical exercise. If you are in school, it still consists of intramural sports. Most of us who played on school sports teams have significantly decreased the level of activity. Those taking desk jobs decrease it significantly, more than physical laborers. Still further may be the decline of those white-collar workers whose job hours are not set and who put enormous additional hours into their jobs, trying to build a career. In the flurry of mental and emotional activity, they forget how few calories brain and stress work burn per hour (usually fewer than five).

Those of you who stay at home fare no better, being near the television and the refrigerator all day. Eating may become your primary source of physical activity. And it too burns very few calories per hour. We often come to confuse the work and responsibility we have as adults with living an active life. While it may be mentally active, it is very low in physical activity.

Exercisewalking can minimize the periods of low activity, helping you maintain a moderately high level of fitness throughout your life, simply because it does not disrupt your life. Learning at an early age that the active life is the best life—and that exercisewalking can keep you active, painlessly, throughout your years—can keep you happy and fit.

15

THE LIFETIME
PRESCRIPTION

I was flabbergasted when I heard about the walking habits of one of America's greatest long-distance runners. He shall remain unnamed but I'm sure this story about him will make him even more famous. After a 12–20-mile workout in Central Park Mr. C steps back into the limousine that brought him there and takes him back to his hotel. This elaborate pick-up-and-delivery system for a well-funded amateur athlete is apparently designed to save him a few steps of walking back and forth to his hotel. And, of course, the reasoning goes that if he runs 80–120 miles a week he's done more than enough exercise. Yet this super-trained athlete, in many ways, is no better off physically than the businessman who sits in a cab for 30–60 minutes trying to get crosstown when he could have walked.

Many Americans, despite the fitness trend, avoid walking at all costs, whether a sedate executive or a superstar athlete. Yet the walking action provides an exercise that is natural and unlike any other and one that will lead to the atrophy of many bodily functions if not practiced even by some superathletes. If nothing else the one in our story has cut himself off from the world by

getting around in his limousine and not taking the time to discover the world around him. Later, when his running career
fades, he may be at a loss maintaining an exercise program.
That's when the lifetime prescription of walking would be useful
for him.

Probably the most important initial requirement for any fitness
seeker is the proper attitude. Without that, exercisers will have
no lasting motivation to continue in any fitness program. The
word *lasting* is essential here and undoubtedly represents one of
the basic components of the exercisewalking prescription.

The failure of many exercise prescriptions lies in the fact that
they encourage participants to work themselves into a frenzy of
enthusiasm at the start and urge them to strive for incredible
improvements in fitness. Of course, no one can sustain this
motivational pitch for long. Consequently, the exercise program
is soon abandoned, and the disillusioned exerciser often immediately turns to another program, only to experience the same
sequence of events.

The key to success in any fitness-oriented program is *moderation*. A review of recent trends in American lifestyles shows,
unfortunately, that our society rarely encourages this approach
to anything. Recent fads or trends are rife with examples. The
jogging boom is one. Many Europeans were surprised to see so
many Americans adopting this fad: after all, it obviously was not
healthy to run or exercise on a hard surface amid the exhaust
fumes of passing cars and trucks. It simply didn't make sense to
exercise in this way. Of course, Americans continue to run this
way out of convenience, redesigning their jogging shoes to make
them more shock-absorbent and conducting tests to show that
the auto fumes are not absorbed into the aerobically working
body but processed and exhaled with other carbon dioxide exhaled while exercising. This can-do approach is not to be deni-
grated, for it shows its effectiveness in other areas. But in the art
of living it gets a grade of C at best. For the initial commonsense
reaction to jogging has proved true: about 60 percent of jogging
exercisers are injured and many of the injuries to the lower back
and joints come from the jolting action of the jogger on a hard
surface. A few years of lab tests cannot supersede the commonsense rules about health and fitness that have evolved over
centuries of history. The bottom line is that any new exercise

trend, including jogging, should be treated with a measured response. *Moderation* is best. Another example of this can be seen in America's infatuation with mineral water. In the name of health, many of us have given up alcohol altogether in favor of Perrier water. Ironically, it may have been this extreme reaction to liquor that has spawned the research that has shown that *very* moderate consumption of alcohol (about one ounce a day) may actually *benefit* the heart. Again, a more moderate approach to liquor may be indicated. Quick health fads designed for dramatic results simply do not work.

This probably sounds like something your father or grandmother might have lectured you about, but it is a conclusion reached not only from life experience but in the hundreds of years of human exercise physiology research. Common sense, balance, and moderation should govern our approach to exercise and health—it's the surest and safest bet. In the case of exercise it means that a moderate return is probably the best return because that's the return you can hope to get for the best part of your life.

In connection with walking as the best exercise perhaps John Burroughs' 19th-century prescription, made for Americans on exercise and walking in his work, *The Exhilerations of the Road* (Winter Sunshine) says it best: "A man must invest himself near at hand and in common things, and be content with a steady and moderate return, if he would know the blessedness of a cheerful heart and the sweetness of a walk over the round earth."

Components of a Lifetime Prescription

From the perspective of exercise-oriented walking, there are two components to health and fitness that must be directly addressed in a lifetime exercisewalking program: cardiovascular training (intensity of exercise) and walking for miles (amount of exercise). Factors such as flexibility and muscular strength are built into these components, but weight control may be something that needs to be addressed since your needs in this area may affect how you can approach the rest of the lifetime program. Therefore, the following three sections of this last chapter on the concept of exercisewalking will cover cardiovascular training, walking for miles, and weight control.

Cardiovascular Training

If, like Thoreau, you are already walking 10–12 miles a day every day of your life, you still may not have reached the highest level of cardiovascular endurance because you have concentrated only on one aspect of training—walking training. If, as a 10-mile-a-day walker, you do all your walking miles at a moderate pace, you probably would reach only your level III or IV in cardiovascular fitness, whereas your leg muscle and buttocks muscle strength may be at level V. That's an example of how even walkers can have too much specificity of training.

While you do get more aerobic benefits from endurance training, and longer walks are worth more than shorter walks, unless you train your heart rate at 60–85 percent of maximum, you will probably not rise much above certain average levels of fitness. For most people that's good enough. So if you want to maintain a high level of aerobic fitness, you will have to spend at least three times a week walking or doing some other aerobic training with a 2–30-minute period each time. This means following the advanced routines in Chapter 12 or the leg lifting or walk climbing exercises of Chapter 11.

While an aerobic walker need not always be walking fast, or even sweat if it's cold weather, you can tell when you're training aerobically by the rate of your breathing. It's heavy and there's really no way to hide that fact. However, aerobic walking is also not merely speedwalking. With weight-loaded limbs or a heavy backpack I can walk at 1–2 mph, in effect strolling along on city streets and still be working as hard as someone running at a six-minute-mile pace. My cardiovascular training is just as effective, and I can avoid the jolting effect or more exaggerated movements of the faster-paced exercises. As the training effect develops I can increase the speed, the weight load, or even the work effort by choosing to walk up and down inclines—all of this at only a 1–2 mph pace. The conditioning part or cardiovascular part of any exercise program involves ideally three or four 20-minute workout periods a week.

However, in total, aerobic exercise is only half of the exercise value of your total program. The other two exercise components—strength and flexibility—will be derived first from the leg and arm repetitions of the miles walked on a weekly basis and second from the stretching and strengthening exercises you do before and after your walking workout or before and after your walking day.

Walking for Miles

Again, conditioning really has two parts. The cardiovascular conditioning is for the lung/heart system, and the result is that the body performs work overall without experiencing fatigue. The skeletal muscular conditioning part is achieved when you apply training to particular muscles in order to strengthen, tone, or build them. This kind of conditioning may or may not train the heart/lung system while it is doing its major work on the muscles. In walking, the muscle conditioning of the legs, buttocks, stomach, and back muscles come from the repetition of the walking action itself. Each mile represents between 1,000 and 1,500 repetitions of the legs' muscular contractions, and these are accompanied by rhythmic and systematic straight- or bent-arm swinging motion, including rotation of the shoulder muscles. If you add weight directly to the moving limbs, you can enhance the muscular training effects. Weight added to the trunk or backpack will enhance the value of the leg and stomach action work effort.

So, your walking exercise program needs two, really three, basic components: aerobic conditioning, muscular repetition, and flexibility training. You get cardiovascular conditioning from the vigorous walking workouts of increased speed or work effort. They can be short and built into your regular walking activities without having to isolate them in a track or gym workout. Walking for miles, while it will contribute to basic aerobic fitness, has its real benefits in the lower and middle body muscles and perhaps the upper body, in weight control, in stress control, in general health and age retardation, and in minimal flexibility. Many of the walking routines in Part IV can be used as walking-for-miles programs. It's usually the self-paced or moderate-paced routines that are most adaptable to muscular fitness improvements.

To summarize, an exercisewalking prescription for overall fitness provides aerobic or cardiovascular fitness along with muscular strength and flexibility. Walking for miles can fill that prescription.

The walking-for-miles concept is based on the fact that exercisewalkers must think not only in terms of miles-per-hour intensity but also in terms of the amount of exercise done—the total miles walked in a day, a week, a month, a season, a year, and even a lifetime. Miles are the basic unit for walkers. Runners also use miles, but they usually think of their workouts in terms of hours or minutes run. While the quality of miles walked is important, it is the absolute numbers that carry the most weight over long periods of walking.

Many people look at their walking from the point of view of the time spent doing it: "I walked for three hours." For exercisewalking purposes it's best to look at miles walked first. Hours are often misleading, particularly if you stopped to watch and explore along the way. So, while you were standing a lot, your miles walked amounted to little.

We know that many people fool themselves into thinking that they walk many miles when they are actually just standing a lot. There's also a kind of low-quality walking—back and forth to the kitchen, for example—that some people count to show that they walk a lot of miles. While it is certainly valuable in rating your level of activity, this is really more of a basic activity level than a walking exercise level. Doing a lot of back-and-forth work on your feet will surely bring you closer to the "fair" than to the "poor" category of fitness, but this is not to be confused with walking on errands or occupational walking. That type of walking is full-range walking, where the stride length is at least normal and the number of steps continuous over a long range.

As introduced in Chapter 7, you can look at your fitness goals as a quota of miles to be walked per day:

Fitness Levels	Miles per Day
I (poor)	0–1.99
II (fair)	2–3.99
III (good)	4–5.99
IV (very good)	6–7.99
V (excellent)	8–10 or more

Some comments are in order about the upper and lower limits of these daily miles walked averages.

On the upper end of the daily-average scale the distinction between aerobic and muscular workout walking is obscured. It's hard to avoid being aerobically fit at a 10-mile-a-day walking rate. When measured in terms of running fitness, it may not reach the IV and V fitness levels, but in overall terms it is certainly more than adequate.

When averaging walking miles, you count every day of the week and of your life using the daily average. If you are starting your program after one-third or one-half of your life is over, then multiply the total miles per lifetime (mpl) column by the fraction of your life that remains. Knowing how long your grandparents and their brothers and sisters lived will give you a life-years estimate. Otherwise you can use the national average of 70.

It's hard to make up for years of inactivity; an argument can be made that cumulative inactivity will tend to shorten your life. As we have seen previously, inactivity ranks high in the causes of accelerated aging and the onset of various diseases. Ideally you shouldn't let a year in which you haven't met your walking-for-miles quota slip by for it may be one of the seeds to your physical decline.

It's interesting to have your whole life in front of you from time to time. It keeps your daily life in perspective and helps you get more out of life. Human years are a limited commodity. So too are the number of miles you can walk for exercise and pleasure. Walking more than 10 miles a day would really be the habit of a professional walker because the average time spent on such daily

Walking-for-Miles Lifetime Program

	Level I	Level II	Level III	Level IV	Level V
Miles/Day	0–2	2–4	4–6	6–8	8–10 +
Miles/Week	0–14	14–28	28–42	42–56	56–70 +
Miles/Month	0–60	60–120	120–180	180–240	240–300 +
Miles/Season	0–180	180–360	360–540	540–720	720–900 +
Miles/Year	0–728	728–1,456	1,456–2,190	2,190–2,920	2,920–3,650 +
Miles/Lifetime (68 years)	0–50,000	50,000–100,000	100,000–150,000	150,000–200,000	200,000–250,000 +

mileage is 2½–3 hours. Of course, a racewalker in top shape could do them in little over an hour. A self-paced walker could take as many as four hours.

There's another way to look at this walking time: as active time, time spent in action or being active. Then four hours of being active, when compared with 20 hours of being sedentary, is not much to ask from your time schedule, particularly when it is easier to integrate walking into your daily life than any other exercise.

Walking for Weight Control

While studies (Gwinup) have shown that you can lose weight by walking without any dieting, the weight loss will be gradual—particularly if you practice self-paced walking, i.e., walking at normal speed. Further the weight loss is greater and faster if you are 20–60 pounds overweight rather than only 5–10 pounds. The reason for this is that a substantially overweight person uses up a greater number of total calories while walking because of the weight carried. Walking, in fact, is the only safe exercise for such overweight persons because it is of a low enough intensity to permit immediate accessibility. According to Weight Watchers, which has a walking program called Pep Step, overweight people prefer walking because they don't feel embarrassed or awkward doing it. They can still appear poised and composed while doing their exercises.

Walking can be an important factor in controlling or maintaining your weight. Regular daily walking is the minimum activity level you need to keep your metabolism working normally so it burns at a higher level. You can balance out any additional food intake on a daily or weekly basis with additional miles of walking. Dr. Katahn in his book, *The 200-Calorie Solution*, suggests that 200 calories of walking a day is the minimum amount of walking needed to maintain this balance. Depending, of course, on your weight, 200 calories a day is about two additional miles of walking a day.

Dr. Katahn also suggests that weight control problems for most Americans, contrary to the conventional wisdom, are not based on poor eating habits (e.g., lack of self control) but rather on a reduced level of activity. If we could raise the basic level of activity, overweight problems for most Americans would go away. Walking seems to be the best single activator for this purpose and Dr. Katahn recommends it in his book and in his weight control program at Vanderbilt University. Walking has in fact become the basic exercise of many weight control programs.

My own opinion is that besides a low activity level there is also one other major source of overweight in America and that is processed foods, i.e., any food prepared with extra ingredients, such as fast foods. These prepackaged food items contain two or three times the number of calories that ordinary food contains. Processed foods contain extra sugar, even in the meat sauces, salt and other calorie ridden ingredients designed to enhance taste (and appetite!) but add a disproportionate amount of calories. Thus we are not only less active but eating food with unnecessary extra calories.

It's no wonder that the average weight—or rather fat—on American bodies has increased 42 percent since 1910. Interestingly, 1910 is a good base year for Americans because it was also a year before the widespread use of the elevator, escalator, and telephone when Americans did two or three times as much daily walking than they do today. They did this walking not necessarily as a sport or exercise but inadvertently as a basic activity to get from place to place.

Another recent diet book, the *Dieter's Dilemma* by Dr. William Bennett and Joel Guerin has shown that our appetites are a natural function of our present weight and body size. So our body sends the hunger signal to our stomach because the calorie consumption rate we have has been set like a thermostat. The only way to lower that thermostat (the authors of the book say) is to increase the level of activity through exercise. They recommend walking.

Finally, another factor in overweight problems for many is compulsive eating behavior due to stress. Walking helps relieve stress. You can take a walking stress break and often avoid the need to eat something to overcome the same stress. The timing of your walks will help control your appetite and nervous tension. Whenever you feel either overcoming you, try to take a short walk and you will see some amazing results.

The number of calories per mile a walker burns will vary according to body weight, weight load, and work effort. Walking an incline will burn more calories at the same distance than on flat ground. Generally, walking speed will not change the calories per mile burned although it will change the calorie per hour burned, since the faster you walk the more miles you can walk in a given period. (There is, of course, an exception with racewalking, which involves exaggerated upper body movements.) For the calorie-counting walker, *miles walked* rather than *miles per hour walked* is the basic counting unit.

While 200 calories may be the recommended minimum, you have read throughout this book about daily walking routines which can burn 500, 800, and even 1,000 calories a day—enough to balance the effects of even the most ravenous appetite.

My prescription is to look at walking as both a long-term weight reducer and the basic way to keep your weight under control on a day-to-day or weekly basis. It can also help bring yourself back when you have slipped. Rather than counting, eating, and matching calories to exercise calories, it's better to think of maintaining a certain level of activity through your total sum of walking exercises.

The following tables provide sufficient information to help you write your own exercisewalking prescription for weight control. The first table lists calories burned per minute while walking according to speed and body weight. The other table suggests daily amounts of exercise calories for each fitness level.

Number of Calories Expended by Walking (per hour)

Walking Speed in mph	Weight in Pounds						
	100	120	140	160	180	200	220
2	130	160	185	210	240	265	290
2½	155	185	220	250	280	310	345
3	180	215	250	285	325	360	395
3½	205	248	290	330	375	415	455
4	235	280	325	375	420	470	515
4½	310	370	435	495	550	620	680
5	385	460	540	615	690	770	845

Calories of Exercise Per Day

I	0–199
II	200–300
III	300–500
IV	600–800
V	800–1,000

Building an Annual Walking Program

A yearly walking program consists of daily, weekly, monthly, and seasonal or quarterly walking periods. Each will contribute to your physical fitness.

Daily Walking

On a daily basis, you should have two goals: increasing your mileage from your baseline or present number of miles by 25, 50, or 100 percent, and walking aerobically at least 20 minutes a day or every other day. Most of your daily walking will be done at normal walking pace. As a rule of thumb, you should increase your daily mileage by 3–4 miles with walks to work, lunchtime walks, and after-dinner and prebreakfast walks. Your aerobic walk should be a 4½ mph or a faster brisk walk of at least 20 minutes at least twice a week on nonconsecutive days.

Weekly Training

Assuming a daily increase of 3 miles, your weekly average increase would be 21 miles. By keeping track of your daily shortfall, you'll know how to supplement it with weekly walking activities including hiking, strolling, and walking to appointments. It is difficult to accomplish all the walk activities on a daily basis, but they can be fit in at least once a week.

You can supplement your daily shortfall with a long weekend half-day or day hike, a Sunday morning stroll, or any other walking activity which can occur on a weekly basis. You should walk aerobically a total of one hour a week, or two times at 20 minutes each. A workout of one hour of walk sprints on the weekend could help you catch up on the week's shortfall. Provided you walked aerobically on at least one other occasion during the week, you can retrieve your aerobic walking for the week. A shortfall in any week cannot be recovered by a monthly aerobic walking effort. Remember that aerobic walking is any walking with a work effort that trains the heart including brisk walking, weight-loaded walking, climbing, and long-distance walking.

Monthly Walking

Monthly walking opportunities can make up the weekly shortfalls. These consist of weekend hikes and camping trips and walking while waiting to travel.

Seasonal Walking

Seasonal walking consists of walks taken during vacation periods or business trips. One or two weeks of vacation walking could add up to as much as 30–40 miles each season or 120–150 miles annually.

By making a chart of your daily, weekly, seasonal, and annual walking opportunities measured according to miles, you can keep

Suggested Mileage Rates and Increases

	Base Line/ Old Rate	Total (50%)	Increase	Total (100%)	Increase
Daily	4 miles	7.0 miles	2.35	9.4	4.7
Weekly	28 miles	49.3 miles	16.45	65.8	32.9
Monthly	120 miles	211.5 miles	70.5	282.0	141.0
Seasonal	480 miles	634.5 miles	211.5	1,046.6	523.0
Annual	1,456 miles	5,380.0 miles	846.0	4,184.0	2,092.0

track of your shortfalls in each category and make up lost walking opportunities. Thus, you can reach your new walking goals by substituting miles walked in one category with those in another.

After you've determined your baseline daily walking mileage, divide your potential walk opportunities into daily, weekly, monthly, and seasonal (vacation) goals. Set your goal to increase your miles 50 to 100 percent. The following chart indicates suggested rates for each period.

You might be thinking that improved walking requires you to be a mathematician. Throw away your calculator and slide rule because walking mathematics is simple arithmetic which you can do in your head, and you'll find your estimates satisfactory.

PART VI

EQUIPMENT FOR WALKERS

John Muir, one of America's greatest long-distance walkers (he was originally from Scotland) and best known for his thousand-mile walk from Wisconsin to the Gulf of Mexico, once gave his plan for preparing for a long-distance walk: "I throw a loaf of bread and a pound of tea in an old sack and jump over the back fence."

We all know that preparing to go on a short or long walk can be that simple: Just start walking. If you're missing something, you can get it along the way. Or, if your pack's too heavy, you can send it back home by parcel post. If your shoes are too tight, you can get a new pair and break them in, gradually increasing your mileage. As a real walker you'll be distinguished from a tramp or other drifter by your purposeful gait and your lofty goals: "To go the distance, on foot!" People all over the world welcome, help, and respect the walker.

If you are a serious backpacker, and as Colin Fletcher says, "you carry your house on your back," then your equipment problems become quite technical and also technological.

In general, the exercisewalker's equipment is designed and selected with the exercise movement in mind. It's generally lighter and allows freer movement, in the case of clothing and footwear. The equipment is also constructed to support you in your quest for more miles walked. Walkers start with feet first since the feet tend to get sore and break down way before the rest of the body. Next, the variability of the weather and terrain makes walking wear a seasonal choice. Finally, certain aids, supports, and medicaments as well as new-fangled measuring devices make the job of getting and computing exercisewalking activities easier, more efficient, and more modern. The next three chapters will give you all the information you need to prepare for the exercise part of your walking activities.

16

WALKING SHOES AND WALKING FEET

In many respects leather shoe manufacturers are still in the 18th century, or perhaps in the Middle Ages, when it comes to proper shoe design. Until recently leather shoes and boots were designed with just two considerations in mind: durability and protection against the elements. It was not until the running shoe revolution that shoe design took a giant step into the 20th century.

It was the marketing forces behind the jogging boom that spurred researchers to look closely into shoe design. They tested shoes in the laboratory for strength, endurance, flexibility, and support. They also studied runners' biomechanical movements and applied this knowledge to guidelines for shoe design. Perhaps the testing and rating of shoes by running magazines did the most for shoe design. Once their brands had been rated, shoe manufacturers were motivated to make further improvements to increase their ratings. This kind of competition led not only to the production of much lighter shoes but also to new patents for many shoe designs and the use of new construction materials. Now that the jogging shoe boom has leveled off, engineers and manufacturers have trained their sights on walking and hiking shoes.

In 1980–81, 15 new walking shoes appeared; more were produced in 1982. In 1983, 100 new walking-style shoes for men, women, and children will be on the market. Walkers will have to make a choice among hundreds of special brands. In addition to new brands, many existing shoes are designated as walking shoes and include comfortable casual shoes, running shoes, and hiking boots.

You may decry all this marketing attention given to your favorite pastime, but I contend it will be for the better. Many of us, particularly those who wear the so-called stylish shoes and ladies' shoes, have been influenced by style makers who have made styles to suit their ego needs over practical health needs. These shoes are often too narrow for the feet, pinching them and preventing much physical movement without pain and distress. Molding the foot to style trends has become destructive to our feet and health. I predict that the fitness boom will revolutionize all shoe design and create a more demanding customer who puts the health of his feet and body before style considerations. We already see the change in tennis and jogging shoes. In fact, these shoes have themselves set a new sporty fashion trend. Many people wear their sport shoes and training outfits as casualwear even when they aren't exercising.

I predict that the impact of a walking shoe boom will be greater than jogging because walking shoes, like exercisewalking styles, have greater variety and can be produced in all shapes and styles for work, home, play, hiking, and racing. A walking-type shoe can be used for any activity. You'll be able to do your exercisewalking at any time or place and to have a proper walking shoe for every occasion. You needn't wait for a walking shoe boom to find walking shoes—they already exist. You just have to look hard and be more discriminating in your method of shoe selection.

Finding the Perfect Walking Shoe

During my 1,100-mile walk I tried out different styles of walking shoes, including jogging shoes, hiking boots, and low-cut leather shoes. I read all I could on shoe design and even visited shoe factories to see firsthand how shoes are made. I also experimented with walking shoe design by making my own prototype with which I walked 300 miles.

You may not yet be able to find the perfect shoe, but you should be able to evaluate existing shoes to find the best one for you by using the following criteria. I have listed them in their order of importance. If you have foot problems, I suggest that you first get advice from your foot doctor and review my guidelines with him.

1. *You must be able to comfortably fit all parts of your foot into the walking shoe.* The "toe box" should have enough room for your toes to wiggle and spread out and to expand. Unless you have a very narrow foot, narrow pointed toes are out. Any bit of pressure on the front or side of the shoe is dangerous since the tightness will turn to pain and blistering once you start to walk a lot. While experts generally say to avoid too much room to keep feet from slipping back and forth in the shoe, my experience has shown that you're better off erring on the side of more room than less. Your feet tend to grow longer and wider when you do a lot of walking. They become particularly large while you're walking and then shrink afterward. The growth comes from the additional circulation of blood in the feet and from the strain of walking many miles. Give your feet some room to grow with you as you increase the amount of walking you do. I found that an additional pair of socks and a hard support or insole cushion will take up some of the extra space until your feel begin to expand. While there is some shrinkage, the growth I felt from a lot of walking lasts a long time. Even months after my 1,100-mile walk, I still did not fit into my old pair of dress shoes comfortably.

2. *The shoe must be flexible in the sole and the top to assist in the walking motion.* The sole should flex at the ball of the foot and be stiff only in the shank area. Bend the shoe and see if it is flexible. The force it takes for your hands to flex the shoe will be the same force needed to flex your foot muscles during each mile walked. While it's true that you can break in a shoe through use, you should not let your feet do this extra work. Besides, a shoe that must be broken in to be flexible has a tendency to bend the wrong way. Such shoes often look curled when not being worn.

3. *A cushioned sole is mandatory for walking long distances.* I recommend a great deal of cushioning for the insole and outer sole. If the shoe doesn't have enough, you can add an orthopedic

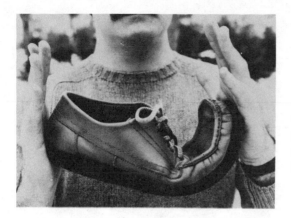

The shoe must be flexible
in the sole and the top to
assist in the walking
motion.

device. Cushioning is the key to preventing blistering, the biggest
problem of the exercisewalker.

4. *There should be good support at the heel and arch.* While
keeping the shoe from collapsing, good heel and arch support will
also keep your feet positioned correctly while you are walking. If
your shoe does not have arch supports, you can add foam rubber
supports.

5. *The upper part of the shoe should be made of material that
will allow the shoe to breathe.* I found leather and nylon mesh to
be the most comfortable. The more air you can get to the foot
while walking, the more comfortable you will feel, and your foot
will remain drier. This, too, will help prevent blistering. The
upper part of the shoe should be made of a lightweight soft
material with no seams inside the shoe. I found that the feet
swell more on the top surface if you have a stiff upper that rubs
and irritates the top of your feet as you walk. Nylon uppers seem
to be the lightest and airiest; however, leather uppers are best for
hiking in inclement weather. Laced shoes are best for holding the
foot in the shoe and control the way the shoe fits around the foot.
If possible, you should have padding in the uppers, particularly
in the tongue portion.

6. *Whenever possible, shoes should be lightweight.* Even hiking shoes made for walking are tending toward a lighter weight.
Avoid a stiff and high heel collar. This will impede your walking.
Only the most rugged mountain conditions require such heavy,
stiff boots.

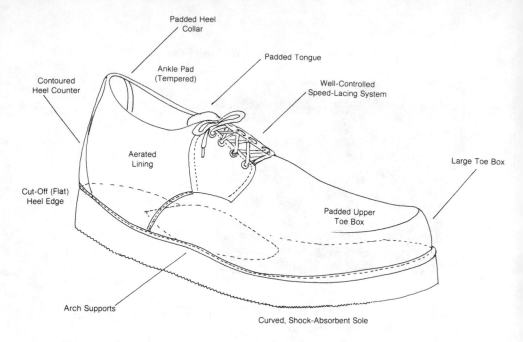

Padded Heel
Collar

Padded Tongue

Ankle Pad
(Tempered)

Well-Controlled
Speed-Lacing System

Contoured
Heel Counter

Aerated
Lining

Large Toe Box

Cut-Off (Flat)
Heel Edge

Padded Upper
Toe Box

Arch Supports

Curved, Shock-Absorbent Sole

What to Look for in a Walking Shoe.

7. *The ideal walking shoe should have a curved sole.* A curved sole will facilitate the rolling foot of the heel–toe action. Few shoes have this innovation, but it will come.

To evaluate individual shoe brands would require a book in itself; therefore, I leave this task to you. I have found that no one brand or style is the perfect shoe for walking. Many say that jogging shoes are. In fact, they say they're better designed for walking than for jogging. This is not altogether true. While such support shoes may be good for asphalt surface walking, they do not withstand variable weather and terrain conditions as good leather shoes. Jogging shoes are not yet acceptable office wear. Thus, the better approach is to have a variety of comfortable walking-style shoes that can be used for work, weekends, outdoor, and special activities involving walking and sports.

Shoe Maintenance

You've probably noticed that, like everything else, the cost of a pair of shoes is a tidy little investment. While buying and using shoes designed for specific walking purposes increases this investment, your shoes will last longer if they are properly taken care of.

Here are some ways to prolong the life of your shoes. First of all, improving your walking techniques should bring about less wear on the heels of your shoes. Second, putting on shoes and taking them off with care continues a cycle of basic shoe maintenance that many people ignore. Third, you should apply special conditioning on your shoes to keep them in good shape.

Although the second point is obvious, let's compare notes on what *I* do when I put on and remove a shoe and what you do. When putting on my shoes, I sit down, pick up one shoe, pull apart the sides with my thumbs to loosen the laces, and pull back the tongue. Then I use a shoe horn to protect the heel collar and to slip my foot into the shoe. That is the essential procedure I follow for each shoe. If I don't have a shoe horn available, I use my index and middle fingers to protect the heel collar. Because I loosened the laces—without unthreading them, of course—there is ample room for my foot to ease into the shoe.

Sitting is optional when removing the shoes. Untie the laces, pull out the sides to loosen them further, and pull back the tongue. Grasp the heel of the shoe, pull your heel out, slide the shoe away from your foot. By loosening the laces in the removal of each shoe, it is simple to put it back on with just a shoe horn.

The point of this elaborate description is that cramming your feet into your shoes causes unnecessary wear, and stepping on the heel and forcing your foot out while the shoe is still tied *damages* a shoe. I haven't revealed an utterly new secret technique our parents forgot to teach us as kids, but sometimes haste rules out common sense. Get into the habit!

My third point about shoe maintenance hinges on the type of materials used by the shoe manufacturer. When you buy a shoe, make sure you know what kind of treatments to use to keep the material in good condition. Whenever your leather shoes show signs of drying out—becoming brittle, for example—clean and dry them, then apply the recommended dressing. If the leather becomes very wet, dry it slowly—never put wet leather shoes near a direct source of heat, like a fire or heat radiator. Stuff the shoes with newspaper, paper towels, or tissue to absorb internal moisture.

Quality shoes should last a long time if cared for properly. High cost does not guarantee high quality, but if you invest a lot of money in a pair of walking shoes, it just makes good sense to attend to their care and make them last.

Foot Care

Blister prevention is the exercisewalker's number one foot care concern. While in most cases you can continue walking with blistered feet, tender feet do slow down your progress.

It is a myth to think you can permanently or completely toughen your skin so that it is blister-free. Even though you are constantly walking, there will always be a tender spot where a blister forms—even between your toes. In addition, the skin constantly renews itself. Thus, the fight against blistering by trying to harden the feet is, to a large extent, a losing battle.

The first defense against blisters is keeping your feet dry. Moisture softens the skin and makes it sensitive to friction. Well-padded shoes will also help prevent blistering. Padding should be in all areas—top, sides, heel, and even over the toe box. After designing a prototype walking shoe with plenty of padding, I discovered that padding and sole cushioning may be the secret to a blister-free walking shoe of the future.

If your shoe has little padding, you can compensate by wearing an extra pair of socks. You should change the inner socks often with either a fresh pair or by switching them with the outer layer. It is good to have extra pairs of socks along to switch off during the walking day. There are now several walking socks (called Wick Dry) that absorb moisture and carry it to outside of the sock. Others have special padding on the heel and the foot that help in cushioning. Both Wigwam and Klondike manufacture socks that are very suitable for exercisewalking.

Another suggestion that seems to help prevent blisters is to coat your whole foot with petroleum jelly and rub it in well, especially between your toes. This feels strange at first, but after you put your sock on and start walking, you won't notice it. Another idea is to carry moleskin or ordinary adhesive tape with you on your walks, and at the first moment you feel a blister forming, stop immediately and put a piece on that area, before it turns into a blister. The tape will come off easily enough in a hot bath. If you are on a walking trip lasting several days, you may wish to replace the moleskin or tape on the sensitive area before you rub your feet with petroleum jelly each morning.

If blisters do occur, and they inevitably will, you can drain them by piercing them with a sterilized needle and cover them

Socks for different hiking needs—hunting sock made of 65% Creslan Acrylic, 20% wool, and 15% Nylon; hiking sock made of 90% wool and 10% Nylon; running sock made of 70% Acrylic, 20% wool, and 10% Nylon; and liner sock made of 100% Herculon®.

Foot Massage for Aching Feet

Follow these steps for each foot:

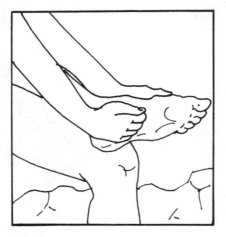

Work closed fist into sole of foot in a circular motion.

Work your thumbs in the heel and arch area.

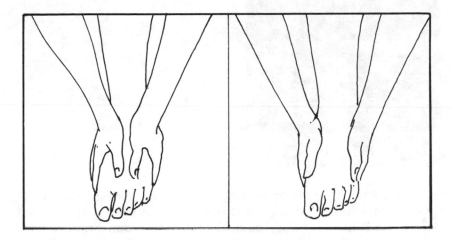

Squeeze each foot with both hands, sliding your thumbs down to the edge of the sole.

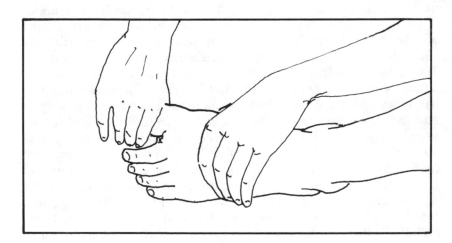

Hold each toe (one at a time) with thumb and index finger, gently pulling and allowing your fingers to slide off.

During a rest break on the trail,
take the time to care for your feet.

with a sterile dressing or leaving them alone and simply cover
them with a Band-Aid. Be sure the dressing is sterilized because
an infected blister is very painful and can be dangerous. Don't
cut the skin off the top; it will expose an even more tender layer
of skin. You may not want to drain some blisters because they
provide your foot with cushioning, but others will be painful
because of the pressure they cause in tight-fitting areas of your
shoes. Try to keep the blisters covered by a Band-Aid or tape
with a piece of gauze. I find it's possible to walk with blisters.
After awhile my feet seem to become numb to pain. I usually
drain my blisters before bed and find that they harden overnight.

There are also some medicines on the market for preventing
and healing blisters. Tincture of camphor has been described as
the best blister relief. There are also sprays and creams, such as
Tough Skin, which toughen the skin temporarily.

You can massage your feet during your hourly breaks and give
life to aching, tired feet. Foot massage is also a soothing way to
end the day. Another refresher is to put your feet up and let the
blood circulate in the opposite direction while taking the pressure off your feet. If you adapt a walking exercise lifestyle, your
feet will become the center of attention. You should give them all
the tender care they deserve. Keeping them clean and dry will be
a priority. Trimming toe nails will also prevent snagging and
bruising. If you've walked all day, try to stay off your feet at the
end of the day and keep them elevated. A warm foot bath is also
quite good for the feet.

There are special foot soaps, such as Johnson's Foot Soap,
which I found worked wonders on my feet and the whole body
after 30 miles of daily walking.

17

WALKING WEAR

From head to toe, "walking wear" is any piece of clothing that will help your walking in all terrain and weather conditions. It is generally lighter than most clothing because the walker generates a great deal of body heat. Preferably it should be layered so that in cold weather it can be removed in stages as the body warms up. It should be loose-fitting and allow the arms and legs to swing in full arcs. However, as with many sport exercise trends, walking wear, while functional, begins to take on a style purpose of its own. A walking enthusiast of the 1980s can be spotted in a crowd not only by his purposeful, brisk pace and his upright posture, but by the style of clothes he wears.

Headgear and Sunglasses

Headgear and sunglasses have the function of shielding the eyes from the sun's rays. I usually wear either one or both (if the sun is particularly strong) when walking for more than one hour. Continuous exposure to the sun causes headaches, dizziness, and temporary vision impairment unless you shield your eyes from direct sunlight. The sun's effect is even stronger on the eyes, reflecting from below as well as above, when you walk near smooth surfaces like asphalt, water, and even some dirt roads.

Although there are various types of sunglasses, I find that the ones with mirror coating on the top and bottom seem to take care of the harshest rays.

In warm weather, a walking hat should have a rounded crown with air pockets above the head to allow air to pass between your head and the top of your hat. The walking hat for cold weather should be a knitted material like wool to hold in the body's heat, which mostly escapes from the head. A hat not only protects eyes from the direct sunlight, it also prevents the sun from burning your forehead and, if your hair is thin, the top of your head. Protecting this body part closest to the sun is more important than it sounds. My walking experiences show that fatigue and even headaches come much quicker during walking exercises when I didn't wear a hat and sunglasses. Such headaches can cut short a walking day. A well-worn walking hat has become the symbol of the fashionable walker, as faded jeans symbolize the cowboy. I imagine that some day fashion designers will be selling artificially worn-out walking hats.

Upper Body Wear

Cool and Cold Weather

As with Nordic skiing, the layered approach to cool and cold weather clothing is the best one. While walking will warm up the body relatively quickly, you should start with two or three layers of warm clothing, which you can peel off and put into your backpack as you warm up. If it's really cold, a wool scarf is useful to shield exposed areas of the face and neck from frostbite. If it is also windy, a wind jacket and perhaps wind pants serve well. Under a lightweight sweater, you can also wear a long-sleeved or short-sleeved T-shirt. I find that turtleneck shirts are less useful for me because they tend to trap too much hot air and make the body sweat more than it needs to.

When doing your exercisewalking in wet cold or cool weather, you also have to be concerned with staying wet too long. If your

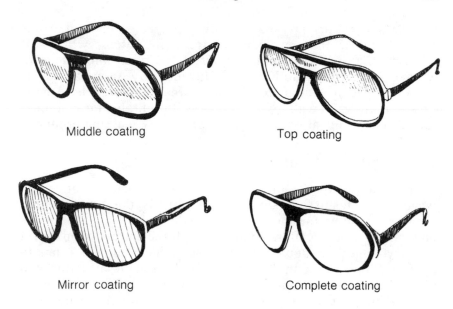

Middle coating   Top coating

Mirror coating   Complete coating

Coated Sunglasses

clothing becomes soaked through, your body may cool down too fast, producing hypothermia. This is a condition in which the core body temperature drops drastically, and your system is unable to regain its natural temperature. The condition can easily be fatal, so you must not allow the clothing you are wearing, particularly those pieces touching the skin, to remain wet too long. Change to drier clothing immediately. Also try to keep the inner clothing layer dry.

The overall factors in walking wear are lightness and maneuverability. The body must be able to function with maximum efficiency, even while carrying outdoor clothing. It must also stay as dry as possible and allow the skin to breathe while you are exercising. Traditional materials like wool and down are certainly suited for outdoor wear. Wool breathes well and absorbs moisture in a way that keeps the body from cooling down, so you won't freeze if you get wet. There are, however, also new synthetic materials, "Thinsulate" and "Gore-Tex," which make outdoor wear even lighter while maintaining its breathability. Thinsulate insulates the body while limiting the thickness or bulkiness of other materials like down, polyester, or wool. Gore-Tex is a fabric that repels water from the outside while still allowing the air to circulate. Many of the new innovations in outdoor and walking clothing are being made by American manufacturers who are stimulated by the increased interest by Americans in hiking and walking. This makes it profitable for manufacturers to experiment with introduction of new walking products.

Warm and Hot Weather

Upper-body wear requirements are much easier for warm weather. A T-shirt or shirt with straps is the best clothing because it allows for the greatest freedom of all for the upper-body motions while allowing air to reach the body to keep it cool and dry. Clothing should be seamless or have outside seams to avoid rubbing the skin. T-shirts should be made of cotton and washed a number of times to be most comfortable. I often wear my "walking T-shirt" under my regular shirt so I can remove my outer shirt when doing my walking exercises during the business day. Since the T-shirt will also absorb the sweat, I remove it before putting my regular shirt on again. T-shirts come in a variety of colors and some even contain slogans and pictures if you want to be colorful or outrageous. For the more conservative, solid-colored shirts are best. Black is a good color for keeping you warmer on chilly days when the sun is shining. Light-colored T-shirts are the coolest in hot weather. A word of caution: regular white undershirts are not appropriate walking wear because they make you look underdressed, and you will stand out in a crowd.

For maximum flexibility and speed, bare-chested walking (for women a halter top) may be best of all, but use plenty of suntan lotion or sun block to protect your skin from the drying and burning effects of the sun and wind. A sunburned upper body not only makes exercise movements uncomfortable but may also cause sun sensitivity and make it impossible to stay outdoors on a sunny day.

A poncho may serve a walker well in rainy weather. Even though the rubber or plastic material does not breathe well, air flows in and out from underneath and on the sides. A poncho also allows room for a pack underneath as well as unrestricted leg movement and, to a limited extent, arm movement. Ponchos are also practical as improvised ground cloths or even a makeshift tent. Finally, if it is really hot and rainy, an umbrella is perhaps the most useful device in keeping the rain out while letting the body remain cool. Some walking sticks are built with umbrellas attached.

Pants

Walking shorts are best of all. They facilitate easy leg movement and protect against rubbing and chafing between the legs and thighs. The thighs of many novice walkers rub together because they are still flabby and need toning. Others are just built naturally with heavy or muscular thighs. If this is a problem for you, it sometimes helps to get a lining for the area rubbed the most or use outer patches before or after the pants have started wearing through. Because of varying weather or temperature conditions, you'll often find yourself using long pants. These should be selected for their softness and looseness, particularly in the seat and crotch areas. The pants should be fitted for or chosen so they allow for the full flexing of the leg muscles and the walker's stride. Tight-fitting designer jeans are the least appropriate walking pants. If pants are tight in the seat and crotch, they will hinder your movement unless they stretch. Walking pants will last longer if they are double-stitched or stitched with strong threads at the outer seams.

18

EXERCISE AIDS AND SUPPLIES

Because a whole book could be devoted to hiking and mountaineering equipment (going into the wilds can involve complicated logistical planning), this chapter will concentrate on walking supplies and equipment that facilitate walking as an exercise. Lightness and flexibility are the watchwords that should dictate your choice of exercisewalking equipment.

Backpacks

On one-day hikes and short weekend workouts away from home, a small backpack is useful even if it only carries your first-aid items, a change or two of socks, and cold weather wear, if appropriate. Generally, the smaller your pack, the less you are likely to carry with you. Consider using a fanny pack, which straps around your waist like a belt rather than hanging from the shoulders. By setting it over your rear end, the fanny pack will generally not pull your weight back so you will be able to walk upright. You can also strap a few small items such as canteen and camera to the front of the belt to improve your balance further.

240

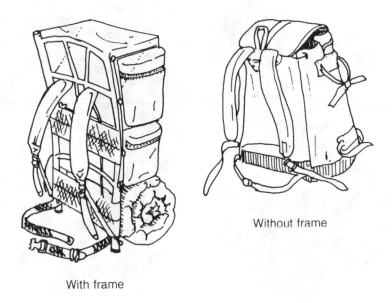

Without frame

With frame

Backpacks

Of course, carrying a heavy pack is unavoidable when mountain climbing or hiking in the wilderness. A heavy backpack tends to pull your body back, forcing you to lean forward to counterbalance the weight while walking. You should transfer the weight away from your shoulder to your hips by using a back frame and waist belt. Many hikers, especially day hikers, carry too much weight and too large a backpack and hinder their flexibility, speed, and posture. However, by walking with additional weight, you're strengthening your muscles and burning more calories. If training with weights is your goal, you will be better off placing the weight on your ankles with a weight belt than placing it on your back.

Measuring Devices

A watch or chronograph, pedometer, a pulse-measuring device, and compass constitute a complete set of walking measurement devices. Of course, if you want to save money or want to walk freely, most of these devices are not absolutely necessary. You

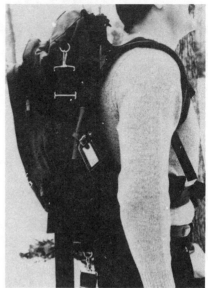

A combination pack that can be converted from a soft suitcase into a backpack is offered by many manufacturers.

can measure your walking program using only a watch, your feet, and your brain. Because of the increased attention that will be given to the sport of walking in the future, the walker who is trend-conscious or technologically oriented should be aware of the devices that make the job of measuring more accurate.

The Pedometer

The pedometer is a much underrated and sometimes criticized device. It is actually a very useful tool; when used correctly it can keep track of your walking-for-miles exercise. The pedometer is placed in the belt or attached to the wrist and measures the number of steps you take. It will record the number of steps you take and translate this number into miles. You can set the pedometer for your step length of 2, 2½, 3, or 3½ feet.

As you continue your exercisewalking training, your stride will probably grow longer, and you can adjust the pedometer for

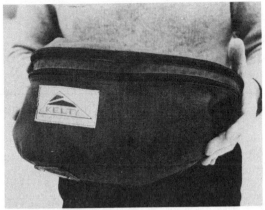

This clever fanny pack goes around the waist and can be expanded into a good-sized daypack when needed.

any changes. You should also monitor your stride for different kinds of terrain. On flat terrain, your stride will be longest, while it will tend to shorten with climbing. Measure your stride by taking a natural-sized step and freezing in position.

Mark the distance on the ground and measure it with a ruler or tape measure. While doing your walking training, it's a good idea to check the pedometer's mileage over a known distance such as one mile. This will tell you if your setting was wrong or if you have changed the length of your stride.

Persons with exacting requirements have criticized the pedometer as not being absolutely accurate. The accuracy, of course, is only in the number of steps taken. Step length can vary during the same walk, particularly over uneven terrain. The pedometer cannot be absolutely perfect, but, it's a tolerable kind of imperfection since the total miles measured tend to average themselves out. After walking with a pedometer for 1,100 miles, I found that it compared favorably to the distance measurements on the road maps I followed. It was also a good supplement to determine the distance I walked when I left the road and followed the coast. At that time I was grateful for a record of the bonus miles I got from walking the uneven coastal contours.

Pulsometer

We have already discussed simple methods for measuring heartbeat like taking a six-second finger pulse measurement. While this pulse rate measurement method is certainly adequate for the average exercisewalker, some of you will want to measure your pulse rate continuously to determine if you have reached, and remain in, your training zone for the exercise period in question. The heart exercise computer shown on page 245 attaches to your wrist and finger and measures your pulse while you exercise. It allows you to program your upper and lower training zone limits into the computer. When you exercise too hard or too little, a beeper will sound to tell you to speed up or slow down. The heart computer also records how much time you spend exercising in your heart training zone.

Creams, Jellies, and Medications

Generally, the body will recover completely from short walking workouts of less than one hour; however, longer workouts and long-distance walks put the body under stress. When this stress is continuous, pain relievers can be a significant aid to being able to stick to a vigorous walking program. I found that "body ache," a condition of stiffness in which many muscles hurt from overuse, can be kept to a minimum by taking two aspirin

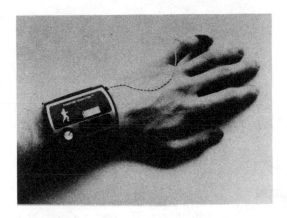

Exercise computer, which fits on the wrist, can be used to measure pulse rate as well as keep you aware of whether you're training too hard or too little.

every four hours while walking and right before bed. In the evening, a glass of wine or a stiff drink can take the place of the aspirin. There are also body creams, such as Ben Gay and Infra-Rub, that help bring heat and relief to marathoners' sore muscles. I've tried walking long hours and long distances with and without these medications, and found that they make a big difference not only in your feeling of well-being, but also in your ability to keep walking at maximum speed and strength day in and day out. Even though they are often uncomplaining, many walkers in pain have a tendency to cut short their walking day or to walk slower.

Creams and jellies are an important component of an athlete's kit. Like muscle pain, sunburn and windburn tend to slow your training program no matter how hard you try to be brave and fight it. Blistex will help protect your lips from burning and swelling. Suntan lotion or a total sunblock, if you have extremely sensitive skin or will be out in the sun for extended periods of time, is a must to prevent sun rays from reaching overexposed areas of the skin like the nose, forehead, and back of the neck. Even if there's a cloud covering, harmful sun rays get through to the skin. Remember your worst sunburn and try to think how unpleasant it would be to exercise with it on a sunny day. If chafing is a problem for you, it's a good idea to rub some petroleum jelly on your nipples, under your arms, along the side of your chest, on the inside of your thighs, or on any other problem area to prevent chafing.

Edward Payson Weston, 1836-1929, believed that walking could actually make a man "improve with age and never go stale." And he lived to age 93.

In 1861 at age 22, Weston walked from Boston to Washington in ten days, as part of Lincoln's inauguration. He missed the ceremony by half a day, but launched a professional career in long-distance walking.

At 70 he walked 512 miles in 12 days breaking a world record. At 74 he walked 1,500 miles from New York to Minneapolis in 60 days. He also walked across the country in his seventies, breaking no records but thrilling thousands.

Walking Sticks and Staffs

Walking sticks and staffs can be useful for walk climbing and walking through places where rocks are loose, and they seem to be helpful in giving both physical and psychological support. Some confirmed walkers believe a walking stick helps them maintain their balance while walking, particularly when carrying a heavy backpack in a mountainous region. Walking sticks also serve as a pacing device by transferring a hand movement pace to the ground in front of the feet. Doctors recommend sticks as a useful extra support for a person recovering from an injury or illness or for those who have weak legs or bad balance. I found a walking stick most useful as a weapon against dogs who often try to menace walkers who come too close to their perceived territory. Finally, walking sticks may become a walker's calling card or symbol and become as fashionable as they were at the turn of the century. Pedestrian Edward Payson Weston used a walking stick in his long-distance walking.

Treadmills

These are conveyer belts for walking. Motorized and nonmotorized treadmills simulate flat as well as uphill walking conditions. They are also good for observing and testing your walking action. Nonmotorized treadmills usually require a greater work effort to keep moving.

Despite the apparent inconsistency, many walkers do not or

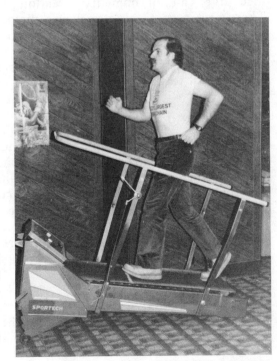

Non-motorized treadmill can be used for walking indoors.

cannot enjoy the outdoors, so they must confine their exercise to the indoors. This is particularly true for those in winter who fear falling on the icy walkways. But it is also true for persons who must stay at home to watch children or whose business interests do not allow them time to exercise. These latter have gotten used to working out in home gyms or in front of the television and so forth. For all these exercises a treadmill for walking is recommended. If nothing else, it will supplement any walking done outdoors.

I have used treadmills both indoors and outdoors (I use it in my exercisewalking clinics and demonstrations) and have found it to be a great aid for four types of exercisewalking: speed work, duration and distance workouts, weight-load walking, and walk climbing.

You can walk your fastest on the treadmill, up to 10 mph or even more, and no rock or other obstruction will ever get in your way to break your pace. The treadmill's instrument panel will also give you an immediate readout of your walking speed. There's no need to stop, measure distances, or count steps per minute. The speedometer gives you an immediate reading and helps you with your speed work. It's especially good for walk sprints, which not only train your heart but help you increase your overall walking speed, even when you are outdoors.

Distance and Duration Workouts

The treadmill will keep track of the number of miles you walked at any stride length. This is particularly good because you can vary your speed and stride length during a particular workout and you don't have to do any complicated calculations. A mile walked on the treadmill is a mile, regardless of your pace or step length.

I find that the treadmill is particularly useful for making up miles missed in a walking-for-miles program.

Weight-Load Walking

The treadmill is a great piece of weight-training equipment for a weight-training program you can do while walking. You can keep track of the number of repetitions and even use the braking system, causing resistance that leads to a greater work effort. A simple weight-training program uses a backpack and baggies or soft drink cans, each filled with a pound of sand. If you're overweight, you won't need the sand but can count the pounds over your limit as the extra weight. This is a great weight and fat loss system, too.

Walk Climbing

A unique feature of the same treadmill is the ability to slope the angle of the treading platform. This enables you to create conditions for exercisewalking similar to climbing hills, stairs, and even mountains. If you add a backpack to your walk climbing routine, you can prepare for trekking and mountain climbing ahead of time without having to find a workout mountain.

EPILOGUE

As walking is studied further, new, advanced walking techniques will emerge. For example, weight-training programs are now being developed with their central focus on the walking action. More sports activities like roller skating and bicycling will be combined with walking. Advanced walking techniques are being developed from racewalking and long-distance walking experiences, and new equipment and shoes and clothing styles will emerge to facilitate these techniques.

I predict that walking as an exercise will continue to grow by leaps and bounds in the 1980s. I am planning to write a second volume that will deal with advanced exercisewalking techniques and the new walking boom. In the meantime, I would appreciate comments on your results in applying these walking techniques to your exercise programs. You can write to me directly at this address

Gary D. Yanker
EXERCISEWALKING PROGRAM
PO Box 888, FDR Station
New York, NY 10022

APPENDIX: FITNESS RATINGS AND ENERGY EXPENDITURE TABLES

Fitness Ratings Based on Blood Pressure and Heart Rate

Men Aged 20-29

Blood Pressure Measurements	I (Poor)	II (Fair)	III (Good)	IV (Very Good)	V (Excellent)
(a) Systolic	136-140	128-135	120-127	112-119	94-111
(b) Diastolic	88-90	80-87	80	72-79	61-71
Resting Heart Rate	72-80	66-71	60-65	54-59	40-53
Maximum Heart Rate	179-183	182-191	192-197	198-200	201-214

Women Aged 20-29

Blood Pressure Measurements					
(a) Systolic	120-130	118-120	110-117	101-107	90-100
(b) Diastolic	80-82	78-80	72-77	68-71	56-67
Resting Heart Rate	75-84	70-74	63-69	59-62	48-58
Maximum Heart Rate	172-180	181-186	187-190	191-198	199-213

Men Aged 30-39

Blood Pressure Measurements	I (Poor)	II (Fair)	III (Good)	IV (Very Good)	V (Excellent)
(a) Systolic	132-140	124-131	120-123	110-119	96-109
(b) Diastolic	90-92	81-89	80	74-79	60-73
Resting Heart Rate	72-77	65-71	60-64	55-59	40-54
Maximum Heart Rate	174-180	181-186	185-191	192-198	199-210

Fitness Ratings Based on Blood Pressure and Heart Rate (continued)

Women Aged 30–39

Blood Pressure Measurements

(a) Systolic	122–130	118–121	110–117	104–110	90–103
(b) Diastolic	82–90	80–81	74–79	70–73	60–69

Resting Heart Rate

	76–82	70–75	65–69	58–64	48–57

Maximum Heart Rate

	170–176	177–182	183–185	186–192	191–210

Men Aged 40–49

Blood Pressure Measurements

	I (Poor)	II (Fair)	III (Good)	IV (Very Good)	V (Excellent)
(a) Systolic	138–142	126–137	120–125	111–119	96–110
(b) Diastolic	90–98	84–89	80	76–80	60–75

Resting Heart Rate

	72–78	65–71	60–64	54–59	42–53

Maximum Heart Rate

	164–171	172–180	181–185	184–191	192–205

Women Aged 40–49

Blood Pressure Measurements

(a) Systolic	130–138	120–129	112–119	105–111	90–104
(b) Diastolic	82–90	80–81	75–80	70–74	58–69

Resting Heart Rate

	76–80	70–75	64–69	60–63	43–59

Maximum Heart Rate

	158–166	167–173	174–180	182–186	185–208

Fitness Ratings Based on Blood Pressure and Heart Rate (continued)

Men Aged 50-59

Blood Pressure Measurements	I (Poor)	II (Fair)	III (Good)	IV (Very Good)	V (Excellent)
(a) Systolic	140–150	130–139	122–129	116–121	98–115
(b) Diastolic	90–100	86–90	80–85	78–80	60–79
Resting Heart Rate	72–77	65–71	60–64	55–59	42–54
Maximum Heart Rate	150–160	161–170	171–176	177–183	184–200

Women Aged 50-59

Blood Pressure Measurements					
(a) Systolic	140–148	130–139	120–129	110–119	90–109
(b) Diastolic	90–92	82–89	79–81	70–78	58–69
Resting Heart Rate	75–83	69–74	64–68	60–63	45–59
Maximum Heart Rate	152–160	161–167	168–173	174–180	181–202

Fitness Ratings Based on Blood Pressure and Heart Rate (continued)

**Men Aged 60
and Over**

Blood Pressure Measurements	I (Poor)	II (Fair)	III (Good)	IV (Very Good)	V (Excellent)
(a) Systolic	150–160	140–149	130–139	120–129	98–119
(b) Diastolic	90–98	84–89	80–83	76–80	60–75
Resting Heart Rate	72–77	65–71	60–64	55–59	38–54
Maximum Heart Rate	131–145	146–159	160–165	164–175	174–195

**Women Aged 60
and Over**

Blood Pressure Measurements					
(a) Systolic	142–160	136–141	128–135	120–127	110–120
(b) Diastolic	88–98	80–87	80	75–79	66–74
Resting Heart Rate	74–79	66–73	62–75	57–61	46–56
Maximum Heart Rate	126–140	141–150	152–155	156–165	164–178

Energy Expenditure in Various Walking Styles and Related Activities

Activity	Weight in pounds						
	110	117	123	130	137	143	150
Climbing hills							
with no load	6.1	6.4	6.8	7.1	7.5	7.9	8.2
with 11-pound load	6.5	6.8	7.2	7.6	8.0	8.4	8.8
with 22-pound load	7.0	7.4	7.8	8.3	8.7	9.1	9.5
with 44-pound load	7.4	7.8	8.2	8.7	9.1	9.6	10.0
Cycling							
leisure, 5.5 mph	3.2	3.4	3.6	3.8	4.0	4.2	4.4
leisure, 9.4 mph	5.0	5.3	5.6	5.9	6.2	6.5	6.8
racing	8.5	9.0	9.5	10.0	10.5	11.0	11.5
Golf	4.3	4.5	4.8	5.0	5.3	5.5	5.8
Marching, rapid	7.1	7.5	8.0	8.4	8.8	9.2	9.7
Running, cross-country	8.2	8.6	9.1	9.6	10.1	10.6	11.1
Running, horizontal							
11 min, 30 s per mile	6.8	7.2	7.6	8.0	8.4	8.8	9.2
9 min per mile	9.7	10.2	10.8	11.4	12.0	12.5	13.1
8 min per mile	10.8	11.3	11.9	12.5	13.1	13.6	14.2
7 min per mile	12.2	12.7	13.3	13.9	14.5	15.0	15.6
6 min per mile	13.9	14.4	15.0	15.6	16.2	16.7	17.3
5 min, 30 s per mile	14.5	15.3	16.2	17.1	17.9	18.8	19.7
Sitting quietly	1.1	1.1	1.2	1.2	1.3	1.4	1.4
Skiing, hard snow							
level, moderate speed	6.0	6.3	6.7	7.0	7.4	7.7	8.1
level, walking	7.2	7.6	8.0	8.4	8.9	9.3	9.7
uphill, maximum speed	13.7	14.5	15.3	16.2	17.0	17.8	18.6
Skiing, soft snow							
leisure (F)	4.9	5.2	5.5	5.8	6.1	6.4	6.7
leisure (M)	5.6	5.9	6.2	6.5	6.9	7.2	7.5

				Weight in pounds					
157	163	170	176	183	190	196	203	209	216
8.6	9.0	9.3	9.7	10.0	10.4	10.8	11.1	11.5	11.9
9.2	9.5	9.9	10.3	10.7	11.1	11.5	11.9	12.3	12.6
9.9	10.4	10.8	11.2	11.6	12.0	12.5	12.9	13.3	13.7
10.4	10.9	11.3	11.8	12.2	12.6	13.1	13.5	14.0	14.4
4.5	4.7	4.9	5.1	5.3	5.5	5.7	5.9	6.1	6.3
7.1	7.4	7.7	8.0	8.3	8.6	8.9	9.2	9.5	9.8
12.0	12.5	13.0	13.5	14.0	14.5	15.0	15.5	16.1	16.6
6.0	6.3	6.5	6.8	7.1	7.3	7.6	7.8	8.1	8.3
10.1	10.5	10.9	11.4	11.8	12.2	12.6	13.1	13.5	13.9
11.6	12.1	12.6	13.0	13.5	14.0	14.5	15.0	15.5	16.0
9.6	10.0	10.5	10.9	11.3	11.7	12.1	12.5	12.9	13.3
13.7	14.3	14.9	15.4	16.0	16.6	17.2	17.8	18.3	18.9
14.8	15.4	16.0	16.5	17.1	17.7	18.3	18.9	19.4	20.0
16.2	16.8	17.4	17.9	18.5	19.1	19.7	20.3	20.8	21.4
17.9	18.5	19.1	19.6	20.2	20.8	21.4	22.0	22.5	23.1
20.5	21.4	22.3	23.1	24.0	24.9	25.7	26.6	27.5	28.3
1.5	1.6	1.6	1.7	1.7	1.8	1.9	1.9	2.0	2.1
8.4	8.8	9.2	9.5	9.9	10.2	10.6	10.9	11.3	11.7
10.2	10.2	11.0	11.4	11.9	12.3	12.7	13.2	13.6	14.0
19.5	20.3	21.1	21.9	22.7	23.6	24.4	25.2	26.0	26.9
7.0	7.3	7.5	7.8	8.1	8.4	8.7	9.0	9.3	9.6
7.9	8.2	8.5	8.9	9.2	9.5	9.9	10.2	10.5	10.9

Energy Expenditure in Various Walking Styles and Related Activities
(continued)

Activity	Weight in pounds						
	110	117	123	130	137	143	150
Snowshoeing, soft snow	8.3	8.8	9.3	9.8	10.3	10.8	11.3
Standing quietly (F)	1.3	1.3	1.4	1.5	1.6	1.6	1.7
Standing quietly (M)	1.4	1.4	1.5	1.6	1.7	1.8	1.8
Walking, normal pace							
asphalt road	4.0	4.2	4.5	4.7	5.0	5.2	5.4
fields and hillsides	4.1	4.3	4.6	4.8	5.1	5.3	5.6
grass track	4.1	4.3	4.5	4.8	5.0	5.3	5.5
plowed field	3.9	4.1	4.3	4.5	4.8	5.0	5.2

				Weight in pounds					
157	**163**	**170**	**176**	**183**	**190**	**196**	**203**	**209**	**216**
11.8	12.3	12.8	13.3	13.8	14.3	14.8	15.3	15.8	16.3
1.8	1.9	1.9	2.0	2.1	2.2	2.2	2.3	2.4	2.5
1.9	2.0	2.1	2.2	2.2	2.3	2.4	2.5	2.6	2.6
5.7	5.9	6.2	6.4	6.6	6.9	7.1	7.4	7.6	7.8
5.8	6.1	6.3	6.6	6.8	7.1	7.3	7.5	7.8	8.0
5.8	6.0	6.2	6.5	6.7	7.0	7.2	7.5	7.7	7.9
5.5	5.7	5.9	6.2	6.4	6.6	6.9	7.1	7.3	7.5

SOURCES AND FURTHER READING

American College of Sports Medicine: *Guidelines for Graded Exercise Testing and Exercise Prescription.* Lea and Fibiger, Philadelphia 1975.

American College of Sports Medicine: "The Recommended Quantity and Quality of Exercise for Developing and Maintaining Fitness in Healthy Adults." *Sports Medicine Bulletin* (July 1978)

Atzler, E., and Herbst, R. Arbeitsphysiologische Studien. Part 3. Pfugers Arch. 215:291, 1927.

Bar-Khama, A., Shoenfeld, Y., Schuman, E. *The Israeli Fitness Strategy.* New York: William Morrow and Company, Inc., 1980.

Belloc, Hilaire: *The Path to Rome.* Thomas Nelson & Sons, London and New York, 1970.

Bennett, William M.D. and Joel Gurin, *The Dieter's Dilemma*, Basic Books: 1982.

Calder, Jean. Walking: *A Guide to Beautiful Walks and Trails in America.* William Morrow & Co., New York, 1977.

Cavagna, G.A., and Kaneko, M. "Mechanical work and efficiency in level walking and running" *J. Physiol.* (Lond.) 268:467, 1977.

Conrad, C.C. "How Different Sports Rate in Promoting Physical Fitness." *Medical Times*, May 1976.

Cooper, K.H. *The Aerobics Program for Total Well-Being.* New York: M. Evans and Co., 1982. Endurance points, pp. 123,139.

Dean, G.A. "An analysis of the energy expenditure in level and grade walking." *Ergonomics* 8:31, 1965.

Dill, D.B. et al.: *Training: youth and age.* Ann. N.Y. Acad Sci., 134:760, 1966.

Durnin. J.V.G.A., and Passmore, R. *Energy, Work and Leisure.* Heinemann Educational Books, London, 1967.

Fletcher, C. *The New Complete Walker.* New York: Alfred. A. Knopf., 1978.

Gayle, R., Montoye, H. and Philpot, J.: "Accuracy of Pedometers for Measuring Distance Walked." *Research Quarterly*, 1977.

Gehlsen, G. and Dill, D.: "Comparative Performance of Men and Women in Grade Walking" *Human Biology*, September 1977.

Greive, D.W., and Gear, R.J. "The relationships between length of stride, step frequency, time of swing, and speed, and speed of walking for children and adults." *Ergonomics* 5:379, 1966.

Gwinup, Grant: "Walking." *Harper's Bazaar*, October 1973.

Hirschberg, G.G., and Ralston, H.J. "Energy cost of stair-climbing in normal and hemiplegic subjects." *Am. J. Phys. Med.* 44:165, 1965.

Inman, V.T. *Human Walking*. Williams and Wilkins: Baltimore, 1981, p. 71.

Jacobson, H. *Racewalk To Fitness*. New York: Simon and Schuster, 1980.

Kasch, F.W., and Wallace, J.P.: "Physiological variables during 10 years of endurance exercise." *Med. Sci. Sports*, 8:5, 1976.

Kasch, F.W. "The Energy Cost of Walking and Hiking." *The Physician and Sportsmedicine*, July 1976.

Katahn, M., Ph.D., *The 200 Calorie Solution*. New York, London: W.W. Norton and Company, 1982.

Luria, M.H., and Koepke, K.T. "The Physical Conditioning Effects of walking." *Journal of Sports Medicine* 15, 1975.

Marey, E.J. *Movement*, Translated by E. Pritchard. Appleton, Century, Crofts, New York, 1895 & Marey, E.J., The Animal Machine (1873)

Margaria, R. Sulla fisiologia e specialmente sul consumo energetico della marcia e della corsa a varie velocita ed inclinazioni del terreno. Vol. 7. Atti Reale Accad. Naz. Lincei. Giovanni Bardi, Rome, 1983.

Marsden, J.P. and Montgomery, S.R.: "A General Survey of the Walking Habits of Individuals." *Ergonomics*, 1972.

McArdle, W.D., Katch, F.I., and Katch, V.I. *Exercise physiology* Energy, Nutrition, and Human Performance. London: Henry Kimpton Publishers., 1981. pp. 120, 430-443.

McDonald, I. "Statistical studies of recorded energy expenditure of man." Part II. "Expenditure on walking related to weight, sex, age, height, speed and gradient." *Nutr. Abstr. Rev.* 31:739, 1961.

Menier, D.R., and Pugh, L.G.C.E. "The relation of oxygen intake and volocity of walking and running, in competition walkers." *J. Physiol.* 197:717, 1968.

Molen, N.H., and Rozendal, R.H. "Fundamental characteristics of human gait in relation to sex and location." *Proc. Kon. Ned. Akad. Wet., Ser. C* 75:215, 1972.

Molen, N.H. "Problems on the Evaluation of Gait." Thesis. Ph.D., Health Sciences. Vrije Universiteit, Amsterdam, 1973.

Murray, M.P. "Gait as a total pattern of movement, including a bibliography on gait." *Am. J. Phys. Med.* 46:290, 1967

Murray, M.P., and Clarkson, B.H. "Vertical pathways of the foot during level walking." *J. Am. Phys. Ther. Assoc.* 46:585, 1966

Murray, M.P., Drought, A.B., and Kory, R.C. "Walking patterns of normal men." *J. Bone Joint Surg.* 46-A: 335, 1964

Murray, M.P., Kory, R.C., Clarkson, B.H., and Sepic, S.B. "Comparison of free and fast walking patterns of normal men. *Am. J. Phys. Med.* 45:8, 1966

Murray, M.P., Kory, R.C., and S.B. "Walking patterns of normal women." Arch. Phys. Med. Rehabil. 51:637, 1970.

Passmore, R., and Durnin, J.V.G.A. "Human energy expenditure." Physiol. Rev. 35:801, 1955.

Pollock, M.L. et al.: "Frequency of training as a determinant for improvement in cardiovascular function and body composition of middle-aged men." Arch. Phys. Med. Rehabil, 56: 141, 1975.

Pollock, M. L., Miller, H., Janeway, R., Linnerud, A., Robertson, B. and Valentino, R.: "Effects of Walking on Body Composition and Cardiovascular Functions of Middle-Aged Men." Journal of Applied Physiology, January 1971.

Popova, T. Quoted in Issledovaniia po biodinamike locomotsii, Chapter 3, vol. 1: Biodinamika khod'by normal'nogo vzroslogo muzhchiny, edited by N.A. Bernshtein. Idat. Vsesoiuz. Instit. Eksper. Med., Moscow, 1935.

Ralston H.J. "Energy-speed relation and optimal speed during level walking," Int. Z. angew. Physiol. 17:277, 1958

Ralston, H.J., and Lukin, L. "Energy levels of human body segments during level walking. Ergonomics 12:39, 1969.

Schwartz, L. Heavyhands: the Ultimate Exercise System. Boston: Little, Brown and Company, 1982.

Shephard, Roy J., M.D., Ph.D. Physical Activity and Aging. Yearbook Medical Publishers: Chicago, 1979.

Strydom, N.B., Bredell, G.A.G., Benade, A.J.S., Morrison, J.F., Viljoen, J.H., and van Graan, C.H. "The metabolic cost of marching at 3 m.p.h. over firm and sandy surfaces." Int. Z. angew. Physiol. 23: 166, 1966.

Stutman, F.A., M.D. The Doctor's Walking Book. New York: Ballantine Books., 1980.

Sussman, Aaron and Goode, Ruth: The Magic of Walking. Simon and Schuster: New York, 1967.

Wilmore, DR. J.H. The Wilmore Fitness Program. New York: Simon and Schuster, 1981.

Wyndham, C.H., can der Walt, W.H., van Rensburg, A.J., Rogers, G.G., and Strydom, N.B. "The influence of body weight on energy expenditure during walking on a road and on a treadmill." Int. Z. angew. Physiol. 29:285, 1971.

Zarrugh, M.Y., Todd, F.N., and Ralston, H.J. "Optimization of energy expenditure during level walking." Eur. J. Appl. Physiol. 33:293, 1974.

INDEX